Assignment Moscow

Assignment Moscow

Reporting on Russia from Lenin to Putin

James Rodgers

I.B.TAURIS
LONDON • NEW YORK • OXFORD • NEW DELHI • SYDNEY

I.B. TAURIS

Bloomsbury Publishing Plc

50 Bedford Square, London, WC1B 3DP, UK

1385 Broadway, New York, NY 10018, USA

BLOOMSBURY, I.B. TAURIS and the I.B. Tauris logo
are trademarks of Bloomsbury Publishing Plc

First published in Great Britain 2020

ISBN:	HB:	978-0-7556-0115-8
	ePDF:	978-0-7556-0117-2
	eBook:	978-0-7556-0116-5

Typeset by Integra Software Services Pvt. Ltd.
Printed and bound in Great Britain

To find out more about our authors and books visit www.bloomsbury.com
and sign up for our newsletters.

Dedicated to the memory of Ian Leverton, 1947–2009
A great teacher who inspired and encouraged both my love of journalism, and my
lifelong fascination with Russia and its literature.

Contents

List of Figures

Acknowledgements

My thanks go first to the Society of Authors for a generous grant which enabled me to travel to Russia, to refresh my knowledge of a country I had not seen for some years and to gather new impressions which were invaluable to my research. I would also like to thank my employers at City, University of London for permitting me to take sabbatical leave from the Journalism Department while I finished the book.

I would like to thank Joanna Godfrey at I.B. Tauris for commissioning the book, and Olivia Dellow and Tomasz Hoskins for seeing it through to publication. I am grateful to Robert Dudley of the Robert Dudley Agency for his assistance in preparing the proposal. Chris Booth, a former BBC colleague, read drafts of large parts of the manuscript. His comments were invariably well observed and very helpful.

An earlier version of part of the section in Chapter 1 on John Reed was published in the *British Journalism Review* in June 2017 (Vol. 28, No. 2). An article I wrote offering a more extensive analysis of the British newspaper reporting of the February revolution was published online by the journal *Media History* in June 2019, DOI: 10.1080/13688804.2019.1634526.

Valentine Baldassari provided excellent research assistance, especially in transcribing and preparing interview material. Kevin Cummins helped me prepare photographs for publication. Many thanks to them both.

Stephen Penton and Alex Asman from the library at City, University of London gave me very useful advice: Alex in particular on electronic access to newspaper archives. Els Boonen at the BBC written archives in Caversham was extremely helpful, answering any questions I had, and also in suggesting material I had not thought to request. Dominic Marsh and his colleagues at the Guardian Archive at the John Rylands Library at the University of Manchester made research there a pleasure. I would also like to thank Anne Jensen for her help during my visit to the Times Newspapers Archive, and the Bishopsgate Institute where I was able to read the papers of Sam Russell.

I would like to thank all my contributors for giving generously of their time, and for their enthusiasm for my project. My thanks to Andrew Wilson for also allowing the reproduction of one of his photographs. Families of former correspondents have also been very helpful, and I would like to thank in particular Gavin and Mish Weaver, son and daughter of Shelley Rohde, and Ruth Müller, daughter of Sam Russell. My thanks also go to Nicolas Werth for permission to cite from his father's work.

Having first gone on assignment to Moscow in 1991, I have worked there with many different colleagues over the years. I was lucky enough to be part of the teams of some great Bureau editors, both for Reuters TV and the BBC: Ralph Nicholson, Sara Beck, Kevin Bishop, Alan Quartly. I benefitted greatly from conversations with other correspondents, in particular Allan Little and Steve Rosenberg. I would also like to thank Suzanna Woods, Marie Frail, Sue Jamieson, Vladimir Bomko, Zoya Trunova, Jonathan Charles, Zurab Kodalashvili, Duncan Herbert, Andrew 'Sarge' Herbert, Andrew Kilrain, Linda Mottram, Konstantin von Eggert, Leonid Ragozin and Patrick Garrett for helping to make even some of the most challenging times enjoyable and rewarding. An evening with Chloe Arnold and Christian Lowe, while I was visiting Moscow in March 2019, was memorable not just for their hospitality, but also for the insights into how things had changed, or not, since my last posting. A special mention should go to Jamie Coomarasamy, Nanette van der Laan, Duncan Knowles and Wendy Sloane, all of whom I met in Moscow in the early 1990s – great colleagues then, they remain close friends. I would like to remember Peter Martini and Yury Bomko, who sadly are no longer with us – victims of Russia's terrible record on road safety. Wesley Eremenko-Dodd, Artyom Liss and Daria Merkusheva were all great producers during my final assignment as BBC correspondent; cameramen Anton Chicherov, Alek Gregorian and Jon Hughes were a pleasure to work with. Without Mikhail Ivanovich Bykoff, the BBC Moscow bureau could never have negotiated the bureaucracy of post-Soviet Russia as it did.

My wife, Mette Jørgensen Rodgers, a Danish foreign correspondent in London, has been nominated for awards for her reporting, and still found time to listen to my ideas for this book. My love and thanks to her, and to our daughters, Freya and Sophia.

Assignment Moscow. Numbered list of illustrations for publication, with chapters.

1.1. Winter Palace (author's own photograph). Chapter 1

1.2. British journalist Morgan Philips Price (1885–1973), the Labour MP for the Forest of Dean, 1935 (photo by Bassano/Hulton Archive/Getty Images). Chapter 1

3.1. 'Boarding her dispatch from Paris, Mrs Marguerite E. Harrison, a Baltimore newspaper woman has been arrested in Moscow by the Soviet government and imprisoned there. Mrs Harrison is charged with being a secret agent of the State Department of the United States according to a report. She has been doing newspaper work in Russia for some time. The photo shows Mrs Harrison, close up' (Bettmann/Contributor). Chapter 3

3.2. Portrait of American reporter and war correspondent Floyd Gibbons (1887–1939), who lost an eye covering the battle of Belleau Wood during the First World War and who was later the announcer on some of the first regularly scheduled national radio news broadcasts for CBS and later NBC, as he wears an Army uniform and stands with his arm in a sling, 1918 (photo by Pictorial Parade/Getty Images). Chapter 3

3.3. *New York Times* correspondent, Walter Duranty, wearing a black suit, sitting and leaning on his elbow, and puffing on a cigarette (photo by Edward Steichen/Condé Nast via Getty Images). Chapter 3

5.1. The Moscow Radio Tower, designed by Vladimir Shukhov (author's own photograph). Chapter 5

7.1. Soviet press pass issued to the author for the Gorbachev-Bush summit, Moscow, July 1991 (author's own photograph). Chapter 7

8.1. Grozny, Chechnya, April 1995 (author's own photograph). Chapter 8

8.2. 'Curfew pass issued to the author by the Moscow military authorities, October 1993' (author's own photograph). Chapter 8

8.3. 'The author with the Russian army in Chechnya, March 2000 (photo © Andrew Wilson)'. Chapter 8

8.4. Russian soldiers in Grozny, March 2000 (author's own photograph). Chapter 8

10.1. A Soviet-era crest of Lenin. Volgograd 2019 (author's own photograph). Chapter 10

Foreword by Martin Sixsmith

Many years ago, as a student in the Leningrad of the 1970s, I tried to get into the Soviet spirit. The cult of Lenin was big in those days and I liked the kitschy Lenin teapots and statues, the posters, the films, the Lenin poems and the sentimental Lenin songs. There was one in particular, sung by the Red Army Ensemble with an imposing *basso profundo* belting out the words. It was called 'Lenin Is Always with Us' and it reminded me of going to Liverpool games, standing on the Kop singing 'You'll Never Walk Alone.' If I tell you the words, you'll see why. 'Lenin is always with you,' sings the bass. 'In grief, in hope and joy,' sing the choir. 'Lenin is your springtime, Your every happy day. Lenin is always with us, Bringing joy to the world … ' 'Walk on through the wind, Walk on through the rain … ' (actually, I added that last bit). When I met my first Russian girlfriend we were living in a very communal student dormitory at the Leningrad Polytechnic. I asked if there was somewhere we could be alone, but she told me with a straight face that we could never be alone *potomu chto Lenin vsegda s nami* – because 'Lenin is always with us.'

Being a student in Leningrad was good for my Russian. It also gave me an ear for Soviet-speak – that grotesquely distinctive language used by the regime – and how to interpret it. It tipped me off that the Kremlin sometimes says things that are not strictly true. But I also learnt that with good Russian and a good ear; it is possible to see through the fibs. Most of my Russian friends were experts at it. They pretended – and everyone else pretended with them – that they believed the Kremlin's stories about the incomparable bliss of living under communism. But at the same time, everyone knew we were part of a charade involving two realities – the pure, perfect, socialist paradise we had to pretend we were living in; and the dreadful, miserable, impoverished reality we saw around us.

As James Rodgers points out, some Western correspondents have gone to Russia without acquiring that ear for the truth. The most famous of them, Walter Duranty of *The New York Times*, swallowed Stalin's fairy-tale of Soviet plenty, progress and happiness. It won him a Pulitzer Prize and made him a celebrity in the inter-war years. But it came at a cost. Duranty closed his eyes to the reality of poverty, repression and terror that surrounded him. While Malcolm Muggeridge and Gareth Jones were reporting the famine sweeping Russia and Ukraine, the hundreds of thousands of deaths and the cannibalism, Duranty pandered to pro-Soviet Western liberal opinion and didn't.

It was great news for the regime. Duranty was one of those whom Lenin dubbed his 'useful idiots'. Others included HG Wells, Sidney and Beatrice Webb, and George Bernard Shaw. All of them lauded the USSR for ideological reasons, disillusioned with their capitalist homelands or eager to believe the rosy promises of the socialist utopia. From the revolutions of 1917 to the era of Vladimir Putin, James Rodgers convincingly identifies the motives and failures of those who have too readily believed what they have been told.

As the BBC correspondent in Moscow in the 1980s and 1990s, I tried to spot the Kremlin's lies. 'There are no cases of AIDS in the USSR', they said; but I had met the men who were dying of it. 'The Jews do not want to emigrate'; I knew scores of refuseniks. 'There is no fighting between Armenians and Azeris'; I had witnessed it. 'The Russian mafia is a figment of Western propaganda'; we had been threatened by them. The list was quite long.

In most countries, the media can be a bit of a luxury because there are other ways of discovering the truth. But Russia is different. Russia has been a closed society, in which the Kremlin controls the sources of information. Newspapers, radio and television have been enlisted to serve the state. Before the internet, photocopiers, printers, supplies of paper and carbon paper were obsessively guarded. It made foreign journalists important. Domestic journalists who knew the truth couldn't print it, but foreign journalists could. The problem was that too many of them didn't. In some cases it was a language problem – the Kremlin isn't going to volunteer its secrets to you, and good luck if you're trying to discover them without Russian; it can be a problem of hubris – men like Duranty enjoyed the pats on the back from the Kremlin; or in some cases a problem of professional laziness. Whatever the reason, it mattered.

It mattered because Western journalists have long been the principal way the West has learnt about Russia. In my experience, Western diplomats – who're meant to be finding out the truth for themselves – all too often rely on friendly chats with Western correspondents, then echo their findings back to their governments. As James Rodgers demonstrates, the reporting of Western journalists has had a disproportionate effect in forming people's ideas of the place.

Today, oddly, the journalistic pendulum has swung. Where Duranty and Co. could see no bad in Russia, Western correspondents now declare they can see *no good at all* in anything the Kremlin does and *no truth at all* in anything the Kremlin says. They heap opprobrium on the Putin regime until it reaches comical levels of outrage. Why? Partly because Neo-con Western governments promote their own extremist agenda by sharpening the contrast with Moscow's. It shapes the media to rail against Putin and – like Duranty and the Blockheads in the last century – the media have become the Useful Idiots in ours. When the then British Defence Secretary, Gavin Williamson, told Russia to 'just go away and shut up', he did so with zero knowledge or understanding of Russia. But much of the British press was happy to pander to his inflammatory incompetence. If correspondents go to Moscow with a preconceived agenda in their knapsack, their reports are sure to reinforce the politicians' bile.

Don't get me wrong. There are bad things in Russia. I detest the trampling on civil rights and the pressure applied to opposition voices. We should condemn this. We should absolutely condemn the criminality, the murder of journalists and former spies. But we should recognize that there are worse regimes around the world with whom we happily talk and trade and back-slap.

And it is to our detriment. Russia rarely responds to pressure; there is a Russian machismo that stops them bowing the knee. The Kremlin's campaign of destabilization against the West is a response to this. Much better to negotiate with Moscow – from a position of strength, but recognizing nonetheless the issues that unite us rather than divide us. We have a shared European heritage and history, a shared culture and many shared values. As James Rodgers demonstrates, the best Moscow correspondents have understood this and used that understanding to tell Russia's story. Russia and the West should be prioritizing the problems we could tackle together – international 'Islamic' terrorism, the refugee crisis, the march of global warming that will one day send millions fleeing north to our shores. Together, we could do something; divided, we each shoot ourselves in the foot.

–Martin Sixsmith

Introduction

In our age, telling stories is more prized than ever before – yet those who tell them are increasingly despised. The same governments who spend huge sums of money on public relations companies, and international television channels, at the same time act aggressively towards journalists who seek to communicate news that is more challenging, nuanced or substantial. Journalism has also seen its economic models fail, and yet we need more than ever to understand a world where politics and technology are rapidly changing, and changing our lives.

Few countries have experienced such great change over the last three decades as Russia. In 1990, the Union of Soviet Socialist Republics was still a superpower. Its grip on its socialist neighbours in Europe had weakened as the last century approached its final decade, but Moscow still bore the banner of Marxism–Leninism, as it had since the end of Tsarist Russia during the First World War. In Mikhail Gorbachev, the Soviet Union had a leader who believed that its creaking system could be reformed and made fit for purpose. It could not. Russia went rapidly from communism to a brutal form of capitalism, just as, at the dawn of the Soviet era, it had gone from an absolute monarchy to revolutionary socialism. Journalism thrives on what is changing, on what is new. Russia has frequently given the outside world plenty to think about.

Relatively few Westerners, however, have ever been to Russia to see it for themselves. Those who did in Communist times often went with sympathies for the system. So did some of the correspondents: open about their own political sympathies with the Soviets. Not all of them found that sympathy survived the experience. Other correspondents went because they were fascinated by Russia's history, language, culture or politics – some simply because it was a time in their career when they were seeking a new challenge, and Russia offered it. Yet they all offered perspectives which few outsiders could gain for themselves. Travelling to Russia from Western Europe or the United States has never been as simple as a holiday to a neighbouring country. Distance is only one obstacle. Politics has usually managed to place many more in the way in the form of visa requirements and other bureaucracy. Moscow correspondents, then, have often tended to see and experience that which their compatriots could not. In consequence, their accounts and analysis have tended disproportionately to influence views of the world's biggest country.

Journalism and history

I first went to Russia in 1987 as a language student. I arrived in Leningrad, then the Soviet Union's second city. I first went as a journalist four years later, in the summer of 1991 – the year that Leningrad would change its name, and the Soviet Union cease to exist – as a producer for the television news agency, Visnews. Visnews later became Reuters Television. For Reuters Television, I returned to live in Moscow from 1992 to 1993, when I produced the news coverage for GMTV, then the Breakfast news programme on the UK's main commercial channel, ITV. I joined the BBC in 1995 and was frequently assigned to Russia, covering stories such as the first Chechen war, the 1995 Duma elections and the 1996 presidential elections. I returned to live in Moscow in 1998, working there until 2000 as a BBC producer and reporter. From 2006 to 2009, I was BBC correspondent in Moscow.

This book is not a memoir. I refer to my own journalism only where I believe it contributes to the larger story which I am trying to tell, and where I think reflection on my own work as a journalist may illustrate useful points for readers especially interested in understanding the practice of journalism, in particular, Journalism students.

The biggest challenge in writing this book has been trying to tell a clear story from a vast quantity of sources. More news material and correspondent memoirs have been produced on Russia since the start of the Soviet period than any one person could ever possibly hope to read – and that is just in English. Although I read and have read a lot of history, as I believe any journalist covering international affairs should, I am not a historian. My undergraduate degree was in Modern Languages, my PhD, by prior publication, in Journalism and Media. I have not therefore tried to compete with works of history, so much as to offer an additional perspective. I am indebted to Professor Robert Service's *A History of Modern Russia*, to which, as readers will see, I refer for historical background to the news stories I discuss. Other works of history on which I have drawn are listed in the bibliography. The approach I have taken evolves through the book, depending on the sources available to me. Thus, the opening chapters draw on newspaper reports from the time; correspondent memoirs (the vast number of these which have been published throughout history is a measure of how great audiences' interest in Russia has been); and unpublished archives such as letters and memoranda exchanged between correspondents, editors and others. The archives I have consulted are mentioned in the acknowledgements and listed in the bibliography. For the later chapters, I have been able to draw on the same sources just listed and interviews with former Moscow correspondents. These interviews relate the experience of working in the Russian capital from the 1950s until the present day. From the early 1990s onwards, I have also been able to use my own experience, too. Having been away from Russia for almost a decade after finishing my last correspondent posting there in 2009, I was fortunate enough (thanks to a generous grant from the Society of Authors, and to a period of sabbatical leave from the Department of Journalism at City, University of London) to be able to return for a visit in March 2019, when I travelled to Moscow, Volgograd and Saint Petersburg.

It is in Russia's former, imperial, capital that the book begins. Chapter 1 considers the coverage of Russia's revolutionary year of 1917, and the bitter differences of opinion – and, in some cases, wishful thinking, it provoked among correspondents and editors who found themselves witnessing, and writing about, events that would affect the whole of the coming century. Chapter 2 covers Russia's post-revolutionary conflict, a period which saw Western journalists themselves drawn to take sides and to draw sharply differing conclusions from what they reported. The third chapter looks at one of the most controversial chapters in the history of Western reporting of Russia: the coverage, or lack of it, of the famine which accompanied agricultural reform under Stalin. The following chapter tells the story of the way that the Show Trials of Stalin's enemies, real or imagined, were covered: a spectacle designed to make an impression not only on the Soviet public, but also on the international press.

Chapter 5 covers the reporting from Russia of the Second World War: a pivotal moment in relations between communist and capitalist allies against Nazi Germany. With few exceptions, however – the aftermath of Soviet victory at Stalingrad being one – Western correspondents were kept at a distance from the action – perhaps with lasting consequences for Western understanding of the Soviet role in a victory which has become a sacred memory in contemporary Russia.

Chapter 6 considers the period after the war when relations between Russia and the West so rapidly soured, and the Western press corps dwindled in number as restrictions placed upon them made the value of keeping a correspondent there at all open to question.

The three chapters which follow cover the years when Russia underwent the transition from communism to where it is today, under the successive leadership of Mikhail Gorbachev, who would be the last leader of the USSR; Boris Yeltsin, Russia's first president and first post-Soviet occupant of the Kremlin; and Vladimir Putin's first decade at the top of Russian politics. That last era is, of course, one which continues today – and which has seen the optimism which greeted the end of the Cold War buried in the past as that conflict itself once was.

Each of those periods, from the 1980s until today, saw significantly different conditions for Western journalists working in Russia: their treatment by the Russian authorities symptomatic of the Kremlin's relations with the West at any given time. Under Gorbachev, that meant extended, but still limited, freedom – and occasions when the Western media could be played for internal Soviet political purposes. Under Yeltsin, it was 'free for all', the only limits being, especially in the midst of the haphazard slaughter of the military campaign against Chechen separatists, the correspondent's own courage and sense of danger. Chapter 9 examines the coverage of the major stories of Putin's first two terms as president and concludes with Russia's war with Georgia in 2008 – a conflict during which Russia pioneered media management techniques which, I will argue, have their more sophisticated successors today. It being too early to offer a conclusive version of Russia's treatment of the British and American news media in the Putin era, Chapter 10 takes the form of an essay identifying continuity and change in the experience of Western correspondents reporting on Russia today.

The men and women who have been drawn to report on Russia have told the story of a country known to relatively few outsiders. I argue therefore that British and American reporting of Russia has had a disproportionate influence on the formation of audiences' views of the country. That reporting has hardly been flawless. Yet at its best it has offered insights and expertise which are sometimes lacking in career politicians. The suggestion from the former British Defence Secretary, Gavin Williamson, in March 2018 that Russia 'should go away and shut up'[1] was an example. The journalists who have reported on Russia have not all been experts, but they have often been motivated by a desire to understand other countries which is sometimes lacking in career politicians – especially those who have made up their minds about a place while knowing little of it, and, in consequence, having little idea how to influence it.

As relations between Russia and the West – and my country, the United Kingdom, in particular – have worsened, so Russia has increasingly been seen as good or bad, more frequently the latter. In 2015, The *Guardian* published a letter in which I had written that President Putin's administration had used the Baltic states' admission into NATO to 'fuel his popularity'.[2] A few days later, I received an email from producer at China Central Television's American channel, asking me if I wanted to take part in a discussion about 'Putin the peacemaker'. I agreed, while also explaining that I did not agree that Putin used 'the appearance of strength to forge peace'. I heard no more. Merely by commenting on NATO expansion, I had been taken for a Putin apologist. As a correspondent in Russia, I tried to tell the story as fully as possible, reflecting as many views as possible, and never confining myself to one camp of opinion or another. This book hopes to contribute to a more nuanced and contextual understanding of the story of Russia. Both the country and those who want to learn about it deserve that.

James Rodgers
Chiswick, November 2019

A note on transliteration.

For transliteration from Russian to English, I have tried generally to follow Library of Congress Transliteration rules. There are exceptions. Where there is a recognized form in standard use in English, I have tended to use that: for example, the Russian forename Александр is rendered not as Aleksandr, but as Alexander, and the name of the last leader of the USSR as Gorbachev, not Gorbachëv.

Sympathies in the struggle: Reporting Russia in revolution, 1917

Christ the Saviour told the story of Russia's century. Blown up by the Bolsheviks in 1931, the cathedral on the banks of the Moscow River had been rebuilt in the 1990s, under the presidency of Boris Yeltsin – a former Communist party boss who came to play a crucial role in the collapse of the Soviet Union. Yeltsin's coffin now lay inside the cathedral, where his funeral service was shortly to begin. It was 25 April 2007. Some of us Moscow correspondents had been allowed to enter that morning, before the ceremony. Inside the white walls, bright in spring sunshine, and beneath the golden domes, I had seen the wreaths sent by mourners. There was one from the domestic security service, the FSB.[1] This successor to the Soviet secret police had outlived the president who had sought to curb their power. In Vladimir Putin, they now had one of their own in the Kremlin. For a city of some 10 million people, the crowds who came to mourn, or just to watch, were sparse. Many more had come the previous year to see a Holy relic saved from the godless Communists who would eventually destroy the cathedral. The relic was the hand of John the Baptist. It had been saved by the Dowager Empress Maria Fyodorovna, mother of the last Tsar of Russia. Months after the relic drew such crowds – queues hundreds of metres long, a wait of many hours – the remains of the Empress herself were returned to Russia, to be reburied alongside those of her son, Nicholas II; daughter-in-law, Empress Alexandra; and some of her grandchildren.

The ceremony for Maria Fyodorovna took place in late September in 2006, with the first distant hints of the Russian winter in the damp air. The service was held in St Isaac's cathedral in St Petersburg. Almost ninety years earlier, a revolution had swept the Dowager Empress' son from power. She fled to her native Denmark. The revolutionaries shot her son, daughter-in-law and grandchildren.

In the early afternoon, as I rushed to my hotel room to edit a report for the BBC's
One o'clock News,[2] I tried to think of how to do justice, in a short news story, to
all the history that city had seen, and of which I had been reminded during that
brief visit: the Winter Palace, now the Hermitage Museum – at anchor in the
river Neva, the *Aurora*, the ship which had fired the shot giving the Bolsheviks
the signal to seize power. Approaching deadlines always give a burst of nervous
energy, especially when, as that day, time is short. There was something extra
then: something about being in St Petersburg. The story concerned the fate
of just one of the millions of people – albeit one of the more prominent ones
– whose lives had been forever changed by the revolution of 1917. With each
step, the deadline drew nearer. I started drafting my script in my head, but other
thoughts flashed up, too. What would my counterparts who had covered the
revolution have made of what had happened that day? The matriarch of the
Imperial family, mother of an emperor the revolutionaries reviled as a tyrant,
honoured with great ceremony – in the city where the revolution began. What
would they have made of the tabloid hacks not interested so much in the reburial,
but in whether Crown Princess Mary of Denmark, there to represent the Danish
Royal Family, was pregnant? (She was). Editorial priorities aside, Russia was still
a country which inspired fear and fascination among first-time visitors, and the
reporters and photographers from the Danish gossip magazines fell mostly into
that category. They were the latest of successive waves Western journalists who
had headed east to see and to tell. In doing so, they had helped to shape the
relationship between Russia and the West: ideological adversaries in the Cold
War, allies in two world wars.

During the first of those colossal conflicts, the world that the Dowager
Empress Maria Fyodorovna knew was torn apart around her. Sensing that change
was near, dozens of foreign correspondents were in Russia's imperial capital. At
the same time as it was fighting the First World War, Russia was struggling with
political reforms unprecedented in its history. Those reforms, which followed
the bloodshed of an earlier revolution, in 1905, were hamstrung by the fact
that, for the parties involved, 'the new order' was 'a deviation from the country's
true system, which for the monarchy was autocracy and for the intelligentsia, a
democratic republic'.[3] The Tsar-Emperor's distaste for the parliament, the Duma,
was evident. It took him ten years to bring himself to cross the threshold of
the Tauride Palace where the assembly sat.[4] In the twentieth century, Nicholas
II was still a firm believer in the divine right of kings. This tension was not
lost on those watching the Russian political system, which finally ripped apart
under the strain. 'In Petrograd, early in 1917, everybody felt that a revolution

was impending,'[5] wrote *The Times*' correspondent, Robert Wilton, in his memoir published the following year. John Reed's *Ten Days That Shook the World*, as he called his account of the October revolution which brought the Bolsheviks to power, was still months away, but the end of centuries of autocracy was at hand. The correspondents saw a huge story coming.

Yet when the revolution came – with the abdication of Tsar Nicholas II on the morning of 2 March 1917[6] – Wilton and his colleagues found themselves cut off. Telegraph links with the outside world were severed. An American photographer, Donald Thompson, who had taken on this hazardous assignment promising to write every day to his wife in Kansas, got a warning of what was coming. On 8 March, he wrote that at the telegraph station, 'the old lady in charge […] told me not to waste my money – that nothing was allowed to go out'.[7] No telegraph meant no reports for the newspapers to print. That meant no news. It is almost impossible for us to picture a time when readers were reliant on printed papers for *news*. The results of exclusive investigations are an exception, of course – but who now looks to a printed paper for the headlines of a prime ministerial speech; a transport catastrophe; or a football result? It was not so in 1917. In fact, it is remarkable how little newsgathering had changed in the preceding century.[8] Just two days before it was to celebrate the revolution in its news and editorial pages, the *Daily Mail* was stuck with the headline 'NO NEWS FROM PETROGRAD YESTERDAY'. The news story which followed was barely fifty words, beginning, 'Up to a late hour last night the Russian official report, which for many months has come to hand early, had not been received.'[9]

It must have been infuriating. One senses the editors' frustration in the words 'up to a late hour'. All the hapless writer was able to do, having presumably hung around until the latest deadline vainly hoping for a story, was to hint to the readers, by means of the words 'which for many months has come to hand early', that something out of the ordinary was underway. The reader was left to guess what that might be. For the American papers, the challenge was even greater. In the absence of any news by telegraph from Russia, they were reduced to reporting the fact that the *Daily Mail*, and other London papers, said there was no news. The 'Up to a late hour' non-story even formed the lead paragraph of *The New York Times* report, headlined 'Petrograd silent; London mystified'.[10]

All this at a moment when the rest of the world – in particular, Russia's First World War allies against Germany – was desperate for news. When communication was restored, the Reuters correspondent in Petrograd cast aside all pretence at impartiality, knowing that, to a country weighed down by war and winter, one thing mattered above all. The Reuters special report, carried on the front page of the *Daily Express* and in *The Manchester Guardian* and the *Daily Mirror* on 16 March, began:

> The first duty of a British correspondent in these days of national upheaval is to assure his compatriots that 'Russia is all right' as a friend, ally, and fighter. The very trials she is undergoing will only steel her heart and arms.[11]

When Petrograd emerged from the silence, the emperor was gone from his throne. Russia was taking the first steps along a road which would only fuel further the fascination which Western correspondents already had for the vast land on Europe's eastern edge. Once they could, the newspapers made the most of what their correspondents sent – the delays evident from the datelines. The despatch cited above was datelined in the *Express*, 'Petrograd, March 13th, received yesterday'. Reassuring readers that Russia would remain committed to the cause of war with Germany was a priority. In another delayed despatch from the streets of Russia's revolutionary capital, the *Mirror* told its readers on 20 March, 'The workmen express the determination to employ themselves on overtime in order to make up for all the work that has been lost, and are loud in declaring their intention of carrying on the war to victory.'[12] *The Manchester Guardian* expressed even greater optimism: 'England hails the new Russia with a higher hope and surer confidence in the future not only of this war, but of the world.'[13] Drawing mainly on London newspapers and other sources in the British capital at this early stage, *The New York Times* was caught up in the same bullish mood. Their despatch reported the belief in London that the new government's policy would mean 'the uninterruptedly vigorous prosecution of the war to a victorious end'.[14]

Amidst the optimism – and the wishful thinking was understandable – there were already signs that the assurances to compatriots that Russia was 'all right' might be premature and ultimately inaccurate. Hard news was hard to come by and dangerous to gather. The Petrograd press corps of that time contained some correspondents whose knowledge of Russia, and fluency in its language, was peerless – Harold Williams especially excelled in this latter category. As with so many massive international stories, there were also correspondents, like Thompson, who were new in town. Thompson – who spoke no Russian – relied on Boris, 'a Russian boy who was working at the American Embassy in 1915'[15] to be his 'fixer', as modern journalistic slang would have it. Thompson used Boris to help him interpret not only the language, but what he saw around him. In one of his letters to his wife, Thompson gave an account of the activities of an apparent agent provocateur, a 'Secret Service man', dressed as a worker, 'who was deliberately smashing windows' and 'trying to push soldiers'.[16]

Faced with the constant threat of an explosion of violence, Thompson was resourceful. He became a pioneer of secret filming, saying at one point that he concealed his camera in a bag, in which he had cut a hole, so he could 'get pictures with this gyroscopic camera of mine without anyone knowing what I am doing'.[17] This was a wise move. To walk the streets of the revolutionary capital was to risk your life. Death came violently and suddenly to officers as their soldiers switched sides. An Associated Press despatch from earlier in the week gave such dramatic detail that it received a good run in *The Manchester Guardian* and *The Daily Mirror* despite being days old. 'Regiments called out to disperse street crowds clamouring for bread refused to fire upon the people, mutinied, and (slaying their officers in many cases) joined the swelling ranks of the insurgents,'[18] ran one of its top paragraphs.

As his paper luxuriated in the restoration of communication, *The Times'* correspondent was permitted almost 6,000 words for a story headlined 'History of the Movement'. Even so, in introducing this 'remarkable series of despatches,'[19] *The Times* was forced to admit that 'we are still without news of the first outbreak'. In other words, they were printing what they had, but they were missing the very beginning. Indeed, the first section of the article – headlined, perhaps misleadingly in the light of the admission noted above, 'The First Volley' – the correspondent begins 'The events of Friday were multiplied manifold yesterday.'[20] Robert Wilton was the correspondent at that time although, in keeping with the common convention of the age, he was not given a by-line. His narrative unfolded in a mixture of crisp, tightly written, copy which would be completely at home in a news agency report a century later, and the occasional Edwardian-era flourish. Wilton was born in 1868, so, given that when he covered the world-changing events in Petrograd that year he was almost fifty, it is not surprising that he retained in places some of the approach of a more verbose period in the history of journalism. Once the piece got going, he matched his colleague from the Associated Press for drama and a sense of danger. His punchier lines made his story race along even if the passive voice might jar with some modern editors. 'Warnings not to assemble were disregarded. No Cossacks were visible.' Then Wilton was right at the heart of the action

> as the armoured cars, which all appear to be in the hands of the revolutionaries, have been dashing through the streets around *The Times* office, fusillading the Government machine guns, all attempts to get from one place to another were attended with the greatest risk.[21]

Wilton's account suggested that he made every effort to get around the city even so. His reporting combined accounts of the chaotic danger of armed insurgency with moments of diplomatic nicety. He tells readers that he 'had just called on Sir George Buchanan' – then the British ambassador, who, perhaps rather embarrassingly, had just been on holiday – and 'was walking through the Summer Gardens when the bullets began to whiz over my head'. While even today *The Times*' delight at receiving such colourful eyewitness reportage after days of nothing can easily be imagined, the paper's coverage remained focused on the main reason why the events in Petrograd were so closely followed in London. The shorter piece leading into Wilton's day-by-day account reported that Andrew Bonar Law, then a member of the war cabinet, had explained to the House of Commons that the revolution 'was not an effort to secure peace, but an expression of discontent with the Russian government for not carrying on the war with efficiency and energy'. This may have been reassuring to the political establishment and others involved in the war effort. It also, given the Bolsheviks' later, and ultimate, revolutionary success with slogans such as 'Peace-Bread-Land', suggests a good deal of wishful thinking. Nowhere do the correspondents of the time communicate the sense that offering to prosecute the war more vigorously would gain the revolutionaries greater popular support. Instead, bread supplies seem to be at the heart of the violent day-to-day struggle for existence – suggesting that the Bolsheviks understood the people's wants and priorities all too well.

The *Daily Mail*'s wait for news over, it too triumphantly published the 'Full Story of the Revolution'[22] on Friday, 16 March. A series of reports, as in *The Times*, were published together – with readers informed at the beginning that the section datelined 'Saturday' (and presumably all that follows) was 'transmitted on Wednesday at 9.55am'. Again, the correspondent is not named, but may be assumed, on the basis of reports from the previous month, to be Henry Hamilton Fyfe. Fyfe was not troubled by the fact that walking around was 'attended by the greatest risk'. Unafraid to offer his view, he revelled in watching a revolution. Despatches from the weeks before the abdication of the Tsar frequently spoke of food shortages. This was a time when 'bread had to be queued for, and its availability was unreliable'.[23] As what little order remained broke down, Hamilton Fyfe reported that 'a baker's shop well known for its profiteering had its windows smashed, and the place looted'.[24] It turns out that 'large quantities of bread [were] being kept for richer and more fortunate customers'. Hamilton Fyfe was not shy about offering his opinion. 'Such conduct,' he concluded, 'when people have to stand from 5 till 11 o'clock in a queue deserves punishment.' Going around the city on Tuesday morning, he began 'to meet incongruous sights. Here a soldier, rifle-less but with an unsheathed officer's sword in hand, there a civilian carrying, somewhat gingerly, a rifle with fixed bayonet, and farther on a delighted youth with a carbine'. These examples, selected apparently at random, combine to suggest a pattern of incongruity. The autocracy is over; its systems are collapsing. Elsewhere in the same series of reports, Hamilton Fyfe described a confrontation between a group of newly rebellious soldiers and two officers on horseback. Threatened with firearms, the officers withdrew. 'This slight incident showed what was really happening,' Hamilton Fyfe told his readers. One confrontation became the whole reversal of the old order in miniature.

While there is plenty to admire in the reporting of Wilton, Hamilton Fyfe and others, there is one correspondent whose coverage of this first stage of Russia's most revolutionary year would have been truly fascinating to read. He was not, alas, in Petrograd. 'The March Revolution came like a thief in the night'[25] begins 'The Red Dawn in Moscow', the first chapter of Morgan Philips Price's *My Reminiscences of the Russian Revolution*. Philips Price was in the Caucasus. He returned to Petrograd only in April. As Eric Hobsbawm wrote in the introduction to the posthumous collection of Philips Price's *Dispatches from the Revolution*, 'Talking to peasants, merchants, soldiers, overhearing conversations on Volga boats, Price recorded what he correctly described as "the only true voice of Russia". And he got it right.'[26] His long association with the country – he had gone there originally to look after the interests of his family's timber business – had not only given him a profound understanding of the country and its language. It had also given him a deep sympathy for the revolutionary cause – one that would eventually cost him not only newspaper space, but his correspondent career. Bernard Pares, the pioneering traveller in, and student of, Russia, knew Philips Price then and would later write: 'He took the virus of Bolshevism in the regulation way, suddenly and fanatically.'[27] This soon led Philips Price to confrontation with the Northcliffe papers – implacably anti-Bolshevik – in general and with Wilton in particular. Not long after his return to Petrograd, Philips Price wrote of the 'abominable behaviour of the Northcliffe Press ... especially of its correspondent, Wilton' – even expressing the hope 'the Russian people ... will turn [him] out of Petrograd'.[28] Wilton's work was not only infuriating some. It was worrying others. On 1 May, John Buchan (subsequently known much better as a novelist, then working for British government war propaganda) sent a note to the editor of *The Times*, G.G. (George Geoffrey) Dawson. 'The situation in Russia is very delicate,' Buchan wrote, 'and I cannot think that Wilton's cables and articles have always

Morgan Philips Price (Getty).

been very discreet. Would it be possible for you to keep an eye on him, and perhaps give him a hint?'[29] Attracting this kind of official attention may have been one of the reasons that Wilton was to have difficulties with the British authorities the following year.

The reporters privileged with a front row seat at this particular moment in history formed wildly different conclusions of what they saw. The dedications which Philips Price and Wilton chose for their reflections on the revolution, published in 1921 and 1918 respectively, were a continuation of the war of words which had started when Philips Price wanted Wilton kicked out of Russia. Wilton dedicated his book, *Russia's Agony*, 'to my gallant friends the Cossacks and to the officers and men of the allied armies and navies who have fought in the cause of country and freedom'.[30] Philips Price's *My Reminiscences of the Russian Revolution* was 'to those leaders and to the rank and file who by speech, pen and action have defended the Soviet Republic of Russia against the onslaughts of the international bondholders'[31] – symptoms of the 'virus of Bolshevism'. Wilton and Philips Price's antagonistic views tell us at least two things, things which run through the history of Western reporting of Russia. Firstly, it seemed almost impossible for correspondents covering events which would come to shape the century to step back from them. They were engaged. Secondly, they did not seem concerned about it. Hamilton Fyfe's condoning, or even perhaps supporting, the looting which he witnessed at the hoarding bakery is another example. Both Wilton and Philips Price were clearly drawn into the drama they saw, and their impressions led them to side with opposing protagonists. The dedications of their books, though, strongly suggested that their engagement greatly influenced their writing. Their commitment to the cause was uppermost in their mind as they dedicated their work: rather than a commitment to the task of journalism or indeed to a loved one. Philips Price was aware of the challenges which he faced as a chronicler of the revolution. He writes in the preface to *My Reminiscences of the Russian Revolution*:

> It is generally recognized that a historian, if he claims to be impartial, must write some time after the events with which he is concerned. The Russian Revolution is still too near to the present to make it possible to see it in perspective.[32]

His reflection has a universal significance for the reporting of times of great change, revolutions in particular. Arthur Ransome – better known today as the author of children's books, then a correspondent in Russia for the *Daily News* – showed the same mixture of caution and self-justification in the introduction to *The Crisis in Russia*, published, like Price's *Reminiscences*, in 1921. Ransome had gone to Russia to write a guidebook to St Petersburg, a book of fairy tales, and to escape an unhappy marriage. In Russia, he fell in love with the woman who would be his second wife: Evgenia Shelepina – Trotsky's secretary.[33] 'No book is entirely objective,' Ransome informed his reader, 'so I do not in the least mind stating my own reason for writing this one.'[34] In Ransome's view, this was the duty which fell on 'every honest man, of whatever party' to 'do his utmost to postpone the conflict'[35] which Ransome feared was coming between communist Europe and capitalist Europe – a fear which would be all too well founded as the coming century wore on. Here again, engagement and the obligation to promote understanding, by almost instant analysis, were the correspondent's driving forces. While the historian may wait decades, even centuries, to gather evidence and reach conclusions, the journalist has no such luxury. Their advantage is to be there in the moment during the time of change; their disadvantage is they are supposed to make sense of it. Plenty more challenges lay ahead: challenges that would demand everything of correspondents' knowledge of country and language; their resourcefulness; courage; and commitment to their separate ideas of the direction that Russia should take. For a second revolution would shake Petrograd later the same year. In March, though, as relative calm returned to the capital after the end of the old regime, a Reuters correspondent reported the following scenes as he made his way through the city:

> Between two and three o'clock this afternoon men with ladders began moving the Imperial arms from public buildings and shops … The arms were mostly burned in the streets. Some were hurled on to the ice in the canals.

> There was a burst of cheering outside the Duma when a mounted troop bearing a flag on which was inscribed 'Long live the Socialist Republic of All Countries,' drew rein.[36]

The cheers for the cavalry carrying the socialist flag were a nice detail to add to a report. With hindsight, the despatch also hinted at what was to follow. Russia's revolution was not over.

Nor was the war, although Russia's participation in it would not last much longer. In June, a Russian offensive, aimed mainly at the southern front, failed. By this time, Bolshevism was widespread among certain units of the Russian Army. Agreeing with revolutionary propaganda which portrayed continuing the conflict as serving the interests of capitalists rather than combatants, many of the soldiers were ready to lay down their arms. The forces involved in the advance included 'The Women's Battalion of Death'. The battalion's Commander, Maria Bochkareva, hoped that the presence of her female troops 'would shame the rest of the soldiers into fighting'.[37] It did provide one of the few Western women journalists with a chance to get published in the New York *Evening Mail*. 'RUSSIAN GIRL SOLDIERS MEET WITH LOSSES: RHETA CHILDE DORR WITH DEATH LEGION.' The sexism of the age, however, dedicated that the story appeared under the by-line of a male colleague. The published story, which appeared on 28 July, 'had a two-paragraph lead-in by (William G.) Shepherd and 24 paragraphs of Dorr speaking directly about the battalion'.[38] One wonders if the courage which led Dorr to accompany the 'Death Legion' shamed some of her male counterparts in the way the Women's Battalion's martial efforts were supposed to shame theirs. In the event, for all her dedication to the campaign, one of Bochkareva's final acts in the offensive was to kill one of her soldiers she discovered having sex with a male comrade in a shell hole.[39] Faced with a German counter-attack, some of the Russian soldiers contented themselves with getting drunk on a supply of alcohol they found in an abandoned town.[40] The temptations of lust and strong drink only added to the weaknesses which revolutionary fervour and lack of commitment to the cause posed to morale. The June offensive was in effect Russia's last act in the First World War.

Readers of the newspapers at the time would have struggled to guess that. A Central News despatch in *The Financial Times* of 3 July spoke of the 'success' enjoyed in Galicia by 'well trained Russian troops of high moral standing'.[41] *The New York Times* of 3 July celebrated beneath a stacked headline which included 'Deed Thrills All Russia', 'the brilliant Russian advance'.[42] On 5 July, the *Daily Mail* celebrated in terms of the highest hyperbole 'The Russian Miracle', comparing the 'Offensive Surprise' to 'the miracle which rescued Russia and all of Europe from the greedy clutch of Napoleon in 1812'.[43] To give the newspaper its due, the same page did also carry a report in which the Russians admitted that one of their attacks had failed, but it was given nothing like the prominence bestowed on the account of the 'miracle'. The 'miracle' was one in which the politicians and people of allied countries had wanted to believe, much as they had wanted reassurance that the February revolution would not mean the end of Russia's involvement in the war, even though it eventually did. The Russian offensive had been 'generously supplied with guns and shells by the Allies'. As well as supplying weapons, they were also doing their bit in the propaganda war. 'Lies from London' is the headline used, again on the same page of the *Mail*, to dismiss suggestions circulating in Russia and believed to have their sources in London that 'the British working classes are wholeheartedly opposed to the continuance of the war' and other 'silly' reports.

Yet the true consequences of the offensive were to be played out not on the battlefield, but on the boulevards of St Petersburg. While *The Sunday Times* had, at the beginning of July, written of political manoeuvring in the Petrograd Soviet which amounted to 'a death blow at Leninist intrigues',[44] it was Alexander Kerensky, then minister of war, who had 'gambled and lost'[45] by launching the

failed offensive. Lenin and his Bolsheviks sensed blood. The uprising which
followed was provoked by the government's decision to send more units to
the front – serving the dual purpose of preparing to repel a German counter-
offensive and getting the troops – many of whom had strong Bolshevik
sympathies – out of the politically unstable capital. The troops did not want to
go. Soon the Bolsheviks 'were preparing for a decisive confrontation with the
provisional government'.[46] The newspapers were reluctant to believe that they
were acting independently. Lord Northcliffe's titles in particular were convinced
that Germany was behind the unrest which followed the failed offensive. In the
days that followed, 'manly cheering' of victories died down. Instead, the sounds
of gunfire rang out in the streets of the Russian capital. The proudly Bolshevik
sailors of the Kronstadt naval base 'came up the Neva' – the river which runs
through the city – 'in tugs' as the Daily Mail reported on 19 July under the
headlines 'German-made revolt in Russia' 'Anarchy in Petrograd'.[47] On the same
day, *The Times* blamed 'the Maximalists and the German reactionary agents,
whose tools the Maximalists are' for the unrest, declaring that 'M. Lenin and
his associates are the declared enemies of order'. The July days, as the events
came to be known, were a point of no return. The Bolsheviks – called then by
some Western observers, as in the extract above, the Maximalists (although John
Reed, that peerless chronicler of the October revolution, wrote that this was a
mistranslation[48]) – may not have seized power, but the 'decisive confrontation'
had begun. Historians of the revolution disagree on the extent to which Lenin
actually planned to seize power during the unrest of July 1917. Orlando Figes
quotes Grigory Zinoviev recalling Lenin 'hopelessly paralysed by indecision'.[49]
Richard Pipes, on the other hand, judged the uprising 'Lenin's worst blunder'[50]
and argued that the Bolshevik origin of the attempted seizure of power has
since been covered up 'to absolve themselves of responsibility' for an enterprise
which failed. Northcliffe's reporters, without the advantage of hindsight which
the historians enjoy, preferred to see a German-inspired coup attempt carried
out by their proxies. In any event, it was a hugely exciting time to be covering
revolutionary Russia and the greatest of the writers who reported that world-
changing year was about to arrive on the scene.

John Reed will always have some of the glamour of the rock star or poet
who died young. He left behind a book, *Ten Days That Shook the World*, which
continues to influence the way that one of the most significant events of the
twentieth century is understood. He was just thirty-three when, on a journey
through the ruins of the Russian empire, he contracted the typhus which killed
him. He was buried in the wall of the Kremlin – a rare honour for a foreigner.

Reed's early death meant he never had to offer a view on what the revolution became – so he never had to decide, or to declare publicly, whether the murderous violence of Stalin's Soviet Union, the police state that the USSR was to become for so much of its existence, was to be justified or condemned. Stalin, indeed, is a marginal character in Reed's book, whereas Trotsky, vilified for most of the Soviet period, is central to the action. The official Soviet loathing of Trotsky was so complete – visiting the USSR as a student even in 1987, I remember one of my group asking our guide about Trotsky, and being told he was 'an enemy of the people' – that Reed's 'book was banned along with its hero'.[51]

Reed influenced history, and those who made it, in a way few journalists ever have. In the introduction, Lenin wrote that he had read *Ten Days That Shook the World* 'with never-slackening attention'. Sergei Eistenstein's 1927 film, *October*, released to remember and to record the revolution on its tenth anniversary, used Reed's book as a source and borrowed its title for part of its own. In the absence of documentary footage of the actual events of the Bolshevik's seizure of power, it is this cinematic account which provided the twentieth century with the enduring moving images of an event which was to shape it to such a great extent. Its opening sequence, in which members of a revolutionary crowd attach ropes to a statue of a tsar in order to pull it down, seems to set the standard imagery for a televised revolution long before the medium existed. Yet to someone watching *October* today, the scenes of the solid monument finally succumbing to rebellious muscles cannot but bring to mind the end of the system whose dawn *October* celebrates. As the tsar was dragged crashing down in 1917, so was Lenin in the 1990s. In Ukraine, there was another round of goodbye Lenin in 2014 as that country found itself on the frontline of the latest historical confrontation between East and West. In between, Saddam Hussein was wrenched from many of his numerous pedestals. In the late twentieth and early twenty-first centuries you could not have a revolution without television pictures of statues being pulled down. Reed may have died before the television age, but his account of 1917 inspired the great twentieth-century cinematographer to define the terms which television would use to break the news of future revolutions.

John Reed arrived in Petrograd between revolutions. He was not there at the time of the February revolution, but he was there to see the Bolsheviks seize power later that year. Reed's enduring reputation is built on *Ten Days That Shook the World*. It has tended to eclipse his other work. What remains of that, though, suggests a talent reaching well beyond his account of the October revolution. In his preface to *Ten Days That Shook the World*, Reed warns his reader, 'In the struggle, my sympathies were not neutral'.[52] Reed did not himself come from the class which he championed. He was educated at Harvard, already determined to be a writer. Even some of the titles of the poems he wrote while an undergraduate presage his involvement in the revolution. Among them are 'October' and 'Aurore'. The latter was written in the first hours of New Year's Day, 1908 – but his use of the Latin word echoes now with 'Aurora', the name of the Russian warship whose Bolshevik crew fired the shot that was the signal for the uprising to begin. Reed writes of encountering sailors from the '*Avrora* and *Zaria Svobody** – the names of the leading Bolshevik cruisers of the Baltic Fleet'[53] on Nevsky Prospect, Petrograd's main street. Despite his education at an elite university, Reed had long supported left-wing causes. In the view of the twentieth-century campaigning journalist Paul Foot, Reed's experience of covering a strike in New Jersey in the years before the First World War left him convinced 'that there were two sides to every story, and he eagerly ranged himself on the side of exploited people everywhere'.[54] This engagement with the injustices of the world in which he worked as a correspondent inspired him as he sought to expose them.

Before arriving in Petrograd, Reed had already been covering the First World War from both sides. Taken by the Germans in 1915 on what correspondents would now call a 'facility' in occupied France, Reed uses the officers' rudeness and cruelty towards conscripts to reflect more widely on the fate of soldiers in the war. 'I should not care to live half frozen in a trench, up to my middle in water, for three or four months, because someone in authority said I ought to shoot Germans,'[55] he says of the conditions in which he sees the French Army fighting. The Russian Army, 'knouted into battle for a cause they never heard of, appeals to me even less,'[56] the experience had left him bitter and angry. 'There is no such thing as "a moderate army" or "an army of defence."'[57] Reed travelled to Petrograd with his wife, Louise Bryant, who was also a journalist. They stayed initially at the Hotel Angleterre, then, in a transition common to the correspondent working for organizations with more modest budgets than the bigger ones, moved to a private house.[58] The British and American press corps in Petrograd were already substantial: Ransome and Philips Price were there, as were Albert Rhys Williams of the *New York Post*; Arno Dosch-Fleurot of the *New York World* (of whom the new arrival, Donald Thompson wrote, 'He does not know what to think of the situation, although he fears serious trouble is at hand. I think he knows a lot that he is keeping to himself.'[59]); Gregory Yarros of the *Associated Press*; and Bessie Beatty of the *San Francisco Bulletin*.[60]

What is striking about *Ten Days That Shook the World*, almost a century after it first appeared, is the energy which it still radiates. Knowing, as we do, what

---

* The second ship's name means 'Dawn of Freedom.'

followed Reed's blissful dawn – Stalin's purges; the costly Soviet victory in the Second World War; the terminal economic paralysis of Marxism–Leninism – it is perhaps hard to share his enthusiasm to the extent to which he displays it. There is much to admire in the text, however. Reed takes pains to give his reader as detailed a political background as he can. The characteristics of the various branches of Russia's revolutionary movement may only be of interest to the specialist historian these days, but the fact that Reed was able to describe them in the way he did speaks of an impressive command of detail. That exists alongside a peerless talent for reportage. What a combination; what a rare combination. Consider this passage about a rally of revolutionaries:

> The meeting took place between the gaunt brick walls of a huge unfinished building, ten thousand black-clothed men and women packed around a scaffolding draped in red, people heaped on piles of lumber and bricks, perched high up on shadowy girders, intent and thunder-voiced. Through the dull, heavy sky now and again burst the sun, flooding reddish light through the skeleton windows upon the mass of simple faces upturned to us.[61]

No wonder Eisenstein used the book as a source. This is literary journalism as cinema, right down to the lighting effect of the sun 'flooding reddish light' onto the faces of the crowd. Reed knows that he is living in extraordinary times. In normal times, people do not perch high up on the 'shadowy girders' of 'a huge unfinished building'. This is a moment of destiny: 'thunder-voiced' seems even to suggest the intervention of a Zeus-like figure, with whose support the cause cannot fail. This is further reinforced by the bursts of sunlight, appropriately 'reddish' like the revolution.

The night that finally came, Reed wrote about the Smolny, 'in Tsarist days a seminary for young girls of good family,'[62] as Bruce Lockhart described it. Reed managed to get there only after paying over the odds for a cab (the first driver refuses the fare because of the 'devils' in the Smolny) and walking the last two blocks.

> The windows of Smolny were still ablaze, motors came and went, and around the still-leaping fires the sentries huddled close, eagerly asking everybody the latest news. The corridors were full of hurrying men, hollow-eyed and dirty. In some of the committee-rooms people lay sleeping on the floor, their guns beside them. In spite of the seceding delegates, the hall of meetings was crowded with people roaring like the sea.[63]

The tension of the moment comes across in the windows 'still ablaze', in the cars' arrivals and departure. Even the sentries' fires are 'still-leaping' – the people around them 'eagerly asking everybody the latest news'. This is how a revolution must be written, especially one which the writer supports so unquestioningly. Reed was honest with his reader when he wrote of his own sympathies in the struggle. As the Bolshevik seizure of power succeeds, Reed is carried away by the crowd, 'Suddenly, by common impulse, we found ourselves on our feet, mumbling together into the smooth lifting unison of the *Internationale*. A grizzled old soldier was sobbing like a child.' It was cinema on a page, designed to carry the reader with it like an audience at the cinematic moment of emotional release when the good cause overcomes adversity – and triumphs. Reed's self-knowledge when he warns his reader of his own sympathies is astute. Not limiting his revolutionary fervour to joining in the *Internationale*, at one point he even talks of arms being 'distributed to us, revolvers and rifles'.[64] While some Western correspondents may have carried weapons for their own protection in more recent conflicts, none has written about taking up arms for a cause, as this in effect was. Reed was not troubled by this, and the detail was dropped in almost casually. Perhaps by this stage – it is relatively late in the book – he felt that he had brought his reader along with him to the extent that they would not be shocked and might even approve the action.

How then should we judge Reed today? Can we? That he was a great writer is surely beyond dispute. He was also influential. His book has a preface from Lenin. Trotsky (who, if his *History of the Russian Revolution* is anything to go by, was a pretty good writer himself) uses him a source on the opinions of the 'diplomatic agents of the Entente' and on the 'frank confessions of the Russian bourgeois politicians'.[65] Access does not get any better than this, when it leads a journalist to be cited by one of the main actors in the story which they are covering. Yet it is Reed's access and his attitude to the cause he is writing about which must be at the heart of how we should see him today. The twentieth-century historian A. J. P. Taylor was in 1964 invited to write an introduction to *Ten Days That Shook the World*. His assessment displeased the Communist Party of Great Britain, which then held the copyright to the book.[66] The parties could not agree and, as a result, Taylor's introduction did not appear in print until 1977, once the copyright had expired. Taylor praised *Ten Days That Shook the World* as, 'not only the best account of the Bolshevik revolution, it comes near to being the best account of any revolution'.[67] Taylor, though, was perceptive as to the nature of covering revolution, especially where foreign journalists are concerned. Of the detail which Reed purported to give of political activity at the Smolny, Taylor noted, 'Reed did not in fact know. He was a foreign journalist, though a sympathetic one, and the Bolsheviks revealed him few of their secrets'.[68] Taylor made a very well observed point about the lot of the foreign correspondents, especially in time of great change or revolution. Unless the protagonists in political conflict wish to convey a specific message to a particular outside power, they may barely bother with foreign journalists whose views cannot influence those involved in the action. If they do decide to give selected information to foreign correspondents, it may also be with the intention to spin or to mislead. It is Lenin, after all, to whom the phrase 'useful idiots' – for sympathetic foreign journalists and other fellow travellers – is so often attributed. Still, Trotsky's points seem to contradict those of Taylor. Taylor pointed out that one meeting which Reed describes – 'with Lenin fixing the rising for 7 November'[69] – did not take place. Trotsky seemed to think Reed's account important enough to mention this, too – although in a more forgiving way, explaining that 'work done in the heat of events, notes made in corridors, on the streets, beside camp fires, conversations and fragmentary phrases caught on the wing, and that too with the need of a translator – all these things make particular mistakes unavoidable'.[70] Were you to read these words today, without knowing the context, you might imagine they came from an editor trying to excuse an error made by a correspondent put on the spot as the world changed around them. Trotsky, like Taylor, pictured perfectly the huge challenge of covering events as they happen, or shortly afterwards, without the time for reflection, the access to archives, the hindsight, which are the privileges of the historian. It is precisely the sense of place, the sense of the moment, which Reed's account still creates, and which demands that it still be read today, a century after the events it describes. Reed's great skill – even if it involved wishful thinking born of his own support for the Bolshevik cause – was understanding, even at the very time it happened, the lasting significance of what he was witnessing. As will be discussed in more detail, this is something which eluded many policymakers at the time – with lasting consequences for the West's relations with this upstart insurgent regime which was to become a twentieth-century superpower. Reed's good fortune – if an early death can really be described in those terms – was like that of the rock star killed in a car crash or as the result of a night of alcoholic and narcotic excess. His work will forever have the burning energy of youth. It will always live in the moment when he witnessed the world being shaken, loved what he saw and was able to use his considerable literary skill to tell the story. The complications; the disillusionment; and, sometimes, as in this case, the terror, which follow revolutions: they were left to others.

Even if he was led to do so because of his own unshakeable belief in the cause which he chronicled, Reed, as Hobsbawm said of Morgan Philips Price, 'got it right'. For what characterizes much of the coverage of the Bolsheviks' seizure of power, and the weeks which followed, is a sense that the new order simply cannot endure – even though it would come to dominate world history and politics for most of the twentieth century. After reporting the initial shock of the Bolsheviks' success, wishful thinking pervaded the newspaper headlines of November 1917. It was combined with the occasional poisonous splash of anti-Semitism. The right-wing papers in particular made much of the fact that some of the revolutionaries were Jewish, attempting thereby to suggest that the whole enterprise was a Zionist conspiracy. Even when they were not – as in the case of Lenin – this was a depth which was still plumbed. 'Zederblum, Alias Lenin, claims Power' was the second headline in the *Daily Mail*'s editorial 'Another upset in Russia' on 9 November.[71] The article reported Kerensky's flight from his post as head of the provisional government and complained that 'as his opponents control the telegraphs, wireless, and censorship, it is their version of events that we are receiving'.[72] Lenin was described as a 'German-paid agent'. Trotsky – his 'alias' given as 'Braunstein' (his family name at birth was 'Bronshtein') – is characterized rather excitingly as 'an Anarchist who has made most countries too hot for him'.[73] *The Times* of the same day was even more dramatic. Stacked headlines announce, 'COUP D'ETAT IN PETROGRAD/ LENIN DEPOSES KERENSKY/ "PEACE AND BREAD."'[74] As if that were not news enough, the adjacent column reproduced the Balfour Declaration under the headline 'Palestine for the Jews. Official sympathy'. What a day for events and initiatives that would shape the twentieth century and the conflicts – hot and cold – which scarred it.

As the *Daily Mail* noted, the British and other newspapers were almost exclusively reliant on the Bolsheviks' 'version of events'. Robert Wilton, presumably to the satisfaction of Morgan Philips Price, was not there. He had returned to England for a break. As November wore on, *The Times* became understandably frustrated at his absence from the story. Dawson wrote to Wilton on 9 November, pointing out that, in their correspondence, Wilton seemed to be avoiding the question of his 'own return to Russia'.[75] In his reply, Wilton rejected any suggestion that he had been 'shirking', but concluded, 'if you think it is necessary for me to return before January, I shall be ready to start in a month's time'.[76] In Wilton's defence, there was a strong likelihood he could not have reached Petrograd anyway – but the attitude was not one to impress an editor, even in those days of longer travel times. The result was that Lord Northcliffe's papers, all implacably anti-Bolshevik as the press baron himself, were reduced to running whatever communiques the Bolsheviks saw fit to share with the world. They had very little else. The 'Coup D'état in Petrograd' story was, with the exception of the three lead paragraphs – here the paper made its views clear on 'the pacifist agitator Lenin' – sourced from 'the text of Extremist documents'.[77] *The Daily Telegraph* took a similar line. This was a 'Coup D'état in Petrograd', Lenin 'the notorious pro-German agent'. They also drew on similar sources: that is, the 'extremist documents' reproduced in *The Times*. The same page had an article headlined 'Russian Crisis: The Opposing Forces'. This was by-lined 'Our Petrograd Correspondent', although, in keeping with convention of the time, the correspondent was not named, nor is it made clear whether or not they were in Petrograd. The opening line, 'until plain news from absolutely untainted sources comes to hand it will be a great mistake to accept the latest Petrograd telegrams at their face value',[78] suggests a writer bereft of reliable sources. Being in the city itself would at least have permitted some eyewitness reporting. Despite this lack of firm facts, the correspondent – no enviable position, this – has to offer readers a degree of interpretation. This amounts to playing down the achievement which Lenin and his followers appear to have accomplished: 'It is impossible to believe

The Winter Palace, Saint Petersburg

that the nation or army as a whole has already gone over to Bolshevism.'[79] There is also an attempt to demonize Lenin, already characterized as 'the notorious pro-German agent' elsewhere on the same page, 'If Lenin is not a deliberate traitor, then he is a crazy visionary.'

All the newspapers' efforts to make sense of what was happening were hampered by their lack of access to communications. If the telegraph was not completely cut off, as it had been earlier in the year, it was not operating normally in the sense that correspondents were able to send their material. Many of the eyewitness accounts appeared only later in books. *The Times* of 10 November did have a lengthy Reuters despatch 'SCENES FROM PETROGRAD. SIEGE OF THE WINTER PALACE'. The Winter Palace had been the Tsar's residence in Petrograd. By November, it was the headquarters of the Provisional Government. Today, it is the Hermitage Museum. Guy Beringer's report for Reuters opened with Lenin reappearing in public, his moustache shaved off as part of his attempts not to be recognized while in hiding. As the day went on, the Winter Palace was cut off in preparation for its storming. 'Owing to the resistance of the Guards of the Palace, which was being defended by officer cadets and the Women's Battalion, two destroyers anchored in the Neva fired four shells.'[80] The women's battalion angle grabbed editors' attention. *The New York Times* reported in its headline that the Palace was 'taken after fierce defense by woman soldiers'. In a reflection perhaps of what an elusive figure Lenin was, he was identified in the despatch as 'Nikolai Lenine'.[81] According to Beringer, the Palace was eventually taken 'about 2 a.m.'

The Reuters despatch is remarkable for some small details, such as 'ordinary life is going on, with almost a tinge of indifference'. It ended 'while the rifle and artillery fire was continuing in the vicinity of the former imperial palace a performance was given as usual at the Narodny Dom, where a large audience assembled to hear Chaliapin'. The paragraph tells us something of Russia's love of high culture: not even armed insurgency could silence the voice of one of its greatest opera singers. One almost imagines the audience tutting as the gunfire spoiled the singing. Beringer was not alone in getting reports into the papers, though. Bessie Beatty's account of a fight for the telephone exchange – 'the most dramatic story yet to reach America of the Bolsheviki revolution'[82] – was given great prominence in the *San Francisco Bulletin*. She was given a by-line, unlike many male correspondents of the era. 'Clearly, the women's being there was seen as part of the news, the novelty.'[83] Morgan Philips Price was in Petrograd, too – although his first despatch was not printed until it came out in *The Manchester Guardian* on 20 November. His main account of his experiences did not appear until his book, *My Reminiscences of the Russian Revolution*, in 1921. It is a shame. This was the October Revolution reported by one who understood the country and the forces which shaped its politics. Hearing Lenin launch an appeal for world revolution, Philips Price watched the audience, 'sturdy, healthy young men from the Baltic Fleet and from the front'. The skilled artisans of Moscow and Petrograd, dressed in their collarless black shirts and with fur caps on their heads, were also well to the fore.[84]

On the face of it, this might read like some descriptive detail, some colour, to add to the report. It is that and yet it is also something more: a suggestion that the Bolsheviks did have the muscle, the support to achieve, if not world revolution, then at least more than their enemies imagined they could. When Philips Price did get something into a newspaper, it was worth the wait. The opening line was a masterpiece of precision, brevity and clarity. 'The government of M. Kerensky fell before the Bolshevik insurgents because it had no supporters in the country.'[85] It was a truth which the British political and diplomatic establishment, together with its allies in the Northcliffe press, would not, or could not, accept.

Even from the early days of Bolshevik power, with negligible sources apart from the Bolsheviks themselves, a number of themes start to emerge in the coverage provided by the right-wing papers: principal among these is that the Bolsheviks, having won power, cannot be expected to hold it. Indeed, the way that the communiques – aimed, after all, principally at the people of Russia rather than those outside – are presented is almost dismissive. A secondary theme is that of the leaders of the uprising, Lenin and Trotsky, being German agents; anarchists; 'crazy'. A glance at headlines from that month shows 'Leninists paralysed'[86]; 'Lenin losing control'[87]; 'Bolshevist split'[88]; 'Washington and Embassy Officials expect Bolsheviki rule to be short'.[89] Even at the end of the week that the Bolsheviks had taken power, *The Sunday Times* declared, under the headline, 'Unlikely to last': 'The opinion of all who know Russia is that the Leninist supremacy cannot last; that a few days, in fact, will see the end of it.'[90] The problem was that those who did know Russia best – Ransome (although he was among the absentees from Petrograd during the October revolution), Philips Price and perhaps Reed – were largely, or at least partly, supportive of the Bolsheviks. Most importantly, they recognized their power and potential. Even some of those who did not support them, such as Harold Williams, saw this. He had warned in September that their influence had 'increased enormously'.[91] Williams at least found himself at an advantage in the period which followed the February revolution – not least because of the prominent role played by his wife, Ariadna Tyrkova-Williams, in Russian politics at the time. It was not to last once that period came to an end. As Tyrkova-Williams was later to write in her biography of her husband, 'Harold knew many ministers of the Provisional Government for years. In the Taurida Palace Harold spoke to the Soviet leaders every day, but he had no connections among the Bolsheviks.'[92] Even if he had no connections, he had at least an understanding. Others did not. Lord Northcliffe was actually abroad during the crucial first days of the October revolution, and those who remained in charge were less interested in Russian politics.[93] In consequence, with Wilton leading the editorial line, 'the newspaper's coverage combined insight with wishful speculation'.[94] The former came from Wilton's time in Russia, and the knowledge he had acquired from covering the February revolution. The latter was plain to see from the numerous headlines predicting the imminent demise of Leninism – an idea which, on the contrary, would, by the middle of the century, come to dominate 'one third of humanity',[95] while scaring or inspiring many among the other two-thirds.

Yet this failure both to understand, and to heed those journalists who did understand, was costly. The enduring idea that Bolshevism was a tool of German influence made for bad policy, as Bruce Lockhart admitted, albeit with the benefit of considerable hindsight, in his 1932 *Memoirs of a British Agent*. 'The British Government was entitled to regard Bolshevism as a scourge and evil. It might make war on it or ignore it severely. But it was sheer folly to continue to regard it as a movement fostered solely for the furtherance of German ends.'[96] The belief that Bolshevism could not last, could be swept away, led to military intervention, which 'intensified the terror and increased the bloodshed'.[97] For all that foreign correspondents covering Russia have allowed their polarized opinions, their prejudices and their personal views to influence their reporting, the best of them in 1917 understood something that the most influential policymakers did not: they understood that Russia had changed irreversibly, and they understood why.

2

'The press is lying, or does not know': Russia goes to war with itself

Russia's revolutions attract the restless. In the early 1990s, as barriers fell, businesses opened and bandits prospered, all kinds of gold and glory hunters headed East to seek their fortune. A decade later, as soaring oil prices flooded the streets of Moscow with money, the more adventurous outsiders were largely supplanted by bankers, corporate lawyers and accountants. In the early Soviet era, the reverse happened: those wealthy Westerners who had made their money doing business in Tsarist times fled along with the rich Russians who had been their trading partners. Some journalists found their days in Russia were numbered, too. The Russian Empire to which they had travelled had ceased to exist. Its collapse had shocked and shaken the world, which now looked on nervously wondering if, as the Bolsheviks then hoped, the revolution would spread across a Europe weary and angered by the trauma of the First World War. Robert Wilton's departure meant that not only did *The Times* have no one in Russia but also that – on the Bolshevik side, at least – they would not do so again for more than two decades.[1] Harold Williams, stuck for contacts once his allies in the Provisional Government were gone, and with his wife too closely associated with that short-lived authority, soon ended up in London – although his time as a correspondent in Russia was not over, any more than Wilton's would prove to be. Closest to the action, as the new regime was forged in fire, blood and famine were two correspondents who had ended up in Russia more by accident, at least to begin with: one, Morgan Philips Price, to act on behalf of his family's timber business; another, Arthur Ransome, to research a book of fairy tales. The latter is less surprising when you consider his reputation, a century on, endures because of his later success as an author of children's stories. The reporting of both made an extended and persuasive case against military intervention in Russia by the Western powers. Both would eventually be suspected of being Bolsheviks themselves.

Arthur Ransome ran away to Russia. He ran away from an unhappy marriage. 'I did not want to marry anybody else. All I wanted was to bring that marriage to an end. Going to Russia seemed to promise answers to more problems than one,'[2] he wrote later. He was probably not the first, and certainly not the last, foreign correspondent to head off on an adventurous assignment to escape problems in their personal life. Ransome's fledgling career as a writer was marred not only by his marriage, but also by a libel action – successfully defended, but not before it took a great mental toll on Ransome – brought by Lord Alfred Douglas.[3] Fascinated by a collection of Russian fairy tales he had come across in the London Library,[4] Ransome decided to travel to Russia, and learn the language, something at which he was 'remarkably successful'.[5] He was not especially modest with it. 'Russian is one of the easiest of languages,' he wrote later. 'Once the hurdle of the alphabet has been cleared the student will discover that the hospitable Russians have done all they can to make progress easy.'[6] Many of those foreigners who have mastered the Russian language, and those many more who have not, despite trying to do so, would find it difficult to agree. Ransome's hosts, for at least part of his first stay, were Harold Williams and his wife, Ariadna Tyrkova-Williams. Ransome remembered her as 'a woman of dominating character and tremendous industry'.[7]

Perhaps Williams's great abilities as a linguist – he was said to have been able to speak 'between thirty and fifty'[8] – rubbed off on Ransome. The discovery of the book of fairy tales had major consequences. Ransome may have wanted to leave England anyway, but had he not come across that element of Russian culture, and found himself so taken with it, his destination might have been different. The history of Western journalism covering the world's largest country might have been different, too. The way in which Ransome viewed his first journey to Russia is revealed in the title he gave the relevant chapter in his autobiography, 'Journey to the Moon'. Like many ultimately successful foreign correspondents, his career began not with a love of journalism, so much as a love of a place – a love which in turn led to an expertise. He began working for the *Daily News* only because their correspondent was too ill to carry out his work.[9] It was not a great start. His only previous experience seems to have been covering the Oxford and Cambridge University Boat race. Friends had offered him a seat in the press box. Ransome remembered being 'soaked through', while making his 'first experiment in reporting'.[10] Reporting on weightier matters, such as Russian politics in the dying days of autocracy, was literally a headache for Ransome. 'I am no good as a journalist, and never shall be,' he wrote to his mother. 'However, after telegraphing I lie down, and the headache goes as soon as my blood is again evenly distributed.'[11] He got the idea soon enough. A photograph[12] from his years as a correspondent in Russia shows him looking rather sternly at the camera: pipe in hand, mouth obscured by a dark-coloured walrus moustache. He wears military uniform. The Russian letters 'B.K.' (the equivalents of 'V' and 'K' in the Roman alphabet) – presumably standing for 'voenny korrespondent' 'war correspondent' – are visible on the cap. This is Ransome the foreign correspondent as he would perhaps have preferred to be seen. There is no suggestion of the headaches that came with knocking out news copy here. Instead, he almost challenges his observer to match his knowledge of the country he had come to know so well.

Philips Price had immersed himself in Russia's language and culture. In his *Russian Memoirs*, Bernard Pares, despite his misgivings about Philips Price's infection with 'the virus of Bolshevism', also praised Philips Price's earlier work on Russia – in terms which any foreign correspondent in any era would find flattering for the way it portrayed him as both adventurous and successful. Pares wrote of 'Morgan Philips Price, who had already lived among the peasant settlers of the Altai Mountains in Siberia, grown a beard there, and written an excellent book on the subject'.[13] Pares was well placed to judge. It was he who in 1907 at Liverpool opened the first Russian department at a British university,[14] and his lifelong study of the country made him the age's leading expert. A photograph of Philips Price from the time[15] shows him bearded (it is tempting to believe that it is the same beard which Pares says was 'grown among the peasant settlers of the Altai Mountains') and wearing either a fur or Astrakhan hat. He looks serious, perhaps disapproving.

This was certainly true of the way that he saw the work of many of his fellow correspondents. We have seen how he hoped that Wilton would be sent on his way. Wilton, having creditably covered the February revolution, contrived to miss the Bolsheviks' taking of power. He was unable to return: to Western Russia, at least. In May 1920, the British authorities refused him a passport to travel to Finland and Russia.[16] *The Times* sought an explanation for the decision, but was unable to reverse it. Wilton was left to conclude that he had been 'boycotted at the pleasure of the worst enemies of the allied cause', that is, 'Bolsheviks' and, showing the anti-Semitism which even *The Times* would later come to acknowledge, 'Jews'.[17] Wilton was able to travel to Siberia in late 1919 and early 1920, but was forced to do so via the United States rather than from Western Europe. In that sense, Philips Price's wish that Wilton be turned out of Petrograd came true.

Philips Price's knowledge of Russia was combined with deeply held political convictions which, as we shall see, led him eventually into great difficulties.

In the early days of Bolshevik power, it also gave him a clarity of vision, an understanding of the situation which was absent from much of the other coverage – not for him the idea that Lenin's real name was Zederblum; not for him the idea that the Bolsheviks were German agents. *The Times* eventually drew conclusions on Wilton's work which would have pleased Philips Price, even if he might have found them a bit mild. The newspaper found the idea that the Bolsheviks were working for the Kaiser a little harder to let go. *The Times* seemed in fact to cling on to this idea for a surprisingly long time. The volume, published in the 1950s, of the newspaper's official history, did attempt to address some of the failures in their coverage which had become apparent by then. Philips Price, who lived until 1973, would presumably have been pleased to read judgements, such as 'Wilton's service, often important, was erratic,'[18] that the newspaper felt that 'their writer did not command full confidence.'[19] Decades after the events and definitely with the benefit of hindsight, *The Times* remained mealy mouthed about its assertions that Lenin and his followers were German agents. 'Present-day historians deny' – the implication perhaps being that *The Times* still did not share this view – 'the allegation that the Bolshevik party during the October Revolution was in German pay. However, there were at the time contemporary statements of varying plausibility in favour of the allegation.'[20]

Although by the 1950s *The Times* would come to judge Wilton relatively harshly, he spent the early period of Bolshevik power – once he had left Russia and was unable to return – working hard to get his views across. His book, *Russia's Agony*, was his contribution to the interpretation of events in Russia after 1917. Wilton and his publisher, Edward Arnold, rushed it into print with impressive speed, a reflection of the huge public interest in, and likely market for, a book about current events in Russia. It was out by March 1918. The frontispiece showed Wilton – white haired and with a white moustache, his keen eyes looking directly to camera – in military uniform with medals. Did he know he was already seen as erratic, even by some at the newspaper which then employed him? His book seemed from the outset to be an explanation of why he was anything but erratic. He explained in the introduction, 'Few people realized more clearly how little was known about the Russians outside, and how much harm this ignorance caused to our relations with them.'[21] His anti-Bolshevism ran through hundreds of pages. He did note, with a rare note of near sympathy, that Lenin's hatred of the old regime might have been inspired by 'the tragic and violent end of his elder brother,'[22] Alexander, who was executed for his part in a failed attempt on the life of Tsar Alexander III[23] – but Wilton continued by comparing Lenin to a rebellious student who had not outgrown his youthful radicalism. 'Unlike the great majority of Russian revolutionary undergraduates, Lenin remained a revolutionary in his mature years and grew more uncompromising with age.'[24] *The Times'* history also noted that Wilton gained 'in Zionist circles, and even into the Foreign Office,'[25] the reputation of being an anti-Semite. Such a reputation was deserved. Wilton accused 'extremist' Jews of 'provoking' pogroms[26] in the chaos that followed the abdication of the tsar. He claimed that Bolshevism was a Jewish, rather than a Russian, phenomenon.[27] Wilton's own views on the revolution were clear. The volume was after all dedicated to the Cossacks who, he hoped, would sweep the reds from Russia. Wilton's belief, or hope, that this would happen clouded his judgement to such an extent that, even with his vast experience of the country which he was covering, he seems to have been unable to understand Lenin's true strengths.

'The Bolsheviks survived because of their leader and because of their commitment to unbridled force,'[28] wrote the twentieth-century Soviet/Russian historian Dmitri Volkogonov. If this was already apparent in the period which followed the October revolution, it was not apparent to Wilton. *Russia's Agony* may be flawed. It is absolutely not without merit. Wilton, as we saw in the last chapter, was at the heart of the action in the February revolution – sometimes, as when the 'bullets began to whiz over' his head – uncomfortably close. He was also 'an eye-witness of the main events'[29] in July, although, as he added, 'most of my messages to *The Times* were intercepted by the Soviet censor in Petrograd, although they had been approved by the army censorship'.[30] There seems to have been an element of self-justification here. Was Wilton, perhaps knowing that he did not enjoy the full confidence of his editors, seeking to vindicate himself? Some fifteen pages further on, while still discussing the crisis which followed the failure of the Russian Army's July offensive, and having praised the British role in helping the Russians launch that initially successful campaign, Wilton reproduces in full one of the 'messages' which did not make it into the newspaper. It runs to three and a half pages of the book. One of the main arguments put forward in this book is that Russia so excites the emotions of Western correspondents and other visitors that they form strong opinions – good or ill – of the country. Wilton's hatred of the Bolsheviks is clear; his desire to lay all Russia's misfortunes at their door manifest. 'Bolshevism had snatched victory from our grasp, but all hope was not yet lost,'[31] he wrote after the July offensive had turned into a defeat. The 'our' may have been a reference to the British soldiers whose assistance to the Russian Army Wilton had already mentioned so approvingly. It also reads now like a deliberate declaration on

Wilton's part of his support for the anti-Bolshevik forces. Perhaps because he had been out of the country, and lacked the first-hand, eyewitness experience which had earlier served him so well, Wilton seemed increasingly to lose perspective as his account went on. Much of the last section of the book was an exercise in wishful thinking that the Leninist regime simply could not last. As such, it echoed the views stated in so many of the conservative newspapers of the time. Wilton, though, goes beyond that – with a fevered argument that ignores not only the Bolsheviks' control of the major cities, but also their understanding of what Russia wanted. 'Peace-Bread-Land' was a masterpiece of advertising, public relations, propaganda. Howsoever one defines it, it was brilliant both in its simplicity and for its understanding of how to appeal to a populace for whom bread queues and an unpopular war were making life unbearable.

The penultimate chapter of *Russia's Agony*, 'The Hope of Russia' was a hymn of praise to the Cossacks whom Wilton obviously saw as set to restore order. The concluding chapter, 'The New Russia', made confident predictions. 'A new Russia is springing up amid the ruins of the old. The day of Lenin and destruction draws to a close. Do not believe outward appearances.'[32] Alas for Wilton, the outward appearances had much to tell the onlooker. Although he did outlive Lenin, Wilton did not live to see the collapse of the system which that 'revolutionary undergraduate' had founded. This is where the reporting of this stage of Russia's revolution failed. It failed to recognize the zeal and idealism which inspired the Bolsheviks. The nineteenth-century military strategist Carl von Clausewitz wrote that 'war, that is the animosity and the reciprocal effects of hostile elements, cannot be considered to have ended so long as the enemy's *will* has not been broken'[33] (italics in original). The Bolsheviks had this will in unlimited quantities. They combined this with an understanding of what the people of Russia wanted. Even Bruce Lockhart, British agent and unofficial diplomat, in his later memoir of 'men who worked eighteen hours a day and who were obviously inspired by the same spirit of self-sacrifice and abnegation of worldly pleasure which animated the Puritans and early Jesuits.'[34] Wilton's dismissal of Lenin blinded him to Bolshevism's capacity to endure and prevail. 'A new Russia' may have been 'springing up amid the ruins of the old', but it was a new Russia inspired by Lenin, and one which his ideas would continue to inspire for most of the coming century.

If Wilton was unable to disguise the fact that he loathed Lenin, both Ransome and Philips Price struggled to hide their admiration. Ransome's first impressions, however, were different. He was among those observers who, initially at least, when Lenin returned to Petrograd in 1917, failed to understand his potential for taking power.[35] As Ransome's witnessing of unfolding change came to give him a greater understanding, his views changed. They changed not only in the sense that Ransome understood Lenin's and the Bolsheviks' capacity for leadership and power – what Volkogonov might have called 'their commitment to unbridled force' – but in the sense that he came to see in Lenin something almost to worship.

Even if his first steps as a foreign correspondent gave him a rush of blood to the head, Ransome came to understand the importance of the work in which he was engaged. His interview with Trotsky, published shortly after his return to Russia weeks after the October revolution, was the ultimate in correspondent success: an exclusive copied by other newspapers unable to match it. His books, *Six Weeks in Russia* (1919) and *The Crisis in Russia* (1921), read like what they were: the work of the correspondent with an almost missionary zeal to explain to his audience what he felt so strongly that they needed to know. Ransome also had a keen understanding of the role which his work was fated to play in time of revolution and bloodshed, especially as Bolshevik rule became such a pressing and divisive foreign policy issue. The introduction to *Six Weeks in Russia* began with the knowing warning to the reader, 'I am well aware that there is material in this book which will be misused by fools both white and red.'[36] Reflecting further on the role of the correspondent – and almost anticipating A. J. P. Taylor's questioning decades later of the true extent of John Reed's access – Ransome wrote, 'I got, I think I may say, as near as any foreigner who was not a Communist could get to what was going on.'[37] He continued, 'I had overcome the hostility which I at first encountered as the correspondent of a "bourgeois" newspaper.'[38] As a correspondent, Ransome was intensely reflective to the point of being self-critical. He wondered in the introduction to *Six Weeks in Russia* whether he should have included details he had omitted. 'There is nothing here of my talk with the English soldier prisoners and nothing of my visit to the officers in Butyrka Gaol.'[39] In a sense, this seems extremely modern. This is the kind of reflective discussion of the editorial process which has become so much more common since news organizations acquired internet platforms which gave them the space to pursue it. Ransome was not always impressed by what he found. His eye for detail, as he sought accommodation and food, brought to life the novelties and uncertainties of daily existence in the fledgling capital of world socialism. Having finally found a room in the Hotel Metropole, he observed the kitchen catering to all the residents amid shortages not only of food, but even of utensils. 'And all the time people from all parts of the hotel were coming with their pitchers and pans, from fine copper kettles to disreputable empty meat tins, to fetch hot water for tea.'[40]

Ransome was there principally to tell the political story. In the same way that Wilton argued he was so well placed to explain Russia to outsiders, Ransome made his case for the importance of what he was doing. British understanding of Russia was limited for no one was properly 'studying the gigantic experiment which, as a country, we are allowing to pass abused but not examined'.[41] Ransome tried to redress that. He tried to explain to his readers Lenin's charisma. In doing so, he betrayed the fact that he had himself fallen under the first Soviet leader's spell. In March 1918, Ransome saw Lenin give a speech in the Bolshoi Theatre in central Moscow. 'It was a long time before he could speak at all, everybody standing and drowning his attempts to speak with roar after roar of applause. It was an extraordinary, overwhelming scene, tier after tier crammed with workmen.'[42]

Ransome's access during his time in Russia was often excellent. Where ill-judged predictions of Bolshevism's coming collapse had earned the Northcliffe papers hostility and ridicule, correspondents working for more sympathetic titles got closer to the leaders of the new Russia as it took shape. During his *Six Weeks in Russia* in 1919, Ransome was able to interview Lenin:

> If the conditions of the revolution are not there, no sort of propaganda will either hasten or impede it. The war has brought about those conditions in all countries, and I am convinced that if Russia to-day were to be swallowed up by the sea, were to cease to exist altogether, the revolution in the rest of Europe would go on.[43]

From what we can gather of Ransome's views of the Soviet leader 'roar after roar of applause' – and presumably Lenin himself knew them just as well – it is perhaps not too fanciful to suggest that Lenin thought he had found a sympathetic chronicler of the massive transformation he was seeking to lead. A twenty-first-century spin-doctor might admire Lenin's dismissal of propaganda as playing no role. The dismissal is in itself a form of clever propaganda.

Ransome's 1918 pamphlet 'The Truth about Russia' was originally commissioned as a long article by *The New Republic* in the United States. It was later reprinted by the Workers' Socialist Federation, then based in the East End of London. In the British Library in London, Ransome's work is bound together with other pamphlets published by the Workers' Socialist Federation. Among them is *Hands Off Russia*, the text of a speech given by Israel Zangzwill at the Royal Albert Hall in February 1919. The venue is interesting, suggesting obviously that such a speech then could attract a large crowd. As might be guessed from the organization that published his words, it is a forthright defence of the Bolshevik regime. To our eyes, in a political world that is dominated as perhaps never before by media in different forms, it also offers some interesting reflections on the way that the work of Western correspondents then in Russia was seen by contemporary audiences. 'Lenin himself compares newspapers to bombs and guns, and thought it so dangerous that no Government in the world dares leave it uncensored,'[44] Zangzwill told his audience. He went on to regret that Lenin had seen fit to suppress 'the opposition press', but was relieved to learn this was only 'a temporary and extraordinary measure till the new order was firmly in the saddle'.[45] Zangzwill continued:

> It is *our* press that is Lenin's real danger. A Muscovite when he reads that the gutters of Moscow run blood, knows whether the blood is really there, or only invented by the gutter-journalists. But we over here in the fog of peace, can never be absolutely sure that our journals are lying.

Today Zangzwill's political descendants would be on Twitter criticizing the 'mainstream media'. This lack of trust in what they learnt from the other side of Europe seems to have been widespread among left-wing pamphleteers of the time. Another publication from the Workers' Socialist Federation, 'Soviets for the British: A plain talk to plain people' provocatively argued that prominent Russians, including the Imperial family, 'have been bayoneted and buried one week. The next week they rise again, all the better for that. The press, therefore, is either lying, or does not know'.[46]

The political views of the author, L.A. Motler, became clear in the sentence which followed. 'It is true that numerous people have been killed, but as these have been mostly of titled loafing families who would have everything to gain by plotting a counter-revolution, it may naturally be believed that they were found out.'[47] In which case, Motler seems to be telling his audience, they deserved nothing more or less than a bayonet. Although these examples are taken from political pamphlets with a very strong, clear, point of view, they illustrate a wider point. With information about Russia extremely difficult to come by, people were all but forced to resort to guesswork. The information that did get out was heavily censored and therefore unreliable. Much wishful thinking – such as the idea that the Bolshevik revolution could not last – was passed off as considered reporting. Wilton's newspaper may have criticized him later, in its official history, but there is little sense that the faults in his work held him back at the time, even if he was seen as 'erratic'. Northcliffe, owner then of *The Times* and *The Daily Mail*, loathed the Bolsheviks and was clearly happy to see them done down in print.

Ransome too had his prejudices. He was keen to remind his reader of Lenin's influence on the age, 'Whatever else they may think of him, not even his enemies deny that Vladimir Ilyitch Oulianov (Lenin) is one of the greatest personalities of his time', began the section of *Six Weeks in Russia* in which Ransome recorded his recollections of conversations with the Bolshevik leader. His desire to better understand and explain what was happening in Russia did not, however, mean he was blind to its faults. Great foreign correspondents succeed because of their skill in creating a sense of place. They are able to take readers to places where they have never been and probably will never see. This is how readers gain the insight and understanding vital to forming opinions of a place. Unless they themselves were refugees from Russia, few of Ransome's readers could have imagined the scenes which he described shortly after getting to Moscow in 1919. There was much worse than the chaotic squalor of the Hotel Metropole. Ransome wrote of 'a sledge laden with, I think, horseflesh, mostly bones, probably dead sledge horses. As he drove a black crowd of crows followed the sledge and perched on it, tearing greedily at the meat'.[48]

He went on to describe crows forcing their way through hotel ventilators to 'pick up any scraps they could', and noted that the pigeons had 'completely disappeared' from the streets of Moscow which, following the Bolshevik seizure of power, had been restored to the status of capital city. Ransome may have begun his description with the blunt statement that 'there can be no question about the starvation of Moscow'.[49] Yet the way he showed that – the flesh, which cannot be identified and which is in any case 'mostly bones', being fought over by man and crow – completed the picture of a city where food was in frighteningly short supply. The sledge was a peculiarly Russian detail: the horses presumably, even then, in the twentieth century, a familiar enough sight for his readers to compare with their own lives. Ransome is, in a sense, caught between the need to satisfy two objectives. He went to Russia to further his literary ambitions. He wanted more than anything to satisfy his 'hankering after the writing of stories'.[50] Once there, he became a journalist, a committed one, who wanted 'to set down, as shortly as possible, the story of the development of the Soviet power in Russia.'[51] Whether or not he intended it to happen in Russia, Ransome also addressed the other aspect of his life – besides a desire to write – which had driven him to cross Europe in search of new experiences. He found a new wife, Evgenia Shelepina, 'the tall jolly girl

... to whom I owe the happiest years of my life'.[52] She was Trotsky's secretary. Ransome's second meeting with Evgenia – their first had been when he went to interview Trotsky – was occasioned by his need to get a censor to stamp his despatch.[53] The interview, which Ransome had done shortly after returning to Russia in early 1918, had made enough of an impression to be reported as a story in itself in at least one other newspaper. 'Every government in Europe is feeling the pressure of democracy from below,' the revolutionary leader had told Ransome in the account of their meeting which appeared in *The Western Times* on New Year's Day 1918.

The Soviet authorities could have had no objection to seeing sentiments such as those presented to Western readers. In other cases, it was not so simple – and it is here that the real challenges for correspondents' work, and their audiences' understanding, really began. Censorship plagued the reporting of the entire revolutionary period. Before the October revolution, W. P. (William Percival) Crozier, then news editor of *The Manchester Guardian*, had written to the paper's correspondent in Petrograd, David Soskice, warning him that 'we are rather under the impression that some of your telegrams to us may have been suppressed at the Russian end',[54] and asking him to send duplicates by post. Both the Soviets and Western authorities practised censorship. Morgan Philips Price was to fall particularly foul of it. He was not alone. Even his arch enemy, Robert Wilton, felt aggrieved enough to use pages of his book to reproduce in print which did not appear when it was newsworthy. Price's book *My Reminiscences of the Russian Revolution*, which appeared in 1921, burnt with fury at the stories which he had been stopped from telling – in his case, most frequently by the allied censors. It might be hard for us to imagine today how it was possible to cut correspondents off so completely. Proponents of the successes of social media would argue that in the age of Twitter, a tyrant's control can never be as tight as it has been in previous periods of human history. Yet think of how little we saw in daily news reports of life in those areas of the Middle East under the control of so-called 'Islamic State', and we might get a clearer idea of what was possible in the time when the telegraph and telephone were the only means of communication with the outside world. If they were well controlled, so was information.

Some six months after Ransome, having been away from Russia for the October revolution itself, returned to the country, Bolsheviks killed the Russian royal family. While the Tsar's mother, the Dowager Empress Maria Fyodorovna, had returned to her native Denmark, the rest of the royal family had, since the abdication, been under various forms of house arrest. At one time, it had seemed they might be able to go to England, where they could be safe. Subsequently, however, the then King, George V, who was a cousin of the Tsar, 'withdrew his invitation for fear of alienating the Labour Party'.[55] By the summer of 1918, the royal family and their closest and most loyal retainers found themselves in Ekaterinburg, on the edge of the Ural Mountains, where Europe turns into Asia. Even today, Ekaterinburg is not a place frequently visited by foreign correspondents. In 1918, as during the Second World War when industry was moved eastwards out of the way of advancing German troops, Ekaterinburg was a place for the safekeeping of possessions, and people, that Russia's rulers did not want to fall into the wrong hands. When that looked in danger of happening, the local Bolsheviks acted – presumably with the knowledge of their bosses in Moscow. The latter, however, apparently with an eye on how history might one day judge them, were careful not to put their instructions, if indeed they issued them, down in writing. 'Ex-Tsar Shot' announced *The Sunday Times* on 21 July 1918. 'Yet another report of the death of the ex-Tsar of Russia has arrived, but this time it deserves attention from the fact that it has been sent out through the wireless stations of the Russian government.'[56] The paper's circumspection is clear, and apparently, judging from the reference to this being 'yet another' report, well founded. The uncertainty is reminiscent of the mystery that had surrounded the Tsar's abdication the previous year. The caution is even more understandable when one considers the pamphleteer who would, the following year, still include the Tsar's demise in a sneering list of stories of the deaths of people who would 'rise again' the following week. There would be no such resurrection for the Tsar or his family – even though *The Sunday Times* report cited the Russian official message as saying that 'the wife and son of Romanoff have been sent to a place of safety'. They had not, of course. They too had been shot.

It is this kind of uncertainty, of deliberate deception, of confusion which dominates this entire era of Western reporting of Russia – at a moment in its history which was to define the entire century to come. The overriding preoccupation of editors and policymakers during 1917 had been Russia's ability or will to continue to fight in the First World War. As the period after the Bolshevik revolution went on, it became clear that Lenin and his movement would last longer than those in the West who hated them had originally hoped. The Allies were still preoccupied with the war, but this began to affect their views on Russia in a different way. The question of whether or not Russia would continue the war remained relevant. Added to this was the question as to whether the West should intervene militarily to try to stifle Bolshevism if not at birth, then in its infancy. Once the country's new rulers had ratified the Treaty of Brest-Litovsk – the agreement which formally ended Russia's involvement in the First World War – at the Seventh Party Congress in March 1918,[57] it was clear that Russia would play no further part in the fight against the Triple Alliance. Now Russia's former allies in the Triple Entente, Britain in particular, had to decide the part which they would play in Russia's future development. Some journalists, such as Wilton, hoped that Russia would be saved by some version of the old order: Ransome and Morgan Philips Price – the latter in particular – were outraged at the prospect of military intervention. In 'The Truth about Russia', Ransome argued against it – on practical as much as ideological grounds. He wrote:

> If the Allies lend help to any minority that cannot overturn the Soviets without their help, they will be imposing on free Russia a government which will be in perpetual need of external help, and will, for simple reasons of geography, be bound to take that help from Germany.[58]

This is Ransome the practical, the observer – the man with the good contacts close to the centre of power. Yet his pamphlet ends on a much more surprising note, revealing perhaps the reporter who had been caught up in the excitement of the events around him.

> Every true man is in some sort, until his youth dies and his eyes harden, the potential builder of a New Jerusalem. At some time or other every one of us has dreamed of laying his brick in such a work. And even if this thing that is being builded here with tears and blood is not the golden city that we ourselves have dreamed, it is still a thing to the sympathetic understanding of which each one of us is bound by whatever he owes to his own youth.[59]

This is worth citing at length. One quality frequently attributed to good journalism is that the reporter does not make it about themselves. Ransome did not perhaps intend to give his reader his own views on the situation. Instead – as suggested by the informed, well-argued opinion of the extract above – his intention was to present a case which would prevent a course of action leading to bloodshed and unintended consequences in global politics. Perhaps unwittingly, or in haste – Ransome made reference in the piece to the fact that someone was waiting, as he wrote, to take the piece for publication – he laid bare not only his own sympathy for the Bolsheviks, but also an impossibly romantic view of the world and the revolution. 'The Truth about Russia' is not well known today, but this extract arguably gives one of the clearest insights into the way that Ransome viewed the events going on around him. He may have got to grips with covering the murderous chess game that was post-revolutionary Russian politics. He may have been able to weigh up, and dismiss, arguments in favour of intervention. Yet here, with the revolution itself yet young – and perhaps under the time pressure of a deadline – Ransome showed another, perhaps truer, perhaps more enduring side of himself. Invoking Blake's vision of struggle leading to an idealized Jerusalem – down to the 'builded' – Ransome argued that not supporting the Bolsheviks was tantamount to the betrayal of one's own youth. This was Arthur Ransome the writer drawn to Russia for its folk tales, not Arthur Ransome the foreign correspondent covering a revolution. Coming so relatively early in Russia's post-revolutionary history, these lines may be read as an indication of the views and emotions which influenced Ransome's subsequent reporting: this may indeed be Arthur Ransome who, like Philips Price, has become infected with the 'virus of Bolshevism'.

Philips Price, the correspondent in whom Bernard Pares diagnosed that malady, was even more forthright. Censorship had such a hold over the way that the story of Russia was told in the years immediately following the October revolution that correspondents had to turn to book publishers to tell the stories which had not been permitted to pass the censor's pen. That reports such as these were no longer newsworthy in the strictest sense must have been extremely frustrating. They were, though, still current enough for the correspondents in question to claim a degree of vindication, if their stories from the time remained relevant even with the benefit of hindsight. Alas for Robert Wilton, his did not. Nevertheless, convinced that he had plenty worth saying, Wilton allowed himself to reproduce at length despatches which had never made it into the paper. Philips Price found his outlet in longer form, too. Although some of his work was published at the time it was sent, much of it was not.* Price eventually crossed the line so far that he was no longer treated as a reporter so much as a propagandist – but his undoubted skill as a correspondent, and almost unrivalled knowledge of the country, acquired in extensive travel when such trips were possible, meant that he wrote much which is still worth reading today. Take this from *The Manchester Guardian* in early 1918:

> The whole of North Russia is in such a condition of famine and misery that its sole hope is the fear which the Germans must have in occupying such a country. The inhabitants of the towns have nearly all gone to the villages to escape death

---

* Any reader seeking a fuller account of the extent to which Philips Price's work was subject to censorship should see Jonathan Smele's 1995 article 'What the papers didn't say: Unpublished despatches from Russia by M. Philips Price, May 1918 to January 1919' published in the journal *Revolutionary Russia* (full reference in bibliography).

from starvation. These are conditions which only peace, even a separate one, will repair.[60]

Here Philips Price offers a grimly factual account of the state of Russia. Autocracy, and the tyranny which came with it, had gone. 'Peace-Bread-Land' as promised by the Bolsheviks had not been delivered. The threat of invasion persisted. There was no peace. There was no bread, either: then, starvation stalked whole areas of the Russian north. As for land, if people had left the villages, agriculture had been disrupted or stopped. Even if Philips Price raising of 'a separate' peace – the Allies' fear that Russia would eventually leave the war – suggested it is an idea with which he might have had some sympathy, this kind of hard-hitting reporting was no public relations job for Lenin. This was not the kind of despatch a 'useful idiot' would have filed. And yet, though he may have been a great correspondent – remember the striking clarity of his explanation of the causes of the October revolution – Philips Price came eventually to let his own views cloud his reporting to the extent that they polluted it. Gagged by the censor as a newspaper correspondent, Philips Price turned author to tell the story he felt so strongly that the world needed to know. *My Reminiscences of the Russian Revolution* contained many cries of protest against those who had sought to silence him – and against those with whom he angrily disagreed and who had not been similarly gagged. His chapter on allied attempts to influence the course of the revolution was entitled 'International Counter Revolution Assumes the offensive'. Philips Price may not have been a 'useful idiot', but a title such as this might certainly have been seen as useful to the Bolshevik cause.

Philips Price had one failing which led eventually to the end of his career reporting from Russia. Bernard Pares's assessment of the 'virus of Bolshevism' and its effect on Philips Price were just. Yet in judging Philips Price's journalism today, the circumstances in which he was working must be taken into account. He was a correspondent who knew the country better than almost any of his compatriots, perhaps even better than almost any foreigner. He was in effect prevented from sharing that knowledge because of the strict censorship regime to which he was subject. His frustration must have been immeasurable. It was clearly discernible in the most controversial of his publications from Russia, the one which led to his being 'held to be liable for treasonable activities and aiding the "King's enemies"'[61]: 'The Truth about the Allied Intervention in Russia'. It was published in August 1918. Philips Price was able to continue to work in Russia after it had appeared, but he was increasingly starved of funding and denied publication by the censor – to the point that he was all but silenced until he was able to publish his *Reminiscences* some years later. In places, 'The Truth about the Allied Intervention in Russia' was a masterpiece of polemical journalism. As such, for its expertise and eloquence, it bore comparison with the work of another great, engaged, chronicler of revolution, Thomas Paine. In others, it slipped too easily into the language of Bolshevik propaganda, thereby losing the reader looking for what Philips Price declared that he intended to provide: the truth. Then there were the places which led to the accusations of treason. As Philips Price himself noted in his *Reminiscences*, 'the Soviet Foreign Office printed fifty thousand copies of it and distributed it everywhere it could and some got to British troops who were invading North Russia from Archangel.'[62] Even if these troops were not Philips Price's intended readership, they might have imagined that they were when they read passages such as

> to impose fresh tribute on the Russian people, to force them to fight against their will, to still further increase their misery, indescribable as it is at present, that is the task which the British government asks the British soldier to perform when he fights on the Murman.[63,*]

Those soldiers' officers, and more importantly perhaps, their political masters, would not have been impressed to read sentiments such as 'I categorically assert that the anarchy and famine now raging in Russia is the deliberate work of the Imperialist governments of Europe, and in this respect the governments of the Allies and of Germany behave like vultures of the same brood.'[64] It was incendiary stuff. Philips Price must have known it. To lump Britain and Germany together as vultures after the British press had spent four years cataloguing German atrocities in the First World War was designed to shock. In *Reminiscences*, Philips Price sought to defend himself against the allegations of treason which had been levelled at him. 'We were not at war with Russia, and no declaration of hostilities had been made [...] the pamphlet contained no incitement of British troops to mutiny.'[65] His critics challenged him on the latter point. Aylmer Maude, Russian scholar and translator of Tolstoy into English, wrote in January 1919 to C.P. Scott, editor of *The Manchester Guardian*. Maude asked Scott how far informed he was of the activities of Price, 'who is said to be acting as editor of "The Call" the English periodical which the Bolsheviks distribute among our troops and in which they invite them to desert. (Which is obviously treasonable on the part of the English editor)'.[66]

---

* A coastal area of northern Russia, near the city of Murmansk.

My Reminiscences of the Russian Revolution appeared in 1921: soon enough to allow the author to gain some perspective, but too late for his news reporting to have had the impact it might have achieved had it not been censored. In June 1918, as the extent, efficacy and wisdom of allied plans to intervene in Russia were key issues, Philips Price filed to *The Manchester Guardian* despatch warning that 'if the Allies set up in Russia a government only of the Right' then 'the workers, who are now discontented with the Soviet Government, because of the famine, and the peasants, who dislike the forced requisitions, will become doubly so against the allies'.[67]

With hindsight, it read like sound advice as to the likely consequences of an ill-considered intervention. Unfortunately, almost nobody at the time was able to read it – with the obvious exception of the censors who made sure that was the case. In the same way that Ransome made the case against allied intervention on practical grounds – he argued it would drive the Soviets to seek support from the Germans – Philips Price sought to argue that setting up and supporting a government of the right would mobilize Russian workers and peasants who were actually disenchanted with what the revolution had failed to deliver.

In fact, the Allies did not succeed in setting up a government at all, at least not a national one. They did, however, pour massive quantities of men and matériel into supporting the 'White' forces of counter-revolution against the Red ones of revolution. 'In the first six months of 1919', the White Army received 'one million rifles; 15,000 machine guns; 700 field guns; 800 million rounds of ammunition; and clothing and equipment for half a million men. This was roughly equivalent to the Soviet production of munitions for the whole of 1919'.[68] Like Ransome, Philips Price was close to Karl Radek, the Polish Bolshevik who acted as a kind of press officer for foreign correspondents seeking access to Bolshevik leaders. Ransome wrote later of Radek, 'talking with him was for me like revisiting the Latin quarter,' on account of his extensive knowledge of literature and politics. This kind of urbanity seems to have been a common trait of those Bolsheviks chosen to deal with the foreign press. A later generation of correspondents would speak in similarly admiring terms of Solomon Lozovsky, the official who kept an eye on them during the Second World War. Ransome also owed to Radek his 'introduction to many others of the leading Bolsheviks'.[69] For Philips Price, he was an equally important source. 'One thing, however, we will not endure, and that is that Soviet Russia should become a prey to any military adventurer who gets enough foreign money and machine guns,'[70] Radek warned in a conversation which Philips Price reported in *My Reminiscences*. What was Philips Price's purpose here? Was he trying to report truthfully the determination of the Bolsheviks to see their cause through to triumph, trying to give an indication of that spirit of Puritanism, which had made such an impression on Bruce Lockhart, and that will which Wilton so underestimated? Or was he, by reproducing Radek's words – without discussion of whether or not the Bolsheviks would really be in a position to repulse any attack by military adventurers flush with foreign guns and money – acting more as a Bolshevik mouthpiece, even a 'useful idiot'? There was a clue where Philips Price discussed his own despatch, an extract from which is cited above, about the danger of allied plans to set up a right-wing Russian government. 'I sent this telegram in a desperate attempt to rouse the Labour and democratic forces in England to the seriousness of the situation into which the Allies were allowing themselves to drift in regard to Russia,' he wrote. This despatch, 'by some lucky chance, escaped the censorship of the Allies and appeared in *The Manchester Guardian* a few days later'.[71]

At this stage, Philips Price was open about his purpose. He clearly intended that his journalism should not only inform, but also influence, to move to action: 'to rouse the Labour and democratic forces'. He was damning, though, of censorship-driven media campaigns which sought to make the case to reinforce the current policies of allied governments. One such case concerned the fighting in Siberia. Philips Price complained that

> the Havas* agency was giving out messages which were said to have been received from Siberia, via Japan, stating that German prisoners in Irkutsk, led by German officers, had revolted, defeated the Soviet troops and seized authority in Eastern Siberia.[72]

Armed with an official telegram – a copy of which the Commissar for Foreign Affairs, Georgi Chicherin, had given him – Philips Price filed a story saying that the Soviets still held Irkutsk, 'but the telegram was suppressed by the Allied censor, who had an interest in permitting only the provocative falsehoods disseminated from Paris to reach the ear of the public'.[73] Philips Price criticized the 'falsehoods' from Paris, and yet was himself, at the same time, willing to file a story on the basis of a single source from a party with a very strong interest. No trace here of the 'we have not been able independently to confirm the authenticity of this material' which might accompany such a communiqué today.

---

* The main French news agency, later incorporated into Agence France Presse.

My Reminiscences is remarkable for the way it rages against anti-Soviet reporting which must have been published some two years before Philips Price wrote his own account – or, at least, two years before his views could be read by the public. He was writing about coverage in the summer of 1918, and his book did not appear until 1921. Time had not healed. He had not calmed down. He was furious.

> There was no means of explaining to the outside world what was going on in Russia, how grievously the Soviet Republic was being libelled by the hirelings of the Allied press agencies, how treacherously she was being attacked, blockaded and starved by mealy-mouthed hypocrites with unctuous phrases on their lips about 'non-interference in the internal affairs of Russia'.[74]

Such utterances were, of course, humbug. Philips Price must have known at the time of which he was writing. Given the massive commitment of troops and munitions which was to follow, he definitely knew it by the time he was writing. His own commitment to the cause was almost certainly a factor, but Philips Price also managed here to do something which only the best foreign correspondents achieve: he explained, correctly, to his readers what was likely to follow – but was once again gagged.

> 'The Allies are sowing dragons' teeth in Eastern Europe,' I telegraphed to *The Manchester Guardian* by wireless on July 3rd. 'Some day they will grow into bayonets, which will be turned into directions they least desire.' But that message was not taken up, or, if it was, the Allied censorship took care that it did not reach its destination.[75]

The image of dragons' teeth turning into bayonets is striking for its prescience: not simply for the Cold War which was to overshadow world politics for the second half of the twentieth century, but perhaps even into our own age. On a visit to the United States in 1959, the Soviet leader, Nikita Khrushchev, referred to what the veteran correspondent and broadcaster, Alistair Cooke, reported as 'the futile invasion of his country by soldiers of America, France, Germany, Poland and Britain'.[76] Half a century later, the intervention still shaped the way in which the Soviet leadership understood the way that the rest of the world saw it. Mikhail Gorbachev, the leader who presided over the end of Soviet power in Russia, also cited this as an influence. In his 2005 book, *On My Country and the World*, he wrote of his belief that 'nothing [had] been forgotten' since the time when Western powers planned that 'Russia not be regarded as a unitary state'.[77] The allied intervention of 1918 was, for Russia, an experience that led it to see the

West as threatening and bent on preventing Russia from being united and strong. Given the influence which this idea has had on Russian policymakers since – and Vladimir Putin's views of the West's relations with Ukraine seem only the latest incarnation – it is greatly to Morgan Philips Price's credit that he foresaw the longer-term reaction that allied military intervention against the Bolsheviks might provoke. One of the greatest challenges faced by a correspondent at a time of era-defining change is to provide audiences with options of what may come next. It is a vital part of what readers expect and separates simple news reporting from the work of a correspondent who is expected to provide context and analysis. Philips Price admirably achieved this part of his task, but was able only intermittently to get his message to those who most needed to hear it: policymakers; the British political establishment, especially the 'Labour and democratic forces'; the voting population. His warning was an inconvenient truth. He made the prediction on the basis of his years of experience of the country, his command of the language and his extensive travel during the revolutionary era. Few people knew Russia then better than Morgan Philips Price; few people, unfortunately, were able to read what he wrote about the country.

'The Truth about the Allied Intervention in Russia' proved costly for Philips Price. Aylmer Maude's letter to C.P. Scott seems to have hit a raw nerve. Scott, and the paper, went to considerable lengths after the publication of Philips Price's inflammatory pamphlet to distance themselves from him. Five years later, Scott insisted that to call Philips Price a *Manchester Guardian* correspondent was 'extremely misleading', insisting that Philips Price 'sent us letters and occasional telegrams, but he was never a regularly appointed correspondent'.[78] Scott had apparently, and conveniently, forgotten the letter he had written in 1914 introducing Philips Price as the paper's correspondent in Russia.[79]

Alongside the polemic and the propaganda, the pamphlet contained addressed another theme: a plea for the value of journalism – a plea for the correspondent to be permitted to write and to publish. 'One of the most deadly weapons wielded by the ruling classes of all countries is their power to censor the press'[80] was its opening line. In his second paragraph, Philips Price continues:

> Telegrams to my newspaper are suppressed or if passed by the British censor are decapitated [...] All the technical apparatus of the capitalist states of Western Europe is set in motion against those whose duty it is to tell the truth about the Russian Revolution.[81]

This was what Philips Price was trying to do as a correspondent. There was an echo of John Reed's admission that while his sympathies were not neutral, 'in telling the story of those days, I have tried to see events with the eye of a conscientious reporter, interested in setting down the truth'.[82] The extent to which Philips Price was prevented from doing this provides a degree of extenuating circumstances for the severity of his infection with the 'virus of Bolshevism'. With the benefit of hindsight, he implicitly accepted this. 'I must admit, however, that I was undergoing some change in my mental outlook and my writing was becoming less objective and contained more and more Marxist jargon in it,'[83] he wrote in *Reminiscences*. He came to accept that he had abandoned one of the central tenets of Western reporting. He also – somewhat amusingly, given his revolutionary egalitarian sympathies – came to regret ignoring the lessons of his elite schooling, 'I had forgotten how to write the English language as taught me at Harrow.'[84]

Abandoning objectivity is a frequent correspondent response to armed conflict or other extreme situations. Reporters go to observe the wars or revolutions of others and find themselves drawn to take sides. In Russia, it seems to be even more common. Ransome and Philips Price both saw themselves as having a duty to tell the truth. So too did Wilton, although his truth was different from his left-leaning contemporaries. All were involved at one time or another, or in one way or another, in activities that would more properly be considered public relations or propaganda today. Philips Price's article was used by the Bolsheviks to try to undermine the morale of allied troops. In wartime, in 1916, Ransome and Harold Williams had been involved in the work of a '"strictly unofficial news agency," which would place news about the British role in the war in the Russian press'.[85] Correspondents also, given the time in which they lived, and reported from, Russia, existed on the periphery of espionage: the grey area where journalism, diplomacy and intelligence gathering meet to assist or to mislead each other – or both. Lord Northcliffe, patriotic to the point of jingoism, positively encouraged his journalists to get involved if the opportunity presented itself. An American correspondent, Stanley Washburn, left an extraordinary account of his 1914 interview with Lord Northcliffe, during which he was hired as a correspondent for *The Times* in Russia. 'I am very glad you are going to Russia for us,' Washburn later recalled the press baron telling him, 'but'

> if you find you can do anything in diplomacy, in a military way, or through political intrigue, which I gather is a favourite pastime of yours, you are to forget *The Times* and serve the 'Cause,' which is more important to me even than exclusive dispatches.[86]

Arthur Ransome, married to Trotsky's secretary, and 'as near as any foreigner who was not a Communist could get to what was going on,' also dabbled in spying. Arrested at King's Cross station in London on his return from a trip to

Russia in 1919,[87] he was interrogated about his political views. Ransome claimed in his autobiography that he had answered that these were 'Fishing'.[88] Bruce Lockhart, in his memoir of Moscow in 1918 which was not published until the early 1930s, insisted that he had 'championed [Ransome] resolutely against the secret service idiots who later tried to denounce him as a Bolshevik agent'.[89] Bruce Lockhart was in a position to know. As Roland Chambers showed in *The Last Englishman*, published in 2010 and drawing on earlier research by Tim Radford for *The Guardian*, Ransome had actually been recruited by MI6 and was their agent.[90] Lockhart hinted at this in his *Memoirs of a British Agent*, writing of Ransome, 'He was on excellent terms with the Bolsheviks and frequently brought us information of the greatest value.'[91] He also described Ransome as, 'if not a member of our mission, was something more than a visitor'. The relevant documents which would conclusively prove that Ransome actually was a spy, however, were not released until 2005.[92] Given his earlier contribution to the work of the 'unofficial news agency', it is perhaps less surprising that Ransome was willing to cross the line between reporting and spying. It is a blurred line and one on both sides of which many correspondents in history have comfortably operated. What is perhaps surprising about Ransome is that he chose to serve an intelligence service, MI6, which absolutely did not share his willingness to give the Bolsheviks credit where he felt it was due. Bruce Lockhart's assessments of Ransome make interesting reading even today, 'a sentimentalist [...] and a visionary, whose imagination had been fired by the revolution [...] an incorrigible romanticist'.[93] Perhaps it was some of these qualities which led the folk tale-teller-turned-foreign correspondent to turn spy, too.

It is more obvious, as Bruce Lockhart pointed out about Ransome's contacts with the Bolsheviks, to see what MI6 saw in Ransome. As the facts about post-revolutionary Russia were blanketed by the fog of Civil War, correspondents seemed to know more than most others, diplomats included. Even they were sometimes stumped. John Ernest Hodgson's 1932 account of his time with the forces of the White General, Anton Denikin, described the frustrations of the veteran Reuters correspondent, Guy Beringer, 'in despair about getting any information from the staff'.[94] Hodgson's sweeping reflection on the 'character of the Russian' may also raise a smile with anyone who has tried to write about the country: 'He does not regard truthfulness as being at all necessary to the maintenance of amicable social or political relations.'[95] Wilton, Philips Price and Ransome, the three correspondents whose work has been this chapter's principal focus, were all at pains to stress how their access, their presence, gave their journalism an authority which that of their competitors lacked. It was all very well for Bruce Lockhart, writing more than a decade after the event, to quote approvingly the 'brilliant *exposé* (italics in the original) of a Russian who argued of Bolshevism 'that in spite of its dictatorial tyranny its roots were in the masses, and that the counter-revolution had no chance of success for years to come.'[96] Ransome and Philips Price's reporting – had readers actually been able to see more of the latter – would have told people this much earlier. In the case of those two reporters, their own sympathies for the cause may have been a factor in their motivation. If so, it did not mean that they were wrong. Their analysis was correct. Given Ransome's own divided loyalties, and double role, perhaps his own facetious response as to his political views – 'Fishing' – was not so wide of the mark. With the benefit of decades of hindsight and reflection, Philips Price, towards the end of his long life, wrote again of his revolutionary experience. 'I see things in a longer perspective now, but if I had to live my time again I would not do otherwise than I did then.'[97] Along with Arthur Ransome's, his reporting of the years which followed the Russian revolution remains invaluable today to our understanding of what happened then. It deserved a wider contemporary readership than the one permitted by the censors.

3

From 'A wild and barbarous country' via starvation to Stalinism

For centuries, one of the greatest challenges to Western understanding of Russia has been its inaccessibility: distance, visa regulations, political tensions and *pace* Arthur Ransome, the complexity of its language: all have conspired against knowledge of the world's largest country. As a friend from university once remarked to me when I began regularly to travel there in the 1990s, 'I know loads of people who have been to South America, but you are the only person I know who has been to Siberia.' Journalists have gone some way to filling those gaps, but not always to the satisfaction of readers or other writers. At the outset of his *Russian Journal* – his account of his trip to Russia in the late 1940s – John Steinbeck noted, 'There were some things that nobody wrote about Russia.' Food was included in these, twice. 'What do the people wear there? What do they serve at dinner? Do they have parties? What food is there?'[1] Such questions were not only natural human curiosity, but also of great political significance in a country where bread shortages had fed revolutionary fervour, and where the revolutionaries had promised bread. In the first decades of Soviet power, their ability to provide would be tested: with deadly consequences for the people and disastrous consequences for the reputation of some correspondents.

Steinbeck – who travelled with the photographer Robert Capa – saw the USSR in the late Stalin period. The early years of that period were an even tougher assignment. 'For two and a half years at least there was no running water in Moscow. Can you imagine that, you WESTERNERS?'[2] was the sneering challenge which Walter Duranty of *The New York Times* issued to readers of one of his autobiographies. Most, of course, could not – and there were others who would not imagine the kind of privations which scarred the early Soviet period. Instead, they preferred to see a shining new civilization taking shape – often averting their gaze from facts which did not suit that interpretation. In our time, they might have dismissed such reporting as 'fake news'. To report on the early

Soviet period was to overcome Russia's inaccessibility to the outsider and tell the story of what was happening there. Correspondents came away with strong opinions: their own preconceptions altered even as they sought to challenge and shape the views held by their readers.

The bloodletting of the Civil War did not lead to a prolonged period of peace. The Soviet Union's first post-revolutionary decades were cursed by famine and mass murderous political repression. Removed from the revolutionary front line by failing health before his death in 1924, Lenin looked for an eventual successor. Lenin, who 'had always behaved as if his own presence was vital to the cause of the October Revolution'[3] did not much like what he saw. His political testament 'drew pen portraits of six leading Bolsheviks: Stalin, Kamenev, Zinoviev, Pyatakov, Bukharin, and Trotski'.[4] None of them 'emerged without severe criticism'.[5] As good Marxists, those to whom it fell to take up the cause after Lenin's death were wary of lessons from history. If the French Revolution of 1798 had helped to inspire those who wanted to sweep away Tsarist Russia – even down to crowds singing La Marseillaise and describing the Peter and Paul Fortress in Petrograd as the 'Russian Bastille'[6] – then by the 1920s it had become 'a precedent of failed revolution very much on the minds of the party's leaders'.[7] One of the characteristics of that failure, as Trotsky himself noted, had been use of revolutionary violence – in this case, the guillotine – against some of the revolutionaries themselves.[8] Trotsky had good reason to worry. Despite his inclusion on Lenin's list of the severely criticized potential successors, it was Stalin who took over the top job. As he sought to remove Trotsky from the political scene – first by exile, later by murder in exile – some parts of France's revolutionary history seemed to repeat themselves. Ultimately, as Vyacheslav Molotov – a staunch supporter of Stalin who would become Soviet foreign minister during the Second World War – later noted approvingly, 'Many revolutions collapsed. In Germany, in Hungary. In France – the Paris Commune. But we held on.'[9] They did so at a cost of great loss of life, and in a way which divided even more sharply international apologists and adversaries – including journalists covering the USSR's formative years. Some came as believers and left bitterly disillusioned. Others loathed what they saw from the start. Not one of them seemed unmoved.

The enthusiasm which drove them on notwithstanding, the many obstacles placed in their way made reporters' lives extremely difficult during this period – one reason why some chose the trade-off of reaching an understanding with the Soviet authorities which would at least permit them to send some stories, even if it was rarely the full story. For the USSR at this time, still stung and suspicious after foreign support for the counter-revolutionary White armies during the Civil War was not minded to throw open the borders to correspondents eager to see the new world which was taking shape. Western attempts to kill off the Soviet system in its infancy seemed to have created an atmosphere in which all foreigners were seen as threats, correspondents included. Stalin's 'approach to western journalists,' as Shelia Fitzpatrick has noted, 'was that, while a few could be usefully manipulated, their real function was to discredit the Soviet Union, which made them essentially spies.'[10] Yet this was not the only factor which made Stalin and his politburo so hostile to correspondents. Just as Russia has frequently been off limits to foreign travellers for reason of distance, expense or a lack of permission, so relatively few Russians – certainly until the post-Soviet period, when Russia joined the global package tour industry – had been abroad. The exceptions were those sent by the government: whether proudly – as diplomats or military personnel – or in disgrace – as political exiles. While some revolutionaries had fallen into the latter category, and benefitted from their time abroad to develop an understanding of the wider world, Stalin's team were, in comparison, 'hicks who had never lived in Europe and didn't know foreign languages'.[11]

The Soviet government, feeling itself – with some justification – to be surrounded by enemies, was not taking any chances by giving foreign correspondents free reign. Those who did manage to enter during the Civil War period did so, as noted in the previous chapter, without the permission of the Soviets in Moscow and therefore into territory which the Soviets did not control. This lack of access did not suppress reporters' appetites. Unable to get to Russia itself, their journeys tended to terminate in the Latvian capital, Riga. It was here, after travelling across Europe from Paris in the fall of 1919, that Walter Duranty ended up. He struck gold: journalistically and literally.

Riga then was like any city on the edge of a closed border: a magnet for all those who flock to such places in times of war or revolution, trying, as if straining their eyes to peep through a crack in a fence, to find out what is happening on the other side. There were many motives among those who were drawn there: military reconnaissance; political espionage; illicit trading – and reporting. On this occasion, the factors that shape towns such as Riga was then – on the edge of free access, bordering a forbidden territory – fell well together for Duranty. As well as those trying to get into revolutionary Russia, there were those in Riga who were on their way out. A combination of good fortune and doggedness delivered Duranty an exclusive which made *The New York Times* proud. However history may have come to judge him as a person, and however hit-and-miss his own accounts of his life may be, Duranty knew how to grab the reader's attention. The opening paragraph of his 22 December despatch leaps off the page a whole century later. 'A great Bolshevist conspiracy has just been discovered here,' it began, before concluding, after a reference to 100 arrests, 'The object of the movement was to overthrow the Government, and establish Bolshevist rule.'[12] It was the detail which followed in the next paragraph that would ensure that the story continued to run and bolstered Duranty's reputation (while not, at this early stage, endearing him to Russia's new rulers): the tale of a Russian sailor on his way to the United States with a letter to 'comrades', and money and jewels hidden in his boots.[13] A few days later, Duranty, presumably buoyed by enthusiastic responses from his editors in New York, got even closer to the story. In a later despatch from Riga, dated 30 December and published the following day, he gave an account of the hour during which he himself interrogated 'the Bolshevist courier'.[14] Based on his part in the interrogation, Duranty offered his own description of the man's appearance – 'a brutal face, but decidedly not stupid'.[15] Duranty's account brought to life the drama of the period and the kind of details which might thrill and unsettle his readers. He also offered his own conclusion: that the man was 'a genuine Bolshevist agent'.[16]

Presumably not feeling favoured by international coverage such as this, the Bolsheviks kept international correspondents beyond Soviet borders. The arrangement ultimately suited no one. The Soviets could not possibly hope to get favourable coverage when they would hardly talk to anyone. Western readers could hardly hope to understand the USSR when they were not allowed to read about it. The tone of Duranty's 'Red Courier' story – even allowing for journalistic licence and the thrill of having got such a cracking scoop – may be seen, at least in part, as a consequence of this. Russia remained behind a kind of editorial iron curtain *avant la lettre*. Correspondents were stuck on one side of the divide and forced to guess what was going on out of sight on the basis of what emerged. As Whitman Bassow, a former Moscow Bureau chief of *Newsweek*, noted when writing in the 1980s of the post-revolutionary period: 'American editors were forced to rely almost entirely on rumors, gossip, and thirdhand reports emanating from foreign capitals.'[17] In consequence, 'the reporting was so confused, inaccurate, and hostile to the Bolsheviks that no one really understood what was happening inside Russia, let alone why.'[18] But what was happening inside Russia was soon to lead the country not only to announce a shift in policy, but also to be frank about some of its problems and seek outside help in addressing them.

With the bloodshed that had accompanied and followed, the Bolsheviks' seizing of power had come colossal social instability and change. In conditions such as these, economies are inevitably disrupted. Political leaders may have to sacrifice, or at least postpone, principle in order to run the country. In the case of the Bolsheviks, that meant permitting, from 1921, private business under the New Economic Policy (NEP).[19] Then, beginning in 1928, Stalin took the Soviet economy in another direction. The NEP was dismantled. For industry, this meant a 'Five-Year Plan which assigned both credit and production targets to factories, mines and construction sites'.[20] In agriculture, it meant collectivization.

Ninety percent of the Russian population at the end of the Tsarist period had been 'born and bred in the countryside'[21] – so any change to the way that agriculture was administered risked causing significant disruption. It was also to cause widespread death. Aside from the new social order which altered the way that land was owned and administered, war and revolution meant that those who worked the land were often either absent or otherwise unable to function at full capacity. The cities, like the countryside, still needed to eat. Even in the early years of Soviet power, before full-scale collectivization, troops were sent to requisition grain from the bread baskets of the former Empire, among them the Ukraine. Discontent and unrest followed, to the extent that 'in 1920 and 1921 the struggle between peasant forces and Soviet troops in the Ukrainian villages became so bitter and violent as to resemble a Civil War'.[22] With the virtual disappearance of food considered fit for human consumption, famished peasants ate 'grass, weeds, leaves, moss, tree bark, roof thatch and flour made from acorns, sawdust, hay and horse manure'.[23] Others 'hunted rodents, cats and dogs'.[24] Extreme hunger drove some to cannibalism. In some of the starving regions, there were even cafes serving human flesh. Families, intending to consume parts of relatives who had died, resisted attempts by the authorities to remove bodies of the departed. Cemeteries were put under guard to prevent the newly buried being dug up and eaten.[25] The figures behind this terrifying collapse of civilization in the affected areas are themselves shocking. In *The Harvest of Sorrow*, Robert Conquest pointed out that 'the grain crop (including potatoes) had gone down by about 57% between 1909–1913 and 1921'.[26] Russia paid a deadly price for its revolution. Reporting that story was to prove a challenge that divided the Moscow press corps as never since.

By the summer of 1921, the situation had deteriorated to the extent that Russia decided to ask for outside help, although it did not initially do so on an official level, at least not publicly. It fell to the writer, Maxim Gorky, to make the appeal: through international channels including the Western media. He did so hoping that literature, culture and science – if not Russia's brave new politics – would stir the world's sense of humanity. 'Tragedy has come to the country of Tolstoy, Dostoevsky, Mendeleev, Pavlov, Mussorgsky, Glinka and other world-prized men,' his message began. 'Russia's misfortune offers a splendid opportunity to demonstrate the vitality of humanitarianism. I ask all honest European and American people for prompt aid to the Russian people. Give aid and medicine.'[27] The message took a while to reach the West. With would-be Moscow correspondents stranded in Riga, some of the first reports actually appeared from datelines outside Russia – including the Latvian capital. The Soviet government, while desperate for help, were keen to stress that it was not technically they who were asking for it. A stubborn sense of pride dominated even in the face of famine. On 16 July, *The New York Times* headlined a denial from Chicherin that an appeal for aid had been made to a US senator then visiting Russia. His 'denial' was a tortuous contradiction, with a good dollop of ideological disingenuousness. 'We have not appealed to America except through the widespread radio appeals of Maxim Gorky,' Chicherin was quoted as saying in the article 'Says Soviet didn't appeal to America.' He went on to explain. 'We cannot ask for American relief from representatives when we have no existing relations.'[28] The Soviets did not wish to deal with capitalist governments – however much they needed food and medicine. As July went on, the appeal did trickle through to the West – but initially made astonishingly little impact. In London, *The Times* – with an editorial line that was still one of sworn enmity to Bolshevism – did run the story the following day, 18 July. 'Owing to the failure of the harvest, millions of Russians are faced with death from starvation,' ran its news item – but the story was buried at the end of page 9, at the very bottom of a column of brief 'Imperial and Foreign News items.'[29] By the end of that week, *The Times* seemed to have realized that the story perhaps deserved more attention. A despatch from Berlin – 'Russian Pestilence and Famine' – drew on 'official investigations' and an article from the Soviet newspaper *Izvestiya* from earlier in the month to give a fuller impression of the growing disaster.

The fact that the paper could wait until later in the month speaks of an era when policymakers had so much more time to respond to crises. The United States spotted a political opportunity and one which would eventually benefit those correspondents trying to report on Russia from beyond its borders. Official request or not, Washington decided to offer aid to Russia. There were conditions. *The New York Times* reported from Berlin on 23 July, citing other reports from Galicia, that these included 'the immobilization of the Red Army, and the restoration of freedom of the press and personal liberty'.[30] By the end of the month, sufficient progress had been made for the United States to agree to send assistance. It was only then, on 31 July, that Gorky's appeal of more than two weeks earlier was actually published in full – held back, perhaps, by sensitivities to the ongoing negotiation of the conditions under which American aid might or might not have been delivered. Prisoner releases were agreed – among them was that of Mrs Marguerite E. Harrison.[31]

Harrison called her 1936 autobiography *Born for Trouble*. Even though it contradicts versions of the same events given in her earlier book *Marooned in Moscow* (1921) – and leaves the reader wondering what might be true – the title itself seems no misrepresentation. A woman in what was then very much a man's world, Harrison showed remarkable courage, cunning – and questionable journalistic ethics. The combination certainly landed her in trouble and in a Bolshevik jail. She did, though, succeed in crossing into Russia and reporting from there at a time when others failed. The reasons for her success, however, did not begin and end with her undoubted resourcefulness. When she was released, *The New York Times* praised her as 'a brilliant news writer' whose reports were 'for a time [...] virtually the only news received first hand in the United States from the isolated capital of Soviet Russia.'[32] They also hinted, in a report published earlier that year, at one of the reasons why she was tolerated when others were not even permitted to enter the country: she was alleged to be 'a semi official agent of the American government'.[33] These may have been the reported words of a radical activist repeating what the Bolsheviks had told him – a combination unlikely to inspire credulity in that era in the United States – but they were correct. For Harrison had decided, before leaving for Europe in 1918, that she 'was willing to become a spy'.[34] Her decision to take on this extra role – and be caught for carrying it out – can only have played into the hands of the Soviet school of thought that all foreign correspondents were spies. Yet Harrison's decision has to be taken in the context of her time and gender. While there were some women who went from the United States to report on the First World War, they were there to cover stories seen then as being principally of interest to women. In those days, that generally meant hospitals and the lives of housewives. Covering the military and diplomatic progress of the war was much more commonly considered men's work. Writing years later, and giving her fullest account of her time in Moscow (the one that contradicted earlier versions, such as *Marooned in Moscow*, which was presumably rushed out to cash in on her fame as a former prisoner of the Red regime), Harrison was frank about her motivation. Of her decision to leave for Europe in the summer of 1918, Harrison wrote, 'I felt that I was still out of touch with the greatest event in history. I longed to go to France and watch the progress of the war at first hand, but most of all I craved to find out for myself what was going on in Germany.' This is a sentiment that any correspondent would recognize: her determination to get to Russia afterwards, one that any correspondent would admire. Given the constraints placed upon her by her gender, Harrison's claim that becoming a spy was the only way to achieve her aim is plausible – even if, as noted above, her decision was also ethically questionable and would have consequences beyond those which she herself suffered by being jailed.

The New York Times' description of Harrison as a 'brilliant news writer' was backed up by the way she told her story. Her account of crossing the Polish border differs little in the versions she presented in *Marooned in Moscow*, and *Born for Trouble*, fifteen years later. Her eye for detail brings to life a journey which few made then, largely because it was not permitted. Harrison and her travelling companion, Dr Karlin, a Russian who had been living in the United States, made their way from the border to Moscow, passed along a chain of ever more senior Bolsheviks as they progressed. Harrison – showing a commendable correspondent's curiosity – made the most of this opportunity to learn what she could of the country challenging the established global order. She was helped by the fact that she seemed to speak pretty good Russian and had Dr Karlin to help her out when her own vocabulary faltered. Having eventually made it to Moscow on a long train journey of the hardships of which included the near impossibility 'for our orderly to get us hot water for tea from the samovars at the stations'[35] (at least she did not have to try to battle her way to the samovar herself), Harrison was taken to meet an official she names only as Rosenberg, from the Western Section of the Commissariat for International Affairs. She was told that she had 'done a dangerous and absolutely illegal thing in coming to Moscow without permission,'[36] but, surprisingly, was allowed to stay. 'Those who were responsible for your entry into the country will be held to account,'[37] Rosenberg menacingly concluded. The reason for the authorities' leniency became clear only later.

To begin with, Harrison started work as a correspondent, and her memoir recreates not only the world of those few correspondents who were permitted to be in Moscow at that time, but also something of the society which was going upheaval and transition. It was not an easy place to work as a journalist. Rosenberg, Harrison wrote, 'Had no conception of newspaper ethics and regarded journalism simply as an arm of propaganda.' Even if he passed the stories for publication, they still 'ran the gauntlet of approval by Chicherin, who often made changes or erasures, and the "military censorship" – a euphemism for scrutiny by an agent of the Extraordinary Commission.'

The 'Extraordinary Commission' was the Cheka, or secret police, 'Cheka' being a word formed in Russian from 'Ч' ('Che') and 'К' ('Ka'), the initial letters of the Russian words for 'Extraordinary' and 'Committee'. Even gathering what little news the correspondents were permitted to know was a chore. The official bulletin was posted (in French) at midnight Moscow time, meaning that the working day ended only hours after that. This gave Harrison an opportunity to reflect on how safe it was to walk the streets: one of the benefits of living in a police state. Of her nocturnal returns from sending her stories, she recalled feeling 'safer in many ways than I would have felt in a large American city'. She found Moscow a place where 'the most perfect order prevailed' and 'women constantly went about or travelled alone, and in all the months I spent in Russia I never saw any woman spoken to or insulted on the streets'.[38]

With the resourcefulness of a shrewd reporter – and that of a spy – Harrison discovered that the same information posted at midnight could be had from the Russian Telegraph Agency a day earlier.[39] The agency also carried reports of 'strikes, peasant uprisings, meetings and events in the various provinces'.[40] Many of these were too sensitive to appear in the Soviet papers. Harrison knew she would never get them past the Chekist censors. They were, though, 'invaluable' to her for her espionage, a 'report she expected to make in person to General Churchill'.* That had to wait. Some months after her arrival in Moscow, and with everything having apparently gone fine, Harrison was arrested. The Soviet representative in New York, Ludwig Martens, had known all along that she was going for the purposes of spying as well as reporting, and had communicated this to his masters in Moscow. 'The Cheka was playing me like a cat with a mouse, and I was blissfully unconscious of the fact.'[41] This would seem to explain her access to figures such as Felix Dzerzhinsky, head of the Cheka, and perhaps her being allowed to travel illegally to Moscow. The Chekists' toying with her was not over. In order to stay out of prison, Harrison agreed to spy on other foreigners – a deal that she only described in her later autobiography and omitted from the one she wrote shortly after her eventual departure from Russia. The secret police were not satisfied with her performance, however. Accused of not passing back enough decent intelligence, Harrison was arrested again.[42] This time she remained in jail until her eventual release in July 1921, when she left the country in the company of the US Senator, Joseph France, who helped to negotiate her release.

---

* General Marlborough Churchill, Chief of the Military Intelligence Division of the United States Army.

Marguerite Harrison (Getty).

However Harrison might be judged for the fact that her willingness to spy served to confirm Soviet suspicions about foreign correspondents; she did succeed in helping outsiders' understanding of what was happening inside Soviet Russia. She was outgoing enough to get stories where she came across them. Meeting Trotsky at the entrance to a government building, she took the chance to chat with him. Their short meeting ended, according to Harrison, with the Commissar kissing her hand.[43] And even if *Marooned in Moscow* deals less than fairly with the reader from whom it concealed her role as a spy, its afterword was clear-eyed in its advice to the United States, and perhaps even General Churchill and his political masters. 'We may not like the Soviet government, but it is a real government,' she wrote – silencing those who still then believed it would soon collapse. Arguing persuasively that isolation might serve only to strengthen 'the political dictatorship of the Communist Party', she concluded by making the case for the 'cooperation to the fullest possible extent with the Soviet government'.[44] A few days after her release, Harrison was in Berlin. Her former employer, the Associated Press, spotted a story. It was not, alas, an interview to ask for her insights from a country which so few could see, and where she had spent so long. Their story focused instead on her decision to go shopping 'to Repair Russian Ravages Upon Her Wardrobe'[45], as *The New York Times* headlined it.

As Harrison headed West, other correspondents were permitted to go the other way. They arrived in Moscow by train, having taken with them everything they thought they might possibly need. Floyd Gibbons of the *Chicago Tribune* filed a long account of the journey and arrival, which was later also published (presumably to Duranty's annoyance, for he was a couple of days behind Gibbons) in *The New York Times*. His despatch said much about the huge suspicion with which the United States saw the new power in Russia. Gibbons did not travel on his United States passport. He showed officials a receipt for it, issued by American officials in Riga. The reason, Gibbons explained, was that it was 'feared that the Bolsheviki might counterfeit the American passports from photos of the originals'.[46] It seems astonishing today that a receipt should suffice for crossing a border all but closed to correspondents. Gibbons was in his early thirties, but had already made his name for his reporting of the First World War. He had acquired his professional reputation at a cost, having lost an eye on the Western Front – and thus gained an appearance which meant he stood out from the crowd physically as well as journalistically.

Arriving in the same group as Duranty and five others,[47] George Seldes, also of the *Chicago Tribune*, brought 'a canvas bathtub, an electric hot plate, a flashlight, a portable typewriter, and a bulging suitcase'.[48] Other members of the nascent Moscow press corps had come similarly expecting the worst and 'equipped with bedrolls, blankets, and crates of canned food'.[49] No transport other than a lorry was available to take the reporters on from the station. 'Soon, perched high on the top of our baggage and food boxes in the truck, we began our initial trip across the streets of the city that had ruined Napoleon,'[50] Gibbons wrote, reflecting the history of the Russian capital – a history of which he was now witnessing a seminal part. Duranty's first impressions of the city where he

Floyd Gibbons (Getty).

would win a Pulitzer Prize, and lose a reputation, stayed with him: streets full of holes; blocked drains; no shops were open. 'Some of them were boarded up, but in most cases the boards had been torn away and you saw empty windows or no windows at all, just holes, like missing teeth.'[51]

As they all knew then, though, even if it was fascinating to see a city which had been off limits to almost all reporters for a long time, and there were stories to be found there, the real story was far to the south, in the Volga basin, where 'the famine was worst'.[52] It is a measure of the sensitivity of the concession to allow correspondents into the country at all that Lenin sent Maksim Litvinov himself to Latvia to agree the arrangements. Gibbons threatened to fly into Russia without permission (he did have a plane with him). Litvinov had responded by saying the aircraft would be shot down, and Gibbons jailed. Gibbons answered by arguing that jailing an American would put the whole aid deal at risk. Litvinov relented. Gibbons got his head start.[53] He used it well. Even years later, Duranty's frustration at having been scooped was clear. Gibbons, he wrote, was 'beating our heads off'[54] on the Volga famine. The rest of the press corps were still stuck in Moscow with their collapsible baths and boxes of tinned food. Gibbons was sending reports which still impress and shock. He saw a funeral procession for a victim of the famine, 'an open box in which reposed a horrible shrunken figure – matted hair and beard, yellow fangs, greenish skin'. He also described the gruesome spectacle of a boy of twelve chewing fish heads so that he could regurgitate them to nourish an infant in his care.[55] Duranty and the other correspondents were eventually permitted to travel to the stricken region, but not until after Duranty had suffered the indignity of having his own newspaper run the reports of a competitor.

Gibbons left Russia once the famine, and consequently editorial interest in it, began to wane. Duranty stayed, apparently fascinated by the country he had finally reached, and the bold social experiment which was underway there. Duranty's background was very different from that of the working classes whom the Soviet regime lionized. He had been born in Liverpool in 1884, into a family prosperous enough for him to go to one of the elite schools which the Victorian upper classes favoured for their sons: Harrow (the establishment that Philips Price thanked for his English prose). Duranty did not complete his schooling there. He was later moved 'without explanation' to Bedford Grammar School – the move coinciding with a period in his family's history when his father 'dropped from sight entirely' and 'did not rejoin his wife for several years'.[56] Even if the reason for this drastic change in family circumstances has not survived for posterity, it is perhaps telling to note that in *Search for a Key* – 'a watered-down, washed-out version of *I Write as I Please*'[57] in the view of his biographer, S. J. Taylor – Duranty tells his readers on the very first page that his parents were 'killed in a train wreck'.[58] His motives for this untruth are unclear – he might plead that this was semi-autobiographical fiction – but this was not the literary device a devoted son might choose. His parents' fictional fate may have been inspired by the train accident in which Duranty himself lost a leg.[59]

Walter Duranty (Getty).

Duranty had a horror of cliched Western views of Russia. One of the earliest passages of *I Write as I Please* describes his witnessing, as a child, a kind of horror show at a British fairground. Called 'Russian Ride', it was a series of pictures in which a family with five children, travelling in a sledge, was pursued by a wolf pack. The ravenous animals attacked and, as one picture succeeded another, ate the children until only the smallest, a baby, remained. The ghastly spectacle concluded with the parents, having finally reached safety, embracing 'their surviving child'.[60] 'The implications of this story,' Duranty sternly told his readers, 'are obvious enough: Russia was a wild and barbarous country where savage animals could still menace Man; Russians through callousness or necessity do not hesitate to sacrifice lives of others, however dear to them, to save their own.' In common with many successful writers, Duranty guarded jealously his own story. He offered at least two versions of that in his books *I Write as I Please* (1935) and *Search for a Key* (1943). That he was allowed to choose the former title at all shows the sales that his publisher must have expected would flow from his name alone. In *Search for a Key*, the recently graduated Duranty's first steps in journalism are tellingly described, though – and may explain why this Liverpudlian ended up working for a New York paper. Offered a job at *The Daily Mail* thanks to the influence of the father of a Cambridge University friend, his response was, 'I thought the *Daily Mail* and such sensational sheets were unutterably foul.'[61]

Whatever the truth of his life, there are some well-documented factual details that made parts if it read like fantastical fiction. When living in Paris, he knew the occultist Aleister Crowley well enough to take part in sexually charged pseudo-rituals, and to take drugs, with him[62]; he was acquainted with Isadora Duncan in Moscow[63], as the city, newly the capital after the downfall of Tsarism in St Petersburg, thrived as a crucible of artistic experimentation in the years after the 1917 revolution. It was during his time in Paris that his interest in writing about Russia grew and grew. Frustrated – like so many others – by the near impossibility of getting into the country to cover the Civil War, he was reduced to covering from the French capital: picking up what news he could from cables sent from Poland, and from those members of the Russian – anti-Bolshevik – diaspora who had fled there after the revolution. Reading some of his reporting from then, Duranty's sneering dismissal of the wishful thinking of the 'the State Department and the British and French foreign offices', cited above, takes on an additional meaning. For Duranty himself was guilty of this. His Paris despatch published on 1 May 1920 (the date of the Workers' Holiday, as if to make matters worse) concerned the advance of Polish troops fighting Bolshevik forces and was headlined 'Poles' Drive Raises Hopes of Reds' Fall'. The Poles' military success, Duranty wrote, was, 'the first consequence of realization by Soviet Russia's neighbours of the appalling state of weakness to which the Red administration has reduced the country'.[64] Later the same month, Duranty confidently nosed a story on the prediction that 'the rule of the Bolsheviki in Russia is nearing its end, according to information received here from confidential Russian sources.[65] Like *The New York Times'* overreliance on Iraqi exile sources, and members of the Bush administration who were enthusiastic about the 2003 invasion of Iraq, the outcome predicted here turned out to be wrong. *The New York Times* was honest enough later to apologize for having been misled over Iraq. It seems they may have had similar concerns in the previous century about their coverage of Russia. They commissioned Walter Lippman and Charles Merz to produce a study of their coverage. It appeared later that same year, 1920. Their conclusions were clear and unflattering. They included, 'From the point of view of professional journalism the reporting of the Russian Revolution is nothing short of a disaster.'[66] Duranty may himself have felt chastened.

Having finally made it to Moscow, he had a chance to see the new world for himself and write about it. He made himself comfortable, managing to get himself a mistress, Katya, and a house on Bol'shaya Ordynka, near the city centre. In March 2019, the address was home to various businesses including a photo studio, a translation bureau, and a gynaecologist. Duranty witnessed Moscow in mourning for the death of Lenin, the leader who had forged the new regime. His descriptions, written on the day, captured the drama and the mass grieving for a leader who inspired genuine devotion. Duranty described the news spreading through the snow-covered city, carried by special editions of papers which reached the streets in the early evening, producing 'literal stupefaction' in those who read them.[67] Duranty followed the story at length and in detail, reporting later that week that the frozen ground beneath the Kremlin wall had been blasted open by sappers in order to create Lenin's grave,[68] and then on the simple funeral ceremony itself on a day of extreme cold (minus 37 Celsius), even by the standards of Moscow in midwinter. 'Beards, hats, collars and eyebrows were white like the snowclad trees in the little park close to the Kremlin wall, where nearly 3000 communists now lie buried, including the American, John Reed.' Duranty mentions that this 'little park' is the burial place of John Reed, but says nothing more about Reed. Was his a reputation Duranty coveted, and hoped one day to eclipse? Instead, he went on, once more reminding his reader of the life-threatening frost: 'Few dared take off their hats as Lenin's body was borne to its last resting place.'[69] In the same newspaper, in material generated in the United States, Western wishful thinking that the end of Lenin would mean the end of Soviet power was much in evidence. Duranty would have been frustrated by some of the other coverage that *The New York Times* ran that week. 'Lenin lived to see his theories fail,'[70] the headline for Lenin's obituary, published the same day as Duranty's description of the Soviet capital choked with grief, confidently declared. 'Lenin's great experiment: he failed, and no one else is likely to try again,'[71] was the headline the letters' editor chose for correspondence that same week arguing that it was all over for Communism before it had even really started.

It was not of course – but as the decade wore on, some of Lenin's concerns about the field of his possible successors proved to be well founded. One incident in the late 1920s gave a menacing taste of the direction in which Stalin would take the revolution once he found himself in undisputed charge of it.

As at other times in its history – especially those when it was going through significant social change – Russia in the 1920s needed outside expertise. The mines of the Ukrainian coal fields sought the technical assistance of foreign engineers, including from Germany. In March 1928, some of those engineers, together with dozens of their Russian counterparts, were implicated in an alleged plot to sabotage Soviet industry. From the outset, it seemed suspicious. Even *The Times* correspondent – then still reporting from Riga, and so not benefitting from especially good sources – wrote: 'As usual, scepticism prevails about the reality of such a plot, and all kinds of conjectures are current in regards to the motivation for the "discovery."'[72] Duranty, in *The New York Times* a few days later, saw a bigger political agenda: 'There have been hints that the contest for supremacy between STALIN and TROTSKY may have had its repercussions'[73] (capitals in original). As spring turned to summer, the hapless accused were put on trial – a process the outcome of which was never in doubt. As *The Observer* reported in May, 'Twenty of the Russians have confessed their full guilt, while a number of others have recognised their partial guilt.'[74] The alleged sabotage's supposed purpose was to reduce the Soviet mining industry to such a poor state that 'the Soviet Government would be obliged to grant concessions to foreign capitalists'.[75] Its real purpose was closer to home: a threat to anyone who did not want to work the Stalin way, 'a means of intimidating every economist, manager, or even party official who objected to the raising of tempos of industrial growth,'[76] as Robert Service wrote. 'The trial was a judicial travesty. Stalin took a close, direct part in decisions about the engineers.'[77] Duranty was there at the end to hear the verdicts: sending a dramatic account of the 'trial which ended at 1.30am today with eleven death sentences'.[78] In a sign of the changing media world, a 'movie camera clicked so that the whole Soviet Union from Moscow to Murmansk, from Tiflis to Vladivostok, might share in the final scene'.[79] If, however, Duranty had initially suspected political intrigue, his view of the end of the trial was more straightforward. 'Most of the accused, I am convinced, deserve their fate.'[80] If the trial was, as Duranty himself had suggested, part of a battle between Stalin and Trotsky, Duranty's conclusion made clear which side he would be on. His apparent enthusiasm for the way in which Stalin ran Russia was not rewarded as he might have hoped. Stalin's suspicions of foreign correspondents extended to his having very little contact with them. An interview with the leader was the most sought-after scoop in the Moscow press corps. A rival – who was to become a stern critic – beat Duranty to it.

Eugene Lyons was a correspondent who deserves greater renown today. His memoir *Assignment in Utopia* is remarkable for what it says of the way that foreign correspondents worked in the early post-Soviet period; for what it says about life in the country then; and, most of all, for its level-headed reflection on the process of an idealist becoming irreversibly disillusioned. It is testament to the legend that John Reed had become so rapidly after the end of his short life that Lyons, heading for Italy to report on an anarchist uprising in the 1920s, wrote that 'the impending Italian revolution needed its John Reed' – a role he intended to fulfil. Alas, he discovered that 'Italy was brimming all over with potential John Reeds' all accredited to the same radical organizations as Lyons himself. Lyons may have shared some of Reed's talent as a reporter, but he did not share his privileged background. A poor immigrant who remembered 'vermin and vomit'[81] in the bowels of the ship which brought him to America, the promise he showed at school earned him the right to pursue his education instead following his father into the sweatshop – Lyons' brother's fate from age thirteen. 'Ostensibly I was being primed for the law,' he wrote later. 'But my dreams were of writing, not as a means of making a living, but as a weapon on my side of the class war.'[82] His journalism and his Communism flourished together. After five years working for Soviet publications based in New York, Lyons went to Moscow as correspondent for United Press, arriving in early 1928. His memoir, published a decade later, draws on his skills as an observer and as a writer who conveys and interprets his observations. His description of Miss Jmudskaya, the UP Moscow bureau secretary who has endured the vicissitudes of revolutionary Russia, is arresting. 'I never once heard that voice touched with enthusiasm or even bitterness. I was to meet hundreds like her, in whom suffering seemed to have burned out all emotion. Only the charred husks of their character remained.'[83] Duranty – and reading this today we must take into account rivalry and later disagreements – was 'urbane, clever to a fault, a scintillating talker' and 'curiously contemptuous of Russians'.[84] Perhaps Lyons's lack of reputation today is due to his having been an agency reporter, rather than the high-profile correspondent of *The New York Times*, or other August publication. Still, it was he who landed the big scoop that everyone had been seeking for so very long.

Lyons' interview with Stalin, in November 1930, came as such a surprise, and at such short notice, that, suspecting a prank, Lyons made fun of the member of Stalin's staff who called to offer him the meeting.[85] The interview seems to have been granted at least in part because of rumours that Stalin was dead. Lyons, indeed, said that his first question was: 'Comrade Stalin, may I quote you to the effect that you have not been assassinated?'[86] Stalin agrees that he may 'except that I hate to take the bread out of the mouths of Riga correspondents.'[87] In pure news terms, there was not much to the interview. The fact that it had taken place was enough of a story. Lyons asked Stalin about his family – explaining that such matters were of interest to American readers.[88] He was even given a Latin alphabet typewriter to write up his despatch, and tea and sandwiches while he hammered it out. His story's passage through censorship was eased by Stalin's agreeing to sign it, a copy which Lyons, not surprisingly, kept.[89] The interview was published on 24 November and boosted his reputation to the extent that when, the following year, he next returned to New York for a visit, he did so 'his head still haloed in the radiance of that Stalin interview'.[90]

One senses from Lyons's description of Duranty that, however he came to think of him later, he was impressed, if not intimidated, by him. Duranty was presumably at least frustrated, and more probably furious, to have been scooped by such a relative newcomer. He did not have to wait long to catch up. His own interview with Stalin appeared a week later and reads very much better today. It is a hard news story in which Stalin predicts that the Treaty of Versailles, which ended the First World War, 'cannot last'. This, he argues, is because, 'it is a law of capitalist society that the strong must prey on the weak'.[91] Ideologically inspired or not, Stalin's words were hard hitting for their prescience. Duranty knew what to ask and got a real story. It was his intelligence and his insight into the workings of Russia that led him to produce award-winning reporting, coverage for which he won the 1932 Pulitzer Prize for 'Correspondence', 'For his series of dispatches on Russia especially the working out of the Five Year Plan'.

Later that year, a young Englishman joined the Moscow press corps as correspondent for *The Manchester Guardian*. Malcolm Muggeridge's story is especially significant. He came not only as a correspondent, but, like Lyons, as a true believer in Communism. Reflecting on his experience four decades later, he described the ideologically driven preparations he and his wife, Kitty, made for their departure to Russia: getting rid 'of all our bourgeois trappings; my dinner-jacket, for instance, and Kitty's only long dress'. Nor was there a future for 'most of our books, which we considered to be bourgeois literature of no relevance in a Workers' State'.[92]

Nor was this just going to be an assignment. It was a complete new departure to build a new life in a new world: an emigration. 'We were fully prepared to exchange our British passports for Soviet ones; indeed, we were looking forward to making the exchange.'[93] Muggeridge's memoir, *Chronicles of Wasted Time: Volume 1, The Green Stick* (his title a reference to the work of Tolstoy), described his life as a correspondent in Moscow then – a role which Muggeridge saw as 'easy enough. The Soviet press was the only source of news; nothing happened or was said until it was reported in the newspapers'.[94] Once a correspondent had discovered in the Soviet press something that seemed to be of interest, they 'might, if in conscientious mood, embellish the item a little'.[95] In any case, 'the original item itself was almost certainly untrue or grotesquely distorted. One's own deviations, therefore, seemed to matter little'.[96] There was, in other words, scarce opportunity for original reporting of the kind which might bring the new society to life for a reader who had never experienced it and probably never would. There were exceptions. Travel was restricted, but the correspondents could at least observe life in the city in which they lived, even if what they could say about it was subject to censorship. *The Manchester Guardian* of 1 November 1932 carried an article (presumably by Muggeridge, for it seems to show signs of his sharp eye and waspish turn of phrase, but by-lined 'from a Moscow correspondent') about the long queues which formed daily to file past Lenin's body 'the single retrospective gesture encouraged in Soviet Russia. Everything except Lenin is in the future',[97] the writer sagely concluded. Details such as Stalin behaving in public 'with less formality than the average city councillor' and the revelation that Lenin's 'shrunken head rests on a scarlet pillow'[98] helped to bring to life a political system which, having abolished religion, was nevertheless striving to create its own relics and rituals.

Muggeridge's attempts to assimilate into Soviet life did not go well. He could find no suitable accommodation for himself and Kitty, who was pregnant by then. They ended up living in a dacha belonging to Herr Schmidt, a German businessman whom Muggeridge had met at embassy receptions, and whose sources of revenue are never entirely clear. For reasons we will see, he was, by the end of what ended up being a brief stay, deeply cynical by the time he departed – so cynical, in fact, that his memoir published in the 1970s still sneered at Soviet translators, who got 'bras and underwear specially imported for them by their bosses, sometimes in diplomatic bags. Reputedly easy bedfellows who compensated for their deviant capitalistic ways by reporting regularly what they saw and heard to the GPU'.[99,*] There are telling details of Russia newly communist. Searching for a bedpan for Kitty who is too ill to rise, Muggeridge trawls the 'kommisiony' shops, where, having fallen on hard times, the 'relics of the old Russian bourgeoisie brought their family treasures'[100] to sell.

The Pulitzer Prize had helped to cement Duranty's status as the king of Western correspondents in Moscow. Yet Muggeridge was not impressed by Duranty and would later caricature him in a novel *Winter in Moscow*. The two were to fall out, finding themselves on opposite sides of a huge controversy, and perhaps the most shameful episode of Western reporting of Russia in the whole of the twentieth century.

Food played a role in Duranty's rise to fame and in his subsequent – and lasting – controversial reputation. He entered the fledgling Soviet Union as one of a group of correspondents permitted to accompany a famine relief mission; the property he renovated in Moscow became a magnet for those journalists and other foreigners. His reputation in history is such because of his attitude to another famine in the 1930s, and his role in doing down the writer, the young Welshman Gareth Jones, who travelled to Ukraine to bring the story of starvation to the world. Duranty's frequently quoted defence of the harshness of Stalin's regime – made in a poem he wrote, and *The New York Times* published, in 1932 – also has a food metaphor, a curious omen of the way that history would remember him. 'Russians may be hungry and short of clothes and comfort,/but you can't make an omelette without breaking eggs.' This seems to have been a favourite phrase of Duranty's. Jefferson, the character whom Muggeridge included in *Winter in Moscow* to mock Duranty, even translates it into telegraphese in one of his cables. 'Bolsheviks determined harmonize agricultural economy with industrial development plan stop admittedly involves cruelty and other casualties like other forms war but dash putting it brutally dash impossible make omelettes uncracking eggs.'[101] The very fact that Duranty was allowed to file a poem – and, frankly, not a great one – instead of a news report or feature shows the extent to which he enjoyed a status which allowed him self-indulgently to set the rules. He was also keen to stick to those which his Soviet handlers had laid down for him. Stalin, by now without rival at the top of the Soviet power pyramid, was also laying down the rules about the amount of grain the peasants of the Soviet Union had to produce. The quantities demanded, however, were murderously unrealistic. Southern areas of the Soviet

---

* The 'United Main Political Administration', which succeeded the Cheka in 1923 (Service, *A History of Modern Russia*, 131).

Union had, as we have seen, faced famine in the 1920s. It was about to return, carrying off many more dead as it did.

In 1932, Stalin ordered increased grain requisition from those growers who were officially seen as hoarders but who were really just trying to feed themselves, make a living, and save sufficient for sowing. In the view of Robert Conquest, this decree,

> if enforced, could only lead to starvation of the Ukrainian peasantry. This had been made clear to Moscow by the Ukrainian Communist authorities themselves. All through the next months it was, indeed, enforced with the utmost rigour, and local attempts to evade or soften it were sooner or later crushed[102]

Needless to say, the Moscow press corps were not encouraged to cover this crushing of the peasants' attempts to feed themselves. It fell to an outsider to do it.

Gareth Jones was born in 1905. He excelled as a linguist, graduating from both Aberystwyth and Cambridge before embarking on a career which combined political advice, espionage and journalism.* Jones's approach to reporting the Soviet Union of the 1930s was completely different to that of Duranty. While the Moscow press corps stayed put – partly for reasons which will be discussed later, but which later led them to regret their lack of ambition – Jones, aged only twenty-seven (Duranty was two decades older by now and revelled in his role as the elder statesman of the Moscow press corps), gave his Soviet minders the slip and, in September 1931, set off alone[103] to see what he could find. The result was three articles in *The Times* about his experiences. Jones later returned to the Soviet Union as the famine was taking hold, setting off in the late winter of 1933 on 'a difficult and dangerous walking tour',[104] at a time when such travel was completely prohibited. He had used his then status as a foreign affairs advisor to the former British Prime Minister, David Lloyd George, to get access to the country. Knowing, however, that he would not be able to send his material from the Soviet Union, Jones headed for Berlin, where he recounted his experiences. 'Russia today is in the grip of famine, which is proving as disastrous as the catastrophe of 1921 when millions died,'[105] Reuters, in a despatch published in *The Manchester Guardian* on 30 March, reported him as saying.

While the famine itself is one of the episodes which stains Soviet history – principally because of the role Stalinist policy played in the disaster (Conquest

---

* For a documentary film account of his life, see the excellent 'Hitler, Stalin and Mr Jones' broadcast on BBC4 in the UK on 5 July 2012.

called it the 'Terror-Famine) for the colossal loss of life – the controversy surrounding the way it was reported was for a long time forgotten. In recent years, Stewart Purvis and Jeff Hulbert[106] have looked again at the failures and deceptions (their study is a critical assessment of Duranty's role), and thus helped to resurrect Jones' reputation; he has largely been forgotten beyond a circle of dedicated academic admirers. There is no question that he was treated unfairly by the rest of the Moscow press corps, headed by Duranty.

Duranty met Jones. He described him in print as a man of 'keen and active mind' but also declared his judgement 'hasty'. Duranty's despatch instead concluded that 'there is no actual starvation or deaths from starvation', before adding in a phrase which might make even the most amoral spin doctor wince, 'but there is widespread mortality from diseases due to malnutrition'.[107] The despatch also included one of the instances of Duranty's using his favourite phrase 'to put it brutally – you can't make an omelette without breaking eggs'[108] – an especially unfortunate metaphor when the subject was mass starvation.

Duranty's despatch, which has since become infamous, also hinted at one of the reasons why the Moscow press corps decided to 'conceal a famine',[109] as Lyons later wrote. His top paragraph did not lead with 'thousands already dead and millions menaced by death'.[110] That was saved for the end. Instead, it spoke of 'the diplomatic duel between Great Britain and the Soviet Union', occasioned by the arrest of six British engineers on charges of 'high crimes against the Soviet state'.[111] The incident, which came to be known as the Metro-Vickers trial, barely features in some histories of twentieth-century Russia – overshadowed as it is now by the famine, and the show trials which were to come later in that decade – but at the time it was a massive story (and also one on which the author Ian Fleming, then in Moscow for Reuters, distinguished himself with his coverage, his 'descriptive detail gave a hint of the writer who twenty years later was to create the fictional James Bond', according to Donald Read[112]). The Soviet handler of the foreign press, Konstantin Umansky, skilfully manipulated the massive press interest in the Metro-Vickers trial to keep the starvation story pretty quiet. As Lyons wrote later, 'It would have been professional suicide to make an issue of the famine at this particular time'.[113] Instead, the press corps combined to a collective act of 'throwing down Jones',[114] and the story was largely buried. Lyons even went on to describe how the deal was sealed with vodka and snacks in the hotel room, although as Ray Gamache has pointed out, Lyons 'never named any other journalist who was present that evening, nor has anyone ever come forward to corroborate Lyons' version of events'.[115]

For the purposes of assessing the press corps' role, this does not matter too much at this distance. Lyons' contrition is clear, and as good a writer as he might have decided in his regret to embellish his account with a drink-soaked evening, perhaps thus giving physical form to a symbolic truth. What does matter is that this exercise in 'juggling facts to please dictatorial regimes',[116] as Lyons described it later, meant that one of the biggest stories of Russia's entire century was not reported as it should have been. In fact, correspondents even tried to obscure it.

Muggeridge did head south to the famine area. In late March 1933, *The Manchester Guardian* published three of his despatches. Because of the sensitivity of their subject, they did not appear under a 'from our own correspondent' by-line. The three reports ran as a series 'The Soviet and the Peasantry – An Observer's Notes'. Their authorship was attributed to 'A correspondent in Russia'. The first article opened as if it might be a gentle travel piece, describing the way in which 'you breathe again' once given the chance to leave Moscow. Muggeridge, though, was blunt in his assessment of what he saw once he left the train. 'The civilian population was obviously starving. I mean starving in its absolute sense; not undernourished.'[117] Muggeridge described a market in a small town in the Kuban. Aside from chickens, at unaffordable prices, 'the rest of the food offered for sale was revolting, and would be thought unfit, in the ordinary way, to be offered to animals.'[118] It was grim stuff, and clearly, for the way that he recalled it in such detail when he wrote his memoir almost four decades later, distressed Muggeridge greatly. He judged the work of his younger self harshly. 'Reading the articles again, they seem very inadequate in conveying the horror of it all,'[119] he concluded in *Chronicles of Wasted Time*. Muggeridge was not to last much longer in Russia. After a farewell dinner with the Foreign Ministry minder Umansky, at which Muggeridge seems to get drunker and drunker, and an exchange of angry messages with his editor, to whom he wrote, 'I realise you don't want to know what's going on in Russia, or let your readers know,'[120] he left. He journeyed back West as the storm clouds of conflict took shape over Europe. Hitler had just come to power, and the continent would, within years, become a massive battlefield. Muggeridge had decided some months before that he and Kitty had come up against 'the impossibility of settling in the USSR as we had planned'.[121] His dream had ended in a bitter collision with disillusioning reality and would never recur.

He failed to tell the story of the famine; he twisted words to deny its existence; yet Duranty's achievements as a reporter are not in doubt. They are, though, compromised to the extent that, even seventy years after he deservedly won the Pulitzer Prize for his coverage of the Soviet Union, a campaign began to see him stripped of it.[122] In the mid-1930s, though, he was at the height of his fame and reputation: high enough to yell – in capitals – at his readers for their failure to picture real hardship. His admiration for the Soviet system, and for the revolutionary who would emerge as its strongest formative influence, led his 1990 biographer to call him *Stalin's Apologist*.[123] 'Lenin's disciple' might also describe him. Duranty's 1943 book, *Search for a Key*, gave a more reflective account of his being in Moscow at the time of Lenin's death, and of the crowds who passed the coffin in, 'the hall where Lenin's body lay, to pay him their last tribute. Perhaps the greatest man, not excepting Christ or Mohammed, whom this world has known'.[124] The Soviet Union's achievements may have blinded Duranty to its failures, but he also had a scathing eye for some of the wishful thinking in the West which had characterized the reaction to the Bolsheviks' coming to power. He put his first trip to the Soviet border – in 1919 – into context by describing it as the time when Soviet power had 'obstinately refused to fill the prophecies of the State Department and the British and French foreign offices by failing to collapse'.[125]

Duranty's long assignment gave him a chance to live through the time when Stalin turned 'the whole power of his immense capacity for political malice' on Trotsky, who had 'seemed, at least to the superficial observer, the main claimant to the Lenin succession'.[126] Trotsky's prominent role in *Ten Days That Shook the World* meant that Reed's book, despite having a preface from Lenin, spent much of the Soviet period in the shadows. Duranty made no such mistake. In his time in Moscow, ignoring Stalin would have been impossible – but Duranty did not stick simply to reporting the world as it changed around him. He sought to shape the understanding of it too, and is even credited with giving the word 'Stalinism' to the English language.[127]

His contemporaries judged Duranty harshly, but it is hard not to suspect, as with Lyons, above, a degree of grudging admiration in their depiction of his heartlessness. 'He admired Stalin and the regime precisely because they were so strong and ruthless,'[128] concluded Muggeridge. If Muggeridge did envy Duranty in a strange way, he was also happy to launch a snobbish personal attack on him in print many years later: 'Duranty was getting his own back for being small, and losing a leg, and not having the aristocratic lineage and classical education he claimed to have.'[129] Duranty seemed almost to see himself as a kind of latter-day romantic hero, battered about by the world until he became insensitive. Of his experience reporting on the First World War, he later wrote, 'All of this was preparation for Russia, where foreigners are apt so suffer from aesthetic or sentimental shell shock [...] I had been so bitterly scared by real dangers – air-raids, shells, bullets – that these intangible perils did not bulk large any more.'[130] In Pechorin, Mikhail Lermontov created one of the giant characters of Russian literature. In his callous near-seduction of a young princess, he tells his unsuspecting quarry: 'One half of my soul had ceased to exist. It had withered and died so I cut it off and cast it away.'[131] Duranty dismissed 'sentimental shell shock'. He presented himself as a battle-hardened outsider. He had another reason for not upsetting his hosts that spring when famine laid waste to large regions of the southern Soviet Union. Later that year, Maksim Litvinov travelled to the United States for talks that led to Washington's recognition of the USSR. Duranty travelled with him. At the dinner given to honour Litvinov on the eve of his return to Russia, Duranty was presented to the assembled company. 'When Mr Duranty acknowledged the introduction, the guests rose for the first time and cheered him.'[132] It was a triumph, with the great and good of New York recognizing Duranty as not only 'one of the great foreign correspondents of modern times'[133] but also one who had contributed to international diplomacy. Had the famine been reported as it merited, perhaps that might have been put in jeopardy, at least that year – with consequences for his own standing and reputation that Duranty would have been keen to avoid. The plight of the famine victims, to borrow Duranty's unfortunate metaphor, was the eggs which had to be broken for the omelette of his career as journalist and international fixer.

The correspondents in Russia in this period witnessed the forging of a new society, whose ideas were to have a huge influence on the twentieth century. They also saw the pitiless measures which Russia's new rulers were prepared to take to consolidate Soviet power, and to make their revolutionary dream a reality which could endure. If there is a lesson in journalistic ethics to be drawn from the way that famine was or was not reported in the early Soviet period, it is this: trade-offs with the powerful may not bring the desired rewards. For while the famines of the 1920s and 1930s are a scar of shame across Russian history, few now remember the Metro-Vickers trial. Eyewitness reporting and a command of the language are key. The high points of reporting from Russia in this period owe much to both. This was also a decade of disillusionment. Ideologically motivated reporters such as Muggeridge and Lyons ended up broken men; the cynical Duranty broke those who got in his way – and, curiously, ended up almost a believer.

Believe everything but the facts

The dead far outnumbered those who had come to remember them. The group – it could not be called a crowd – that had gathered were mostly elderly: mostly – judging from the way they paused to light candles and place them in the holders which had been set out for the occasion – practising Orthodox Christians. They had come that morning, 8 August 2007, to remember just some of the 20,000 people who had died there, beginning on the same day seventy years earlier: 8 August 1937. That day, ninety-one people were shot. Their names were displayed on boards at the site. Some days, the number of dead ran to three figures. This was the 'Butovo Firing Range' (*polygon* in Russian – the word generally used for a military practice area) – now a quiet corner at Moscow's southern edge, home to a church and a memorial to the victims of the 'Great Purges' who were killed in the 1930s in such great numbers. The site lies a short distance beyond the roaring lanes of the MKAD, the final circle of road which surrounds the Russian capital; the largest and longest of a series of ring roads which begins in the city centre. Butovo itself lies in an area bounded by two major routes heading south: Varshavskoye Shosse (Warsaw Highway) and Simferopol'skoye Shosse (Simferopol' Highway). One is named for a previous possession of the Russian Empire; the other for what has since become a reclaimed city of the Russian Federation, Simferopol' in Crimea – a city, annexed like the rest of that peninsula, from Ukraine in 2014. The names of the roads reflected past history and future ambition – but the real history of the area, that chapter of Russian history, lay buried in a mass grave for the victims of the killing factories that worked to gun down enemies of the people, real or imagined, whose disappearance would also discourage dissent, drunkenness or delinquency among those left behind. Moscow can be unpleasantly hot in the summer, but even as August wears on, the warmest days are behind and fall is felt in the air. That morning was cool; the sun not giving the warmth it might have a couple of weeks earlier. The sky was clear. There was no threat of rain to keep people away, and yet it was only a few knots of mostly elderly women and men who joined the procession from the church to the newly erected pine cross, more than twelve metres high, atop the new memorial that was the centrepiece of that day's ceremonies. Not far away, a display gave brief accounts of some of the thousands who had died there, alongside their prison mugshots. One, Misha Shamonin, was wrapped in a greatcoat that was too big for him.[1] He seemed remarkably calm, but he was about to be shot dead. I remember at the time being reminded of the 'thin, sallow-faced lad of eighteen in a loose coat,'[2] who is in front of Pierre in the line of prisoners due to be shot by French troops occupying Moscow in *War and Peace*. There were two significant differences: firstly, Misha was to be shot not by the troopers of an invading army, but by his own government; secondly, he was only thirteen. I was there to cover the event for the BBC.[3] I was struck by how few people cared enough to turn up. True, it was a normal working day, but it was also in August – never the most industrious month in Moscow, and this was an event held to mark on of the most traumatic periods of Russia's twentieth-century history. A number of those to whom I spoke to ask what the ceremony meant to them turned out to have some personal connection to the killings – a relative, perhaps or a neighbour whose story could be more openly told in Russia's post-Soviet era. One woman, who gave her name as Zinaida, seemed to see her presence as a kind of duty: 'We have to teach our young to remember what it was like, how priests and ordinary people suffered for us,' she explained. 'The earth is soaked with blood here and we should not forget that.' Official presence was limited to the small number of militia (as the Russian police were still called then) officers one might have expected to see at any public gathering. One wore a very large cap with an unusually large double-headed eagle badge, suggesting seniority, but there was no other sign of government representation.

It might be tempting to conclude from that absence that the Kremlin did not care, but it was not as simple as that. Post-Soviet Russia being as keen on history as it is (and on religion, many of those shot at Butovo having been clergy), the memorial had to be marked in the appropriate way. President Vladimir Putin did visit, accompanied by Patriarch Alexei II, then head of the Russian Orthodox Church, some weeks later. The account posted on the presidential website was matter of fact – 'Between August 1937 and October 1938 20,765 people were shot here. So far about a thousand members of the Russian Orthodox clergy, 230 of who [sic] are saints, have been identified'[4] – yet the numbers upon which it drew managed to combine, in a couple of sentences, the cold calculations which characterized this murderous era of Russia's twentieth-century history – when 'vans and lorries marked "Meat" or "Vegetables" could carry the victims out to a quiet wood, such as the one near Butovo'[5] – with older, holier, ideas of martyrdom and canonization. The Kremlin account did not mention Mr Putin's earlier career in the KGB, but it did apportion blame for the deaths to one of that organization's earlier incarnations: 'the NKVD [Stalin's secret police]'.[6,*]

If many of those killed were sent to their deaths, secretly, in grocery vans, others learnt their fate in the most public way then possible, in trials designed as massive media events. The court case against the Shakhty engineers, when a 'movie camera clicked so that the whole Soviet Union from Moscow to Murmansk, from Tiflis to Vladivostok, might share in the final scene',[7] seemed like a rehearsal for what was a carefully prepared press facility. The following decade, Stalin tightened still further his steel grip on Bolshevik power and Lenin's legacy. In 1936, he made Nikolai Yezhov head of the NKVD – an appointment that was to last for the duration of the murderous media circus known as the show trials. 'We will never have a definitive answer to the question of what the Great Purges were meant to achieve. What can be said with some certainty is that to the degree that there was a firm political intention, that intention was Stalin's,'[8] Sheila Fitzpatrick has written. The 'firm political intention' was supported by a presentational intention, a publicity strategy, designed to use the news media as they existed at the time to the maximum possible effect. The movie cameras would click once more. The international press corps in Moscow would also be called upon to play their part in getting the message across. In doing so, they would have a unique opportunity to witness the new violence of the Soviet regime. Twentieth-century Russia had known death on a vast scale in war; revolution and famine. This was something different.

On 1 December 1934 Sergei Kirov, Communist Party chief in Leningrad (as Petrograd, formerly St Petersburg, had now come to be known), was shot dead in his office. The killer, Leonid Nikolayev, was 'a young ex-Zinovievite'.[9] While 'Stalin's complicity in the murder remains unproven',[10] it was 'the murder that gave Stalin the opportunity to settle scores'.[11] Stalin took the opportunity. His first targets were Zinoviev and Kamenev, tried in camera in January 1935 and sentenced to prison terms.[12] The following year, they were taken from their cells for a retrial: in public. The charges this time were more serious, the outcome never in doubt: along with fourteen others, the two former revolutionaries were charged with involvement in a plot to kill Stalin.

---

* 'NKVD' comes from the initial letters, in Russian, of the 'People's Commissariat of Internal Affairs' (Народный комиссариат внутренних дел).

Harold Denny, *The New York Times* correspondent, drew attention to the special Stalinist nature of what 'public' meant in his 'curtain-raiser' article, sent before the start of the trial. 'Although the trial will be public, there will be no room for the general public. Space not filled by the court and lawyers and the sixteen defendants will be jammed with Soviet and foreign reporters.'[13] Denny may have been the correspondent on the spot, but Duranty still managed to muscle in – from Paris. His analysis published in the previous day's paper, 'Proof of a plot expected' showed his own understanding of the workings of the Soviet system, as well as his continuing willingness to take Stalinist claims at face value. 'It is inconceivable that a public trial of such men would be held unless the authorities had full proofs of their guilt, because these are no sabotaging engineers but old revolutionaries.'[14] Denny may not have shared Duranty's conviction that the 'authorities had full proofs', but *The New York Times*' editorial line as to the likely verdict held firm. Noting the numerous demands for the death penalty voiced before the trial even began, Denny wrote of the 'virtual certainty'[15] that those facing trial would be executed. *The Daily Telegraph*, meanwhile, noted that such a sentence, if passed, had to be carried out 'within 24 hours'.[16]

The stage was set for a dramatic story to unfold before the assembled audience – the drama, though, was lessened by the fact that the ending was not in doubt. There was a plot which kept the audience – both in the court and, in the reporting, around the world – entertained: it included instructions given in invisible ink[17]; a secret code using a copy of the *Arabian Nights*[18]; and, as if made for the newspaper which more than any other loved scandal about Bolsheviks, the ex-wife of one of the accused testifying that he had called for Stalin to be killed.[19] *The Daily Mail* – its late proprietor's loathing of the Soviet regime perhaps not helping with access – actually covered some of the story from Warsaw (although it did also print agency despatches filed from Moscow). Distance from the story did not diminish the *Mail*'s appetite for the drama it offered. The *Mail* had previously demonized Zinoviev when, in 1924, it published a letter – supposedly written by him, but now generally believed to be a forgery – calling on the British Communist party to seek opportunities in the current political climate to start 'class war'.[20] During its coverage of the trial, the *Mail* missed no opportunity to remind its readers of this earlier 'scoop'. Every first reference to Zinoviev during the trial was followed by the phrase, 'author of the notorious "Zinoviev letter" of 1924, exposed by *The Daily Mail*'.[21] Not surprisingly, the paper showed little sympathy for the man they had revelled in portraying as the orchestrator of evil worldwide plots to destroy capitalism. When Zinoviev publicly accepted his guilt, his reported words suggest an understanding of the circumstances in which he was being tried. 'I plead guilty before the working class of the world,' he declared through the microphone in front of the witness stand. 'I know that every word pronounced here is universally broadcast.'[22]

The *Manchester Guardian* seems correctly to have judged the significance of what the court had witnessed. Reporting the executions, and noting that, contrary to expectations, every single one of the accused had been shot – the fact that they had confessed had fed a belief that the lives of some would be spared – the paper suggested, in its headline 'The Purge Only Beginning'.[23] Perhaps they should have been less surprised by the fact that all the defendants were shot so quickly. The *Manchester Guardian*'s report two days earlier had described the applause which followed the announcement of the guilty verdicts. Every part played in the trials needed to contribute to the production as a whole, and the clues to what was to come were, perhaps, there in the clapping of those who had been allocated places in court. The Soviet public could not get enough news – literally. The Moscow despatch which reported the executions also reported the militia being called out to control crowds of people trying to buy newspapers. Overall, the coverage of the first show trial did give an understanding of the scale of what was being witnessed. In an age when journalistic slang refers to an article marking the end of a politician's career as a 'political obituary', the obituary page in *The Times* on 26 August makes rather striking reading. In adjacent columns, the life achievements of both Zinoviev and Kamenev were appraised. The opening paragraph of Zinoviev's obituary matter-of-factly advised readers that the execution of the subject of the article was reported elsewhere in that day's edition.[24] The fact that Stalin had started to move against his contemporaries was significant, and it was reported as such. The reaction of the man who was held ultimately responsible for the entire plot was sought. Trotsky, then in Norway, spoke to reporters there to deny any involvement, and even to suggest that no right-thinking person would believe the statements issued by the Soviet government.[25] *The Times*, some days earlier, had said as much – pointing out that only the investigators could really know the extent to which the admissions of guilt were to be taken at face value.[26] The value of the defendants' words in the first show trial was questionable and questioned. The news value was not.

Still, the correspondents were witnessing something designed by the Stalinist government, and which would only work properly if they dutifully played the role which that government had assigned to them. What choice, though, did they have? Stalinist Russia, as we have seen from the accounts of Muggeridge and others in previous chapters, was not a place where free reporting, in any normal

sense of the concept, was possible. Access to officials was minimal. Access
to information was largely restricted to that which was published in official
bulletins or the Soviet press (to a large extent, the same thing). Even in the latter
case, those correspondents (the majority, at least when they arrived) who did not
read or speak Russian well enough to understand sources without a translator
were dependent on their secretaries and assistants to be their eyes on the Soviet
media. The trials were a news event which they could witness – and judge – for
themselves and their readers. No serious journalist could seriously have stayed
away. Nor did they when the second show trial got underway in January 1937.
Later that year – even as lesser figures in the counter-revolution were being
ferried to Butovo in meat wagons, to be slaughtered – a *Manchester Guardian*
correspondent offered a view on the trials as part of a series of articles written
'after many years residence'[27] in Russia. The safety of having left the country
allowed them to be more frank than the censor would have countenanced.
Having reflected at length on the conduct in court, the confessional desire for
self-incrimination, of the old Bolsheviks who found themselves on trial for their
lives under a new regime, the correspondent concluded, 'The Soviets will never
venture to place in the dock on public trial a real enemy of the dictatorship,
of terrorism and rule by force, a defendant who would turn the court into
his forum.'[28] One of the defendants who was on trial this time had previously
been an architect of the Bolshevik public relations machine: Karl Radek. The
circumstances in which he found himself now, having fallen out of favour,
could hardly have been further from the 'Latin Quarter' the literary, cultured,
atmosphere of which his conversation had once reminded Arthur Ransome. His
previous role as publicist for the Bolshevik cause meant that he was personally
known to many of the correspondents who now looked on as he went on trial for
his life. Duranty, back in Moscow, opened his report describing the experience
of seeing a friend in this situation as 'sad and dreadful'.[29] Here as much as
anywhere Duranty deserved the appellation of 'Stalin's apologist', declaring that
he could not understand how men like Radek, and two of his fellow accused,
Yury Pyatakov and Grigory Sokolnikov, 'could continue to follow Trotsky'[30] so
obvious had it been to Duranty, and for so long, that Stalin would prevail in the
struggle to become Lenin's successor. The court case generated massive press
interest. The *Manchester Guardian* published more than thirty items on the
proceedings from when the trial was announced on 20 January until the end
of that month; *The New York Times* published more than twenty. The London
Times was less prolific, an absence explained in part by the absence of their
correspondent, still allowed no nearer the Hall of Columns, where the trial was

taking place, than Riga, for reasons which will be discussed in greater detail below. There were frequent references to Radek's past as a Kremlin spokesman and leader-writer for *Izvestiya*, the Soviet government newspaper – and much as correspondents are often frustrated in their dealings with spokespeople for foreign governments, it must have been chilling to see one with whom they had chatted over tea now at risk of a death sentence. Radek is admired in *The New York Times* for his wit: in the *Manchester Guardian* for his 'grim jest' during cross-examination by the prosecutor, Andrei Vyshinsky. Vyshinsky and the judge, Vasily Ulrich, were together again after first having gained notoriety in international newspaper coverage of the first show trial. This time they heard stories of plans to sabotage Soviet industry, in league with agents of foreign governments, and plans to kill Stalin and other senior Soviet leaders (this latter plot was the subject of Radek's 'grim jest').

Correspondents were able to attend the trial – public spectacle was after all the whole idea – but they had little else in the way of sources. Like their counterparts earlier in the Soviet era, they had mainly to reply on the Soviet media. They knew where to look to learn what the thinking was in the Kremlin. Commenting on the Soviet newspaper coverage which preceded the trial, the *Manchester Guardian* noted that the 'foul Trotskyist beasts' were deemed worse than Fascists: the latter, at least, would not betray their own country.[31] Articles of this sort left little doubt as to the fate that the accused could expect, but that certainty did not cause the crowds to stay away – at least those who could be squeezed into the 'small and stuffy courtroom', including 'ambassadors and leading diplomatists'.[32] *The Daily Mail* managed to turn up at least one angle the other papers did not, although this may fall into the category of stories that elude the competition because they are not entirely true. A few days after the opening of the trial, a 'special correspondent', filing from Warsaw after three days of watching the trial in Moscow, claimed that 'most people in Russia' agreed that the accused Bolsheviks had been led to make such lengthy confessions because of 'hypnotism'.[33]

The pre-ordained nature of the verdict, and likely sentences, did not make their eventual announcement any less dramatic. The *Mail*'s correspondent, still in Warsaw, reported receiving 'by telephone from Moscow' gripping descriptions of the scene in the court when the judges returned after retiring to consider their decision. The despatch included the detail that young couples in the court looked on 'holding hands in nervous embrace. It was for them that this tragic performance was being held, for their edification and as a warning'.[34] In the early hours of 30 January, the accused were led into court to hear the verdict.

Of the seventeen on trial, thirteen were sentenced to death. Radek was among those whose life was spared because, the court decided, he 'had not directly participated in terrorist wrecking and espionage'.[35] The element of carefully rehearsed and choreographed spectacle was not confined to the courtroom. The verdicts having been made public, 'hundreds of thousands of people took part in a monster demonstration' (Conquest is more precise, giving the figure of 200,000, adding that it was −27 Celsius that day on Red Square, where the throng gathered[36]) in support of the death sentences and cursing Trotsky as 'the arch instigator'. The newspapers duly gave Trotsky the right of reply. *The New York Times* published a piece by the exiled revolutionary as the trial got underway, giving him the opportunity to accuse Stalin of falling back on the methods of the Borgias in order to tighten his grip on power.[37] The *Observer*, in an agency despatch datelined Mexico City, reported that Trotsky interpreted the fact that the lives of some of the accused were spared as a sign that Stalin was 'being forced to back down'.[38] It was a hopelessly optimistic interpretation, as the killings in Butovo and elsewhere would show as the murderous year of 1937 went on. Radek may have been spared the firing squad which most of his fellow accused were soon to face, but he had not long to live. He died in prison just a year or two into his ten-year sentence. As was so often the case during the purges, family members were also expected to pay for the sins of the 'foul Trotskyist beasts'. Sonia Radek, with whom Ransome remembered playing in Radek's Kremlin quarters when she was a toddler,[39] got eight years in jail.[40]

There followed a pause of more than a year in the Show Trials. Then, in the midst of the Moscow winter of early 1938, 'suddenly a newspaperman hurried in, displaying all the symptoms [...] of someone who has got a story,'[41] remembered Fitzroy Maclean, then serving in the British embassy in the Soviet capital, in his later memoir. 'News was short in Moscow in those days, and we clustered around him, diplomats and journalists alike.'[42] Having read the list over the correspondent's shoulder, Maclean wrote, he then 'dashed off'[43] to get a pass for the courtroom. When the trial opened a few days later, the same cast was assembled: Ulrich as judge, Vyshinsky as prosecutor. Maclean, surveying the people looking for their places, and recognizing friends, compared it to 'a theatre before the curtain goes up'.[44] The cast list this time had left the outside world stunned, the trial having been announced at a time when it seemed that those the regime wanted to disappear were dispatched away from the public gaze.[45] *The Times*, still reporting from Riga, headlined their first story 'Famous Leaders accused'[46] before listing the names of the twenty-one who would go on trial for their lives. They included Nikolai Bukharin, a former Party theorist, member of the Politburo, and editor of *Pravda* and *Izvestiya*; Alexei Rykov, deputy head of the Soviet government under Lenin; and, in one of the great, cruel and ironic turns of fate in life in the Soviet political elite, Genrikh Yagoda, former head of the NKVD, now found himself going through the unforgiving system to which his own secret police force had committed so many others. *The Daily Mail*, still from Warsaw, declared the case to be 'the most amazing trial of modern times' and bluntly predicted, 'the death penalty is inevitable'.[47] Walter Duranty and Harold Denny were both in Moscow for *The New York Times*. The former, able now to draw on the authority which the knowledge of such a long stint covering the Soviet era had given him, was equally unequivocal, calling this, in a front page story, 'the greatest and most startling of the Soviet treason trials'.[48] The following day, Duranty showed that he understood very well the way that the system worked: commenting first on the media outcry against the accused and reporting on demands coming from sections of the working classes even in the Soviet Union's remotest regions that the accused be firmly punished. 'It is essential not only to crush inner enemies but to make the masses understand that they are crushed,'[49] ran part of his concluding paragraph. Denny followed one of the more remarkable angles of a trial which, he wrote, would be 'much more sensational'[50] than the earlier ones: the fact that one of the defendants, out of twenty-one, refused to plead guilty. Nikolai Krestinsky, a former vice commissar of Foreign Affairs, began his time in the dock by shockingly, and stubbornly, refusing to admit his guilt.[51] The next day, things had changed. Denny reported that Krestinsky 'broke down overnight'. He now accepted his guilt, blaming his earlier refusal to do so on 'the weight of painful shame'.[52] Maclean, writing years later and not subject to Soviet censorship, noted wryly, 'The words were reeled off like a well-learnt lesson. The night had not been wasted.'[53]

Maclean wrote that the Show Trial of 1938 left on him 'a more profound impression than any other experience during the years I spent in Soviet Russia.'[54] That impression was, at least in part, formed by the interpretations offered by journalists. He mentioned in particular A.T. (Alfred Thornton) Cholerton of *The Daily Telegraph*, who 'had been in Moscow for twelve years, and knew more than any of us'.[55] Cholerton's reporting offered an insight, based on detailed knowledge, which other newspapers seem to lack. The length of Cholerton's stay, his understanding of the Soviet system, enabled him carefully to choose words which conveyed to the reader some of the absurdity of what was unfolding. Take the context he offered on the evidence of 'Varvar Yakovleva, the celebrated woman chief of the Petrograd Cheka during the reign of terror in 1919–20'.[56] Cholerton dismissed Yakovleva's evidence as 'hearsay', while explaining to his readers that 'one of the objects of the present trial is to prove that not only all former leaders in this and preceding cases incessantly conspired as enemies of Stalin', but also that they had tried to seize power and arrest and murder Lenin and Stalin as long ago as 1918. Cholerton's reporting also brought to life what must have been a fascinating spectacle – for these cases were as much 'show' as 'trial' – through the exchanges between Vyshinsky and the accused. Bukharin at one point employed the phrase 'utilisation of capitalist contradictions'. The state prosecutor, Vyshinsky, shot back, 'You are here as a criminal, not as a philosopher.' Bukharin replies, 'Perhaps as a philosopher, and a criminal' before Vyshinsky, met this with 'Criminal! Spy!'[57] Cholerton's reporting of Krestinsky's acceptance of his guilt also served to show his detailed understanding of the way that the system worked to drive the accused to incriminate each other. Krestinsky's retraction of his earlier defiant denial of guilt came as Christian Rakovsky – who had been the first Soviet ambassador to London in the 1920s – declared that a letter Krestinsky had written 'announcing that he had abandoned all Trotskyist activities, was a fake'. Cholerton enlightened his readers as to the 'black ugliness of the scene', explaining that Krestinsky had once arranged for Rakovsky, desperately ill with malaria, to be transferred from 'fever-ridden Astrakhan' to Saratov, a move that 'probably saved his life'.[58]

Historians, working with the benefit of many years' perspective, have discussed why the accused were so ready to incriminate themselves. Sheila Fitzpatrick convincingly offers torture and threats to family (a credible explanation for Krestinsky's overnight change of stance), adding, 'But it was also a way of buying a day in court with the world's media reporting every word.'[59] Naturally, this was a subject which came up for the correspondents, too. Cholerton reported Krestinsky's saying, on the day he withdrew his confession, that 'he believed it would be useless to tell the truth unless and until he came into open court'.[60] The *Manchester Guardian* offered two explanations: one that 'coaching' had brought Krestinsky 'back into line'; the other that he decided to have his day in court, 'concentrating foreign publicity on himself, and muddling the issue. If this was his purpose', the dispatch continued, 'he has succeeded admirably.'[61] Duranty informed his readers that all the accused had already pleaded guilty – that was the point at which people came to court in Russia, he argued – and that the purpose of the trial was to determine the degree of guilt and the punishment. In what might be termed full Stalinist omelette mode, he wrote that the trial's true purpose was 'to convince the Russian people that internal enemies are broken, beaten, and lost'.[62] The expected death sentences duly followed, the executions of eighteen of the accused 'in conditions of absolute secrecy',[63] as Cholerton put it, being reported in editions of 16 March 1938. Cholerton further noted that, 'the men shot were people of first-rate importance'. This, ultimately, was the point of allowing the foreign press to watch proceedings. The message was that these 'first-rate' figures, such as Rakovsky and Arkady Rosengoltz, who had been Soviet Charge d'Affaires in London – senior diplomats who had been received in the capitals of world powers – were not immune. No one was. As Malcolm Muggeridge, now reflecting on what he had learnt from his crushing disillusionment with the Soviet Union, put it in a piece for the *Telegraph*, 'Government by fear necessitates everyone being afraid all of the time, not excepting those who govern.'[64] The London connections were obviously of special interest to the British correspondents. *The Sunday Times* of 6 March reported on prominent members of the British establishment being named by one of the accused as British agents who had operated in Russia.[65] The same edition carried, albeit ten pages further on, an advertisement from Intourist, the Soviet Tourist Agency, offering 'cruise tours by Soviet steamers' with 'prices from £1 per day'.[66] The ad did not mention the risks of being suspected of spying while you were there. It is hard to imagine that Intourist's advertising agency, and *The Sunday Times'* Sales department, was pleased by the news coverage that appeared the same day.

In an echo of Muggeridge's analysis, Maclean later concluded that the trial 'would help keep up the nervous tension which, extending to every walk of life, had become one of the chief instruments of Soviet internal policy'.[67] Muggeridge was not in Moscow at the time – his piece was commissioned on the basis that 'he was well acquainted with the work of those political leaders' now on trial for treason. Maclean was in Moscow, but his account – not published until 1949 – still seems to recognize the value of the analytical skills which journalists bring to interpreting events as they happen, rather than later. At least two more sections of Maclean's chapter on the Show Trials bear a close resemblance to parts of Muggeridge's news analysis, printed more than a decade earlier. On the obtaining of confessions, Muggeridge wrote, 'Many theories have been put forward to explain them – Tibetan drugs, hypnosis, the natural propensity of the Slav temperament towards self-abasement.' Maclean suggested, 'People had attributed the confessions of the accused to oriental drugs, or hypnotism, or the workings of the Slav soul.'[68] Muggeridge also noted that the prisoners were 'kept in custody for months, sometimes on and off for years' and 'constantly submitted to intensive cross-examination' – and experience which, he argued, few people would be able to endure without becoming 'unbalanced'. 'Most of the prisoners had been in prison for a year or eighteen months,' Maclean wrote.

'During that time, they would have been cross-examined for days, for weeks, for months on end.'[69] In his praise of Cholerton, Maclean acknowledges the debt which diplomacy can owe to journalism. Waiting, on the last evening of the trial, for the verdict (the judges returned only in the early hours) Cholerton is asked what he makes of it. "'Oh," he said. "I believe everything. Everything except the facts.'"[70] Muggeridge, writing many years later in his 1972 memoir *Chronicles of Wasted Time*, also credits Cholerton with this epigrammatic dismissal of one of the grimmest episodes of Russia's twentieth-century history, although this time it was made to a 'moon-faced' tourist.[71] Cholerton was entitled to repeat such an incisive remark (if indeed he did so, perhaps it had just passed into legend) – at least its being repeated in more than one memoir means that it is more likely to be remembered. Cholerton reported on the trial but, like the best correspondents, was not taken in by the show.

He stayed, however, to see plenty more of what was to come. The American correspondent, Quentin Reynolds, reported from the Soviet Union during the Second World War for *Collier's Weekly*. He related that he was warned, as he sought the assignment, 'Moscow is a pretty fast league. Philip Jordan of the *News Chronicle* is there, and Chollerton (sic) of the *Telegraph*.'[72] By the time that Reynolds was trying to travel to Russia, Cholerton, having arrived in 1921,[73] had been there for some two decades. His standing in the Moscow press corps is obvious from the respect others have paid to him in their memoirs – 'visiting journalists like myself learned a great deal from A.T. Cholerton,'[74] wrote *The Times'* Iverach McDonald – but he was not to join Duranty in becoming a convert to the cause of Stalinism: quite the opposite. Muggeridge wrote of Cholerton that he was tolerated, 'despite his contempt and loathing for the Soviet regime,'[75] and always managed to get visas when they were denied to others. In his account of foreign correspondence between the two world wars, Robert Desmond – who claimed that Cholerton had been in British intelligence before becoming a correspondent – described him as 'notably outspoken, he was warned repeatedly because of his reports, but he was not expelled.'[76] Muggeridge offered the explanation, based on a conversation with a censor, that Cholerton reminded Bolsheviks 'of the good old days of their exile, when they lived penuriously in Geneva or London'[77] – his ability to evoke these happy memories apparently meant that they liked to have him around.

Others were not so welcome. *The Times* was confined to reporting the Show Trials from Riga. It was their only option. Throughout the early Soviet period, censorship of the reports which correspondents were able to send greatly affected their ability to tell the story. This is a technique, as we have seen in earlier chapters, which the revolutionaries adapted from their Tsarist predecessors (remember W. P. Crozier's letter to David Soskice, asking him to send duplicates of all his telegrams by post). In the case of *The Times*, the displeasure which Wilton's anti-Bolshevik reporting had provoked meant that the newspaper was banned from Russia for more than two decades, starting with Wilton's return to England in 1917. The relevant volume of *The Times*' official history, published in the 1950s, recorded that 'the paper had not been given the opportunity of appointing a Correspondent in Leningrad or Moscow'[78] since Wilton's departure. Attempts to resolve this through diplomatic channels were unsuccessful, because the paper did not 'secure the assurance that any Correspondent it sent would be free to say what he wanted'.[79] In consequence, even after two decades of Soviet power, *The Times* was still reporting Russia from Latvia. The correspondent, R.O.G. (Reginald Oliver Gilling) Urch, received *Pravda* and *Izvestiya* the same day; spoke fluent Russian; and had witnessed both revolutions of 1917.[80] *The Times*' official account argued that, as the Moscow correspondents were limited to reporting what appeared in Soviet official sources, Urch 'could and did say what he wanted'[81] – not enough, it seemed, to prevent his becoming 'among English left-wing intellectuals a byword for biased and inaccurate reporting'.[82] Even if *The Times*' history defended Urch from the charge by arguing that he was freer to report Russia from outside, there was also much to be missed. Even if it was hard to report some of the details that one might gather from living in Moscow, even walking the streets to work is an indispensable part of the correspondent experience. The chance to discuss and exchange ideas with colleagues and rivals – during breaks in the Show Trials, for example – is also vital to forming and forging one's own arguments and angles. *The Times*' decision to opt for splendid isolation during this period may be explicable, but it carried more disadvantages than advantages.

The point about the restrictions is valid, however. As the Stalin era wore on, policy seemed more than ever to be influenced by the Soviet leadership's belief that correspondents were 'essentially spies'.[83] Censorship became more and more oppressive. Eugene Lyons devoted a whole chapter of *Assignment in Utopia* to the subject, which included the old word play on the meanings of the titles of the two main Soviet papers: *Pravda* 'the Truth' and *Izvestiya* 'the News' ('there's no truth in the news, and no news in the truth', the joke ran). Lyons' own pro-Soviet views, at least in the early stages of his posting, meant that he found the censors 'reasonable and often positively helpful'.[84] His opinion was not widely shared. From Donald Thompson's discovery that no wires were leaving Petrograd, to W. P. Crozier's suspicion that his correspondent's messages were not reaching him, correspondents faced a constant struggle. By the end of the 1930s, some major news organizations had decided that the game was no longer worth the candle. Further tightening of the censorship regime raised the question as to whether it was worth the trouble of keeping a bureau in the Soviet capital. During the early part of the 1930s, 'much of what a correspondent was actually permitted to transmit was what he and the censor agreed on. Bargaining took place face-to-face, a confrontation that was one of the crucial elements in reporting from Moscow.'[85] Changes to the times at which censors were available, and to the level of language skills which those censors possessed, were coupled with a new policy which meant that Radio Moscow was able to report any Soviet news before any foreign correspondent.[86] Those broadcasts were monitored the world over and went out while the censors' office was closed. By the time it opened, correspondents' news desks already had what they were able to offer. As the censor was unlikely to pass anything which had not appeared in official Soviet media, the correspondents had very little scope for adding any colour, personal analysis or original reporting – even supposing they were able to do it in the first place.

The year 1939–40 saw a series of major newspapers deciding to close their Moscow bureaux. Edwin L. James, managing editor of *The New York Times*, declared, 'The Russians would be pleased if all foreign correspondents got out. It is undignified to keep a correspondent there.'[87] Conditions had finally been deemed right for *The Times* to send a correspondent to the Soviet Union in 1939 (even if the meetings the correspondent had with his sole permitted Soviet source were overseen 'by a silent watchman from the secret police'[88]). Now, late in September 1940, *The Times* correspondent left a few days after the departure of his counterpart from *The New York Times*. A.T. Cholerton was one of the few members of the Moscow foreign press corps who remained, most of them being news agency representatives.[89]

James of *The New York Times* may well have been right that the Russians wanted everyone to leave. Their system of, in effect, preventing any reporting until the story had been on Radio Moscow was a cunning one from the point of view of news management. Even in an age when newspaper sales and advertising revenues gave printed media budgets greater than most enjoy today, they were businesses that needed to make a profit. The conditions imposed by the Soviet government frustrated correspondents, editors and accountants alike. It was not that the USSR wanted no news to leave the country. On the contrary, portraying a positive picture to the world was very important, hence the censorship. This book's focus is the work of correspondents in Russia and the Soviet Union, but in order to provide some context it seems useful here to consider briefly the work of two Western writers who were invited to the USSR in the 1930s, and who, in consequence, got involved in a literary quarrel over their separate works of politically charged travel writing.

The French novelist André Gide's 'Return from the USSR'[90] was published in 1936. In it, Gide described his travels there in a way which was not always complimentary to his hosts and also enraged members of the European left. Gide encountered a 'certain *superiority complex*'[91] and concluded that the Soviet people to whom he spoke wanted the West not to 'inform' them, but to 'compliment' them.[92] He commented on what he saw as the 'extraordinary idleness'[93] of Muscovites. The German writer, Lion Feuchtwanger, published his *Moscow 1937* the following year. While he acknowledged the shortages in housing and clothing which he found,[94] his harshest words were reserved for his fellow writer: 'One is forced to conclude that André Gide has chanced upon exceptionally impudent and stupid young people.'[95] As to Muscovites' alleged indolence, 'it was, on the contrary, the very activity and industry of the people of Moscow which impressed me.'[96] Perhaps the observation of his which has aged least well, however, is that he made upon the second show trial. Having apparently harboured doubts, before his arrival in the USSR, as to reliability of the evidence given in the Zinoviev trial, while attending that of Radek, '[his] doubts melted away as naturally as salt dissolves in water.'[97]

As during the revolutions of 1917, and the allied military interventions which followed, this was an age when the reporting and writing on the Soviet Union were largely devoid of nuance. Those who came to the USSR from the outside left with strongly held opinions. Divisions were growing, too, between the way that those visitors saw Soviet society, and the way it saw itself. Cholerton's verdict on believing everything but the facts built on a correspondent's natural cynicism to shed light on the way that Soviet society was developing. Even Lyons, his recounting of the incident perhaps presaging his own subsequent disillusionment, told the story of a conversation with 'a prominent Russian newspaperman', whom Lyons had asked how much of what the Soviet press printed could be believed. 'If it's printed, it's truth for us. We don't know and don't care about bourgeois notions of facts,' replied the Soviet journalist. 'We don't boast of standing above the turmoil like recording angels.'[98] *Bourgeois notions of facts*: the phrase anticipates the debates of our own time, especially those concerning the information wars between Russia and the West, about multiple truths, or none at all; about changeable and contradictory notions of objectivity. The Russian journalist saw himself and his colleagues as 'pioneers in the job of changing our country': no room for 'bourgeois notions of facts' – or, if they did not serve the Stalinist cause, any facts at all. In Lyons' memoir, published in 1938, he concluded, 'The very memory of an "independent" newspaper, in serious disagreement with the government, has faded out.'[99] Little wonder that this was the era when the Moscow press corps, frustrated by the obstacles placed in its way, began to fade out, too. Newspapers needed news. If there was none to be had, there was no reason to stay. There would soon be a reason to return. This was the dawn of the age of totalitarianism, not just in journalism, but in European politics. The Soviet Union was about to find its brand of totalitarianism attacked by the German version. For a few years at least, Britain, the United States and the Soviet Union would be comrades-in-arms. In an age when technology was changing news reporting, and radio was becoming the dominant medium in a new global conflict, the USSR, its armies and people would be tested as never before – and it would have all the elements to make it one of the stories of the century.

But what a story everything tells here: The Great Patriotic War

The Soviet Union's view of the world west of its borders was formed by war. Russia's greatest gift to world literature, Leo Tolstoy's *War and Peace*, immortalized the fight against Napoleon's invading armies. Attacked by Hitler's armies in 1941, the USSR 'took over the 1812 myth and made it an integral part of Soviet patriotism.'[1] The victory over Nazi Germany, celebrated every year as a public holiday, remains a defining part of contemporary Russia's sense of self. As President Vladimir Putin said in his address on the occasion of the military parade on Red Square on 9 May 2017, 'They fought to the bitter end defending the homeland, and achieved the seemingly impossible by turning around the bloody wheel of World War II, and drove the enemy back to its home whence it dared to invade our land.'[2] Nowhere symbolizes that moment when the course of the war changed more than Volgograd, site of the Battle of Stalingrad, as the city was then called. Crossing the Volga would have given the invader a clear run at the oil fields of the Caucasus, as well as cutting off that mighty river as a supply route. Yet the Red Army, the territory it held squeezed in places to a matter of metres as its soldiers fought with their backs to the water, held out and eventually triumphed. The visitor to the city today – and they were many in the summer of 2018, for it was one of the venues chosen to host matches in the football World Cup – cannot fail to be reminded of Volgograd's violent past. Fans heading to the stadium did so in view of the huge 'The Motherland Calls' statue, towering from the summit of a nearby hill. The hill is honoured as a war memorial. It contains the remains of tens of thousands of dead. Almost the entire city centre was flattened in the battle and had to be rebuilt after the war. One building, a flour mill battered by bullet and shell, was left as a reminder to future generations of how the war had ruined the city. There is another surviving structure: a basement. In January 1943, it was German headquarters. Now it is a museum. Its exhibits include a propaganda leaflet directed at the Italian troops who were fighting with the German forces. On the front cover, soldiers, little more than silhouettes, struggle against a snowstorm. The caption asks, in Italian, 'Why did you come here?' Victory at Stalingrad, together with that at the Battle of Kursk later the same year, 1943, did 'turn the wheel' of World War II, leading eventually to the ruin of Nazi Germany. Where Stalingrad, given its name, would have been a huge symbolic as well as strategic victory for Hitler, it ended with disastrous losses, and the loss to captivity of a field marshal and more than twenty generals. On a rare outing from Moscow, some Western correspondents were taken to Stalingrad to see for themselves those prized prisoners.

The correspondents who covered the Soviet Union's great feat of arms were few. Foreign journalists, where tolerated at all, were largely confined to Moscow. When the capital itself was threatened with capture, reporters were evacuated along with diplomats and Soviet officials. Censorship remained a major obstacle: 'Any correspondent hates all censorship, but the Soviet brand was particularly obnoxious'[3] was the verdict of Quentin Reynolds, of the American *Collier's Weekly*. Those who did endure air raids and evacuation were rewarded with the opportunity to witness and to report, however incompletely, one of the biggest stories of the twentieth century.

The Soviet Union had been taken by surprise in the early hours of the morning of 22 June 1941. The lack of preparedness meant that the German invaders made alarmingly rapid progress. In his book, *Russia at War*, published in 1964, the Reuters, *The Sunday Times*, and later BBC, correspondent Alexander Werth recalled a Pravda editorial from 1939 in which it was argued, 'military thought in the capitalist world has gone into a blind alley', in which 'dashing theories about a lightning war (*blitzkrieg*)' arose from 'the bourgeoisie's deathly fear of the proletarian revolution'.[4] The Soviet Union was about to discover that it too actually had plenty to fear. 'Lightning war' could be extremely effective if the enemy's preparedness was inadequate. The Soviet Union's leadership may have been surprised by the attack, but, eventually, the country fought back and was victorious. It was such a celebrated moment in Russia's history that even today the Second World War is more commonly called in Russian 'The Great Patriotic War'.

Like any military conflict, the Second World War was also a media battle. Radio was now becoming an increasingly important medium for international news distribution. In wartime, that meant propaganda, too. 'Technological developments placed radio at the center of this information war.'[5] In *Munitions of the Mind*, his history of propaganda, Philip M. Taylor argued that this global conflict 'witnessed the greatest propaganda battle in the history of warfare'.[6]

As their use of Radio Moscow regularly to 'scoop' resident correspondents showed, the Soviets, like the other belligerents (for the German Propagandist-in-Chief, Josef Goebbels, radio 'was the most important instrument of Nazi wartime propaganda'[7]), understood the power of this new medium, which 'provided a link between government and those they governed, and between the government of one nation and the people of another.'[8] Philip Jordan, then in Moscow as correspondent of the *News Chronicle*, described in his 1942 memoir *Russian Glory* 'the great lattice tower of the Comintern Radio that hangs above the city like a minaret of the twentieth century.'[9] The striking structure is still there. Based in Moscow from 2006 to 2009, I lived almost in its shadow. In the 1940s, it stood as a monument to changes in global media – a point that Jordan was perceptive enough to appreciate. Finally composing himself some two weeks after the shock of the German attack on the Soviet Union on 22 June 1941, on 3 July Stalin chose radio to address the nation. 'Listeners heard Stalin walk with heavy steps towards the microphone, fill his glass with water and begin.'[10] His message of defiance against the German invader 'rallied morale and strengthened the popular determination to resist'[11] – an effect which would not have been so pronounced without the immediacy offered by the ability to broadcast. Yet the ability to broadcast was something which was either denied or made practically inaccessible to correspondents in Moscow, the challenges it involved making the experience 'a cross between a nightmare and an amusement park fun house'.[12] Charlotte Haldane, the first British woman to report from Russia, arrived in the autumn after hostilities had started. Her account of her assignment, *Russian Newsreel*, appeared the following year. Whatever the challenges may have been for correspondents trying to send material (Haldane's task was made a little easier, as she was invited to broadcast on Radio Moscow itself[13]), they too understood the importance of the new medium. As Haldane put it, 'Every correspondent in a foreign country now, of course, relies on the radio both for news and official propaganda.'[14] She then went on to describe her unsuccessful attempts to get a radio – the Soviet government having 'confiscated all private radio sets',[15] although foreigners were still permitted to own them – at the outbreak of war. Soviet citizens were left with sets that could only receive Soviet broadcasts. Werth, in his *Moscow War Diary*, explained why: the 'absurd tripe' broadcast in Russian from Germany by 'rusty old White colonels, with their alcoholic voices'.[16]

In any case, radios, as expensive manufactured items, were not available to many ordinary Soviet citizens even before the ban was imposed. Perhaps in consequence, Haldane found a Moscow whose residents were desperate for

The Moscow Radio Tower, Designed by Vladimir Shukhov.

newspapers. Politically very much on the left herself – 'when her ship docked at Archangel, she had worked within the Party for nearly five years'[17] – she was impressed by the lack of advertising in the Soviet press, and by the absence of gossip and 'juicy murders'. She was also impressed that the chamber maids in her hotel read the papers – 'heavy and serious as they were' – whenever they got the chance.[18] Haldane saw those maids' fellow Muscovites queuing at the newspaper kiosk visible from her hotel room window, waiting every day for the papers to be delivered. Radio may very much have been the new weapon in this new kind of propaganda war, but it had in no sense replaced print as a means of circulating news: a very different media age from our own when newspapers increasingly expect their readers already to know the news and to look to them instead for interpretation and analysis.

Werth, Reynolds and Haldane were among a small number of British and American correspondents permitted to enter the Soviet Union after the Soviet Union had entered the war. News of the invasion had been broken by Reuters in Berlin – although their 'beat', as agencies term getting the news ahead of rivals, involved a degree of good fortune. (Reuters broke the story early on news that there was to be a broadcast from Berlin criticizing Soviet foreign policy.[19]) The Associated Press did have a Moscow correspondent, but he, Henry Cassidy, was on holiday in the Black Sea resort of Sochi. It took him a while to get back to Moscow (he initially misinterpreted a cable 'Plane immediately' from his assistant to mean that he should expect a colleague to arrive in Moscow by air[20]) – but his two-day train journey did give him material for 'the first wartime descriptive article sent from Moscow' widely printed in American newspapers under the headline 'Ivan goes calmly to war'.[21] For those who were not already in the USSR, the outbreak of war made getting there even harder and more hazardous than usual, even assuming that permission was granted. Haldane considered herself 'one of the exclusive five – and the only woman' who was able to make the journey 'out of the dozens of British correspondents who had been frantically seeking to get to Moscow'.[22] Reynolds described his relief on arriving safely after a freezing and frightening journey by plane.[23] Once there, there were strict limits on what they could do. Stalin's government (especially those old Bolsheviks who had survived the purges of the previous decade) still harboured a strong suspicion of foreign journalists' motives, even if the German invasion of the summer now meant that they were military allies with their ideological foes. The Soviets had grounds for their suspicions. Harold King, whom Reuters sent to Moscow in the spring of 1942, 'rejected an approach to supply material secretly to the British Embassy in Moscow'.[24] Ewan Butler, *The Times* correspondent in Berlin before the war, and later himself in intelligence, told the author Phillip Knightley, 'In those days, journalists and intelligence agents were practically interchangeable.'[25] Still, it led to great practical difficulties. British and American correspondents, where they could get to Moscow at all (*The New York Times* was among those organizations without a correspondent in the Soviet capital), often found themselves frustrated. Rather than being allowed to go to see the fighting for themselves, they had to rely on reports from Soviet media or even interviews with Soviet correspondents who had been permitted to visit front lines. Haldane probably put it mildly when she said such second-hand reporting left correspondents 'naturally discouraged'.[26] The Soviets' decision to allow authors, rather than journalists, to cover the war met with a mixed reception among the Western correspondents. Foreign journalists had to compile their own reports from despatches written in a much more literary style than the conventions of Anglo-Saxon news journalism would allow. 'Curious reading for western eyes',[27,*] Knightley suggested – but not all correspondents agreed. Haldane found Ilya Ehrenburg's reports in *Red Star* (Krasnaya Zvezda) 'superb' (although it should be noted that she too was a contributor to *Red Star*). Werth also praised Red Star 'especially if you know how to read between the lines.'[28]

Those correspondents who made it to Moscow were kept away from the front. 'It's pretty maddening to be in Moscow just now. The truth is we don't really know what's happening,' Werth wrote in his diary entry for 17 July.[29] To Soviet fears about espionage were added fears about security. Jordan recounted the words of the Soviet censor, Solomon Lozovsky. 'I would rather have fifty discontented journalists in Moscow than fifty dead Russian soldiers on the battlefield.'[30] There was an exception to this policy of keeping the correspondents at a distance: a trip to the battlefields west of Moscow in the fall of 1941. The correspondents travelled in a group – not 'embedded' as such, in the early-twenty-first century understanding of the word – but still very much under close supervision. Cholerton, in one of his reports of what he had seen on the trip, wrote that the group had been accompanied by a 'Red Army colonel and a Brigade Commissar' all the way from Moscow.[31] This was not ideal, but it was significantly better than what they had been offered before – so they made the most of it. The party included Margaret Bourke White, the photographer from *Life* magazine who had previously gained the Soviets' trust sufficiently to be permitted to take pictures of the growing industrialization of the 1930s. The first edition of Haldane's *Russian Newsreel* includes some of the pictures Bourke White took that autumn. There is a shot of Red Square being camouflaged: painted to give the appearance from above that it was a built-up area, rather than Moscow's most famous landmark.[32] The trip gave the correspondents, and

---

* Knightley's verdict which will seem harsh to readers familiar with *A Writer at War*, Antony Beevor and Luba Vinogradova's 2006 edition of Vassily Grossman's wartime journalism (in fairness to Knightley, published later than *The First Casualty*).

their readers, something new. In the space of a few days, those lucky enough to get a place experienced a German air-raid (and Haldane really did see being bombed as a piece of luck) and were later given the chance to interview captured German airmen who were supposedly responsible (and examine their damaged plane). The trip lasted six days. The correspondents' relief at being given this chance to see even a little of the war is evident, and from the Soviets' point of view, it was also a public relations success. Cholerton's first despatch in *The Daily Telegraph* talked of the 'excellent discipline' and 'cheerful fighting spirit' of the troops he met. The Soviet ambassador in London would no doubt have been pleased if he read the headline 'Nazis Still Retreat on Smolensk Front'.[33] The ambassador, Ivan Maisky, presumably did read it because, as his diary showed, he paid close attention to the press[34]– and his own assessment of the war was reported in the *Telegraph* the next day, in remarks where he suggested, unsurprisingly, that German losses on the Russian front were many times higher than Berlin had admitted.[35]

As if to back up this Soviet version of events, the six-day tour for the foreign press through recently recaptured territory was well planned. What was presumably not planned was the air raid on the town of Vyaz'ma during the tour. The correspondents were roused from their beds by the sound of explosions; 'there was a thud, and the little hotel shook from head to foot,'[36] wrote Haldane later. Not that she was complaining. 'In Moscow I had never managed to get within miles of an air raid incident. But here I was more fortunate,'[37] she continued. She and Margaret Bourke White, to whom Haldane refers as 'Mrs Caldwell' (she was married to the writer, Erskine Caldwell), went out into the street to see the damage. She saw a family of four who had all been killed in the raid. An old man with a chest wound she feared he would not survive was being carried away on a stretcher. 'What a magnificent morning's work for the Nazi bombers!'[38] Cyrus L. Shulzberger, for *The New York Times*, filed a dramatic account of his experience of the raid: with everyone hitting the floor 'like frogs leaping into a pond at the approach of danger' as bombs blasted all the windows out of the building.[39] Cholerton was more composed, writing of the loss of life and property among the town's residents, while 'we had merely our windows blown in'.[40] The story then took an unexpected turn. Later that day, their Soviet handlers told the correspondents that the crew responsible for the raid had been shot down. The correspondents were invited to watch the interrogation.

Their accounts reflect something which later British and other Western correspondents covering armed conflict have barely known: the experience of reporting on a war in which your own country is directly at risk. One of the

German crewmen, it turned out, had earlier carried out bombing raids over London. Cholerton's report seemed strangely sympathetic: he realizes that the young man, the radio operator, might be exercising caution because there were known to be Gestapo gangs among the German prisoners – gangs who beat those whom they felt had said too much. 'He was certainly no Nazi',[41] Cholerton concluded. Not everyone was so generous. Werth hated what he saw. Perhaps witnessing the destruction of towns and villages in the country of his birth hurt him personally. Those German airmen he had seen 'were certainly disgusting pieces of humanity',[42] he wrote in the next edition of *The Sunday Times*. Commenting on the captives' modest social origins – sons of a butcher, a janitor and a tailor – Sulzberger wrote that their words sounded like the latest edition of the Voelkischer Beobachter, a Nazi propaganda sheet.[43] Haldane, not long out of London where she had also worked as an air-raid warden, wrote that it was the navigator who had taken part in the attacks on London. 'I remembered the corpses of mothers and little children,' she wrote, 'I had inspected as part of my duties, in St Pancras Mortuary.'* The fact that Haldane's memoir was published the following year, rather than, like news reports, in the hours and days which followed the encounter, did not make a difference. Time did not soften her opinion. 'I could not see any hope, in a civilized world, for such as he,' she concluded.[44] The encounter clearly made an impression on the correspondents. Today, those working for Western media would be very unlikely to experience anything similar. The Geneva Conventions forbid exposing prisoners of war to public curiosity, a prohibition usually understood to mean that they may not be interviewed, and certainly not filmed or photographed. This stricture had been enshrined in the Geneva Convention of 1929,[45] although the USSR had not signed. The journalistic value – in wartime – to the correspondents and their newspapers, and the propaganda value to the Soviets, meant that the encounter went ahead. On her return to Moscow, Haldane experienced the new nature of media war. She was invited more than once to broadcast on Radio Moscow (her own Communist views presumably helped here). After returning from the trip to the battlefields, she mentioned on air that she had visited a Red Army Club, the library of which included a volume by the German Jewish poet, Heinrich Heine. This drew a sneering response in a Nazi radio talk. Haldane saw this as proof that Berlin was not in a position to say anything more significant than 'such absurd pinpricks'.[46]

---

* St Pancras is a district of central London.

While the correspondents were busy sending their despatches from the trip, the diplomatic story was developing too. One thing which comes across from Quentin Reynolds's memoir, *Only the Stars Are Neutral*, is the access which correspondents were – occasionally – given in wartime. In the space of a few weeks, Reynolds went on a train journey outside London with Winston Churchill – eating both lunch and dinner with Britain's wartime prime minister – and also enjoyed a Kremlin banquet hosted by Stalin on the occasion of the visit to Moscow of Lord Beaverbrook (Max Aitken, the British Press baron) and the American diplomat, Averell Harriman, who were in the Soviet capital to agree military aid to the USSR. The delegation reached Moscow on 22 September 1941, an arrival reported the following day in an adjacent column to that of one of Cholerton's despatches from the battlefield. The Kremlin menu made such an impression on Reynolds that he got his Russian secretary to translate it in full, for publication.[47] There was plenty to wash this generous spread down with, too, 'red wine, white wine, champagne, and always vodka'.[48] Not everyone was getting carried away. 'Stalin drank every toast. However he drank a light red Georgian wine. No one could call Stalin a tippler'.[49] There was another culinary aspect of this trip, involving another world leader, which was not so diplomatically dealt with. Jordan discovered – he did not reveal his source – that Beaverbrook had spent a large sum of money – £25, according to Cassidy in his memoir[50] – on caviar to take back to Churchill. Jordan protested that it was just the kind of story that the *Daily Express* (which Beaverbrook owned) would like. The Press baron was furious.[51]

Reynolds seems to have developed quite a respect for Stalin and for the system which he created. Despite his criticism, cited above, of Soviet censorship, Reynolds was at pains to stress that this was criticism of censorship, not 'of Communism, or Russia'.[52] He even went so far as to claim that 'no British or American correspondents in Russia' thought that the confessions at the Show Trials had been obtained by torture, and to suggest that if only 'the Low Countries and Poland and Norway and the other slave states' had treated their own 'traitors' in a similar fashion, their fate would have been 'much happier'! He only hoped that one day the United States would 'find a prosecutor as ruthless and relentless as Vyshinsky' to deal with 'Fifth Columnists', before regretting, 'but we are pretty soft'.[53] The brevity of Reynolds's visit gave him a perspective which other, longer-term, and consequently more jaded, reporters might not have been able to offer. Especially illuminating is Reynolds's account of a press briefing given by Solomon Lozovsky, the Kremlin spokesman, to foreign correspondents. It is a masterclass in apparently answering questions while actually saying absolutely nothing – a masterclass which any cynical twenty-first-century spin doctor would no doubt admire. Reynolds, clearly impressed, had already listed the number of languages in which Lozovsky was able to hold a conversation.[54] During the news briefing, however, he wasted time by insisting that questions which he understood perfectly well be repeated in Russian. The correspondents' reliance on the Soviet press as almost their only source comes across, too. As correspondents ask Lozovsky for more details on stories they have found in the Soviet newspapers, Lozovsky bats them away, saying 'if the papers wanted you to know',[55] they would have included the information. Haldane, too, offered an account of what she judged, 'not exactly a Press Conference, as we Anglo-American journalists understood the term'.[56] Her admiration for Lozovsky's wit – especially at the expense of an American journalist 'lacking in intellectual finesse and politically more than a little naif'[57] – shines through her frustration at the lack of information he imparts. She obviously enjoyed Losovsky's responding to the reporter, whom she does not name, with a 'twisty wise-crack'.[58]

The correspondents who dined in such style in the Kremlin were present in Moscow at a turning point in Soviet relations with the West. Churchill had sent with Beaverbrook a letter the final salutation of which was 'with heartfelt wishes for the success of the Russian armies, and of the ruin of the Nazi tyrants'.[59] As the editors of wartime correspondence between Stalin, Churchill and the US President, Franklin D. Roosevelt, point out, some weeks later Stalin even sent Churchill – in Stalin's eyes, 'a capitalist and imperialist' – birthday greetings.[60] The comforts of Kremlin banquets were to be a fleeting treat for the correspondents. As the autumn of 1941 wore on, the advancing German forces drew closer and closer to Moscow. On 16 October, Muscovites woke to 'a sinister snow': the black flakes of documents being burnt so that their owners might hide their membership of the Communist party, along with the ashes of any other paperwork that might be useful to the invader whose arrival Muscovites now expected at any moment.[61] Many senior figures in the government, as well as the diplomatic corps, left the Soviet capital as part of evacuation plans. The correspondents went too 'resentful because we were being forced to leave the best story of the year',[62] as Reynolds wrote. He was not the only one who was fed up. Cholerton was also evacuated, in circumstances he was only able to describe in print almost two weeks later: from Kuibyshev (today named Samara) a city on the Volga River. The correspondents did understand, however, that the danger was real. Jordan wrote that the atmosphere at Kazan Station, from where they departed, reminded him of his time in the Spanish Civil War, 'The smell was dreadful. The smell of fear.'[63] Molotov himself had been charged with getting the foreigners to safety.[64] The British Ambassador, Sir Stafford Cripps, learnt from Molotov – once the group had safely arrived in Kuibyshev – that the evacuation had been ordered because German troops had broken through at Mozhaisk, west of Moscow, on the night of 14 October 'hence the hurry'.[65] Cripps was initially worried that the diplomats had been shifted out of the way and was relieved when it turned out that Molotov too was in Kuibyshev. One of Cripps's main contacts in the Soviet Foreign Ministry was a certain Vyshinsky. Cripps wrote of his 'great thrill' at having 'a very long talk' with him. He did not realize that his interlocutor was the show trial prosecutor.[66]

Cholerton shared Reynolds's dismay at being dragged away from the approach of a major story. It must have been especially frustrating, given that finally the news had come to correspondents who had largely been kept away from it since the German invasion months earlier. Although he admitted, in his despatch sent on Sunday 26 October, and published in the next day's paper, that 'at the time the danger of a German break-through to the capital seemed fairly grave' Cholerton was now 'sorry' he had been forced to leave, and hoped to return as soon as possible.[67] In the following day's paper, Cholerton described Moscow's military preparedness[68] – presumably cursing his luck as, once again, he found himself covering the war from a distance. On their way to Kuibyshev, the correspondents saw the wounds which the invader had inflicted on Russia. Reynolds wrote in some detail of the train journey: the village of Lida 'a mass of smoking ruins'; during a long delay in the city of Ryazan, the party was 'not at all cheered by the sight of a long, bomb-and-machine-bullet-scarred troop train that stood on the next track'.[69] Describing the moment when Kuibyshev finally came into view, Reynolds wrote of his joy at seeing a city not blacked out[70]; on arrival, he was impressed by the fact that the waitresses who served them at the Grand Hotel had 'immaculately manicured nails and waved coiffures'.[71] Not everyone was able to stay in such elevated circumstances. Citing a census from 1935 which gave the city's population as 200,000, Reynolds wrote that it had now grown to a million.[72] He saw the river boats 'unloading pitiful groups of refugees'.[73] Haldane described refugees coming 'down the Volga on open barges, hurrying to get there before the river froze over'. Not for her, though, any joy at seeing a city where the lamps were lit: thoughts of 'the black-out of London, of all Britain' meant she 'could not get any pleasure out of the blazing lights' of this city at a safe distance from the range of Nazi bombers. Covering a war always has its dangers; its moments that can depress people witnessing human suffering. Covering a war when one's own country is at great risk is another matter altogether.

Away from the action, the correspondents were reduced to second-hand reporting. Governments of all shades may resort to the security argument when they want to keep reporters away from a military operation which might not look good in the international press. They may do so because the operation is going badly, or because it involves killing civilians. There were attempts to keep the correspondents in Kuibyshev occupied, to an extent. Cholerton did a good job of writing up a factory visit: 'I saw striking evidence to-day of the Russian strength in arms manufacture in the safe areas'[74]; Reynolds wrote of the visit in his book, published the following year.[75] It is hard to escape the impression, though, that their safety in this case also meant their distance from the story, and the correspondents knew that they were not getting the chance to do their jobs. By December, the threat of Moscow's capture having passed, they were back in the capital.

Moscow might have been safe, but the rest of the Soviet Union was not. As the war continued across other western regions of Russia and Ukraine, the propaganda war was fought with increasing intensity over the airwaves. The BBC was all too aware of this, and, as Britain faced the threat of Nazi invasion, was keen to play its part in the war of words. As Asa Briggs wrote of the BBC during the Battle of Britain in 1940, 'BBC staff felt themselves to be in the front line.'[76] By the time Moscow was in the front line, the BBC was at a disadvantage. In the age when radio was the newest and most contested medium in the media war that was being waged alongside the military conflict, the BBC had no representation in Russia. Internal documents from the time show that the Corporation struggled with political and editorial challenges as they sought to remedy this. Henry Shapiro, who had been the United Press International (UPI) correspondent in Moscow since the 1930s, was considered. In the end, he was apparently judged unsuitable due to 'his lack of BBC background'.[77] The BBC also ruled out approaching Reynolds.[78] He was later invited to contribute, but not as a regular correspondent. He had successfully proved himself to have a suitable voice for broadcast when he recorded the commentary for 'A Day in the Life of Soviet Russia' – a documentary which, even by his own admission, 'was frankly a Russian propaganda film'[79] (he had hoped that taking up the offer of helping with the English language version of the film might assist with his Soviet visa application). Then there were the diplomatic issues. Reynolds hoped that the film 'would show a few pukka Britishers'[80] that Russians weren't born with two heads. Maisky attended the premiere of the film. His personal involvement in the decision whether or not to grant visas to correspondents shows the great importance attached to handling the press in wartime, especially during the early days of the Soviet–British alliance (the United States had yet to join the war). The BBC had to proceed with caution. While this may have been a time when the leader of the Soviet Union might wish the capitalist, imperialist, Churchill a happy birthday, the BBC was not allowed to get carried away as Britain built its relationship with its new ally. There was resistance to playing the *Internationale* – at that time, the Soviet national anthem – on the BBC along with the national anthems of other allies.[81] Later in the war, in Cabinet, Churchill described the BBC as 'a nest of Communists'.[82] Given that the wartime prime minister's battles with the Corporation went back to the 1920s – when he had sought, unsuccessfully, to commandeer the airwaves for the government during the General Strike – the BBC was aware of the possible consequences of falling out with political power.

Still, they needed someone to tell the story from Russia. Alexander Werth was the eventual solution. From the BBC's point of view, he was not a perfect one. Werth's trip to the Soviet Union in the summer of 1941 had been his first visit since his 'boyhood years in St Petersburg'.[83] He returned to London in November. In the spring of 1942, he went back to the USSR again. A BBC internal memo before his departure mentions that 'any dispatches which pay a tribute to the extent of British help' would be 'particularly welcome'.[84] The same memo, however, notes that there have been 'difficulties' with Werth in the past. Additional, handwritten, comments suggest Werth 'was not objective enough in his reporting'.[85] There were technical difficulties, too – problems with the quality and reliability of broadcast links for sending material.[86] This latter challenge was overcome by having Werth send material which was then read out on air in London, often by Joseph MacLeod. This may have solved another problem, too – a BBC memo from as late as 1949 said of Werth, 'he is not, as you probably know, a great broadcaster.'[87]

Whatever the BBC's misgivings, Werth was a significant asset to the Corporation – one without which they could not have told the story of the Soviet Union's 'Great Patriotic War'. Werth, like his fellow correspondents, had to contend with censorship and, with some exceptions, lack of access to the frontlines. Werth seems to have been fairly tolerant of the censors whom he met. He pronounced one 'a jovial-looking fellow'; another 'one of the most handsome youths I have ever seen'.[88] Werth's 'Russian Commentary' formed a vital part of audiences' understanding of how the war was unfolding. Werth may have been away for twenty-four years when he first returned in the summer of 1941, but he understood Russia, and was able to tell the story in a way that few others could, especially given the disadvantages he faced. In a broadcast from London in January 1942, in which he reflected on his experience of the previous year before his approaching return to the USSR, Werth got to the heart of Stalin's approach to raising morale for the fight: 'He knew that Russian public opinion would be hopelessly divided if he had asked them to defend Marxism [...] He said: Defend your country. Defend your Russia.'[89] His despatches bring to life the stories of those who did that: of Olga, the young factory worker who did not like to talk of her two brothers who had been killed at the front, and who herself sometimes worked two or three days on end to support the war effort[90] (Werth noted that she did so 'with red fingernails' – like the manicured hands Reynolds noticed on the waitresses in Kuibyshev, this seems to have been something which impressed correspondents, male ones, at least); the Russian soldiers at Stalingrad who – hopelessly outnumbered and facing a tank attack – strapped explosives to themselves and threw themselves under the tracks of the approaching armour.[91] This latter story, presumably, was gathered second hand – either from a witness, or more likely, given the sources available, from the Soviet press. Werth worked hard, though, to find the stories which he could get at: the shopkeeper whose three brothers were all casualties – one missing; one who had lost part of his skull; one 'badly shell-shocked'.[92] Details like these in his despatches gave audiences suffering with which they, facing their own hardships, could identify. Werth's listeners may have been separated from the Soviet Union by a continent consumed by war, but stories such as these could help them to understand their allies. Reading his work today, there are points at which one understands those who thought his reporting lacked objectivity. The same despatch suggested that Stalin thought 'more of the personal sorrows of millions of Russians than anything else' – a difficult case to make to relatives of the purges of the previous decade.

However suspicious they were of foreign correspondents, the Soviets knew when their own propaganda purposes would be served by giving them some of the access they craved. The trip to Vyaz'ma was an example, allowing access to Stalingrad in February 1943, once the famous victory there was won, was another. 'But what a story everything tells here,' Werth wrote. His despatch combined first-rate eyewitness reporting of the city entirely flattened by bomb and shell: 'One little wooden house – and that's all I could find of normal habitation in a town the size of Manchester'. He described captive German generals, 'with their monocles and iron crosses and new Nazi decorations'. In Werth's eyes, 'behind lock and key they radiated venom'.[93] The BBC's concern that Werth was not objective enough may have been right – but this may have been one of those occasions in the reporting of war where objectivity alone cannot suffice to tell the story. Later in 1943, shortly before it was finally liberated, Werth was able to report from Leningrad – the city which came to symbolize Soviet civilian suffering as Stalingrad did soldierly sacrifice. Before going on to describe the children whose parents had starved to death during the blockade, and the 1,500 shells which had landed in the city the day before,[94] Werth reminded listeners that this was his home town. That may have clouded his objectivity, but it helped him to tell the story.

Reportage such as this showed what those correspondents who knew Russia well could contribute to audiences' understanding of the way that the war was going. Unfortunately, such opportunities were not typical. Other major events, such as the Battle of Kursk, were reported much less satisfactorily because correspondents were not permitted to know, much less to see, for themselves.[95] Western newspapers did understand the significance of the action unfolding in the summer of 1943. *The Times* dedicated an editorial to fighting at Kursk and Orel on 23 July. Its actual reporting, such as it was, was left, like that of *The Telegraph*, to commentators outside Russia. Soviet communiques, rather than correspondent reports, were the sources relied upon for coverage. *The New York Times* ran at least one Associated Press despatch from London, the agency's logic presumably being that the British capital was as good a place as any – in the absence of first-hand material – to draw together the various German and allied sources.[96]

The rare times when the correspondents in the Soviet Union during the war were actually allowed access to the front – albeit under heavy supervision – showed what they could bring to their audiences' understanding, given the chance. Most of the time, they were not given the chance: kept back in Moscow when the frontline lay to the West; removed from Moscow as the frontline drew near. As if physical distance were not enough, the kind of censorship to which they were forced to submit made things even more difficult. Yet the choice was simply to agree to work under these conditions, or not work there at all (it is interesting to note that both Reynolds and Haldane, neither of whom was based in Moscow, decided to leave the USSR from Kuibyshev, without waiting to return to the capital with the rest of the press corps). The correspondents' memoirs – and it is surely a measure of the massive public fascination not only with the story of the war, but also with anything to do with a country to which so few people could travel, that they were rushed into print – all address at length the huge restrictions placed upon them. Solomon Lozovsky was the public face of the Soviet government as far as the correspondents were concerned. Werth wrote later of Lozovsky that with his 'smooth, cosmopolitan veneer … and with his *barbiche* and carefully cut clothes, (he) looked rather like an old *boulevardier*'[97] but this cosmopolitan veneer barely concealed a steely dedication to serving the motherland, and Stalin. While it is easy to understand the sentiment behind his remark about preferring to frustrate journalists rather than see Russian soldiers dead, the terms in which he chose to phrase that sentiment were telling. The correspondents were at their wits' end at apparent absurdities which the censors blithely justified. Reynolds – one of the last chapters in his book is titled simply 'I Hate Censors' – had a row with Umansky in Kuibyshev over a story about Litvinov going to Washington. The story was well known amongst the correspondents, but was censored. Reynolds raised the matter with Umansky – who calmly told him that the story had been on the BBC, who had got it from TASS. Reynolds was left to complain about being beaten by a radio announcer 3,000 miles away 'on the first decent story out of Kuibyshev in weeks'.[98] Reynolds further pointed out that not getting stories would lead to newspapers wondering whether they should keep correspondents there at all, but this probably would not have bothered the Soviet authorities. Jordan's particular frustration was that the censor who was assigned to read his work struggled with the English language, making the task of negotiation immeasurably more difficult. Only after two days' argument was he able to reinsert a word without which the meaning of his sentence would have changed completely.[99] Haldane encountered a different difficulty: the censors' 'chiefly scholastic' knowledge of English. She recounted the story of an argument over the inclusion of the word 'bulldog' to describe the Soviets' determined resistance to the invaders. Only after she explained that Winston Churchill's jaw 'was invariably and complimentarily' described in similar terms was it passed for publication.[100]

If censorship made their job all the more challenging, and the final despatch all the less complete, the correspondents showed a surprising degree of understanding alongside their frustration. This, in general, was an age of censorship. Where BBC scripts today may show the computer usernames of the producer and editor who have approved them, some of the copies of Werth's 'Russian Commentary' scripts which have survived also bear stamps 'Passed for Policy' and 'Passed for Security'. Reynolds, invited to give a talk on the BBC, was asked to take out a script line about hating Germans – although this, according to Reynolds, was mainly because the programme was scheduled for a Sunday, and such sentiment might unsettle churchgoers.[101] Despite his ranting at Umansky, Reynolds was indulgent, suggesting that on censorship the USSR would 'soon learn from the older democracies'.[102] Cassidy was less questioning, apparently convinced that the censors made decisions 'in good faith' and for 'fair' reasons.[103] Jordan, arrived from the UK, wrote that he had been used to a censorship which, unlike the Soviet system, permitted comment. He defended the Soviets' right to follow a different system, if they thought that would help them to win the war. He had a clear understanding of his own situation: 'If I didn't like it, I could go'.[104] Haldane – despite having to argue about 'bulldog' – was also sympathetic, suspecting that the TASS representatives in London might be 'just as heartily infuriated at and disgusted with the Ministry of Information'.[105] Why this acceptance of a system which made their difficult task all the more difficult? In addition to the Soviet censorship they had to endure, there was also, it may be concluded, an element of self-censorship. There were plenty of ways for correspondents to anger their hosts – this alliance between Communism and capitalism was new, after all, and suspicion and enmity could not just evaporate overnight – and doing so would not help with what little access there was or for future visa requests. Not everyone could rely on the old-world charm which saw Cholerton's residency documents renewed. Complaints would not help correspondents to get what they want. In the case of Haldane, there was an ideological strain of self-censorship, too. In her 1949 memoir, suitably titled *Truth Will Out*, she describes a series of events during her 1941 trip to Russia which turned her against Communism for good. The sight of a toddler dead from starvation made her resolve never again to take to a platform in an attempt to convince people 'that the Soviet Union was the hope of the toilers of the world'.[106] This moment of conversion was omitted from *Russian Newsreel*, she wrote in her later memoir, because 'it was neither the time nor the place to furnish the Nazis with material for anti-Soviet propaganda'.[107] Like Haldane, Jordan had also been in Spain supporting the Republican cause. In *Russian Glory*, he was honest from the outset about his loyalties, saying that since Spain, his 'life had been mixed up with Communism and the men of the extreme left'.[108]

Perhaps more than in any other conflict of the twentieth century, British and American journalists readily identified with their nations' war aims. Perhaps more than most other countries they covered, Russia tended to produce contrasting opinions. Even if this was an exceptional time, there were trends which throw light on Western views of Russia as expressed and developed through journalism, and on technological changes in the media: changes which, in turn, were affecting diplomacy and political communication. Cassidy felt he was working in an age 'when news travelled swiftly, making [ambassadors'] despatches dusty with age by the time they reached their governments'.[109] The correspondents in Moscow knew that their presence there was not tolerated out of the kindness of Stalin's heart. Haldane may have found some amusing moments in the press conferences with Lozovsky, but, even in the period of her writing when she did not want to offer Nazi Germany anything of propaganda value, she was frustrated, seeing Lozovsky's briefings as 'a bi-weekly lecture on propaganda for first-year students'.[110] Jordan had a telling exchange with Lozovsky, who apparently saw Western journalism in the same way that Soviet journalism of that era was supposed to function. 'You do not write as journalists,' Lozovsky told him, 'but as politicians'.[111] In her later memoir, freed from the worry that her writing might somehow be of propaganda value to the enemy, freed, too from her own belief in Communism, Haldane was more forthright. '"News" in Russia is inseparable from propaganda; it is angled one hundred per cent from the political point of view, and there is no objective journalistic standard'.[112] Lozovsky's remarks to Jordan showed that the Soviets believed the same of the West. This is a belief which has endured. During my own time as a correspondent in Moscow, officials often made similar remarks. In the war of words which followed the poisoning in the English town of Salisbury of the former Russian military intelligence agent, Sergei Skripal and his daughter, Yulia, in 2018, statements from the Russian Foreign Ministry made it clear that they saw the BBC in the same terms as RT – the Kremlin-backed English language TV channel – was seen in the West.[113]

Despite their hosts' suspicions of their motives, there was clearly a lot of interest in the correspondents' work. Publishers snapped up their memoirs, even in a wartime Britain where paper was rationed. Haldane's, Werth's, Jordan's, and Reynolds' books were all published in 1942; Cassidy's the following year. It is perhaps a reflection of the terms in which an assignment to Moscow was seen that the Penguin edition of Haldane's *Russian Newsreel* was placed by the publisher in their 'Travel and Adventure' category. Alongside her assessment of the military and media wars, Haldane also found space for a chapter on 'Food and Rationing': 'there was plenty to eat in the shops' in Moscow, she wrote, although, 'as in London, there was a more or less chronic shortage of cigarettes'.[114] Werth was not even satisfied with those cigarettes he found. 'Will I have to get used to them?'[115] he asked, after describing what sounded very much like Russian *papirosy* – cigarettes with a cardboard tube instead of a filter – an acquired taste for even the hardened Western tobacco lover. These may not have been the most important details from the point of view of diplomatic or military strategy, but they may have been some of the most memorable for readers who themselves were enduring the hardship of air raids and rationing.

The hardship was mitigated by occasional luxury. While Cassidy did spend the night in a Moscow metro station (as in the London underground, these doubled as air raid shelters), he was able to doze off, having earlier shared a bottle of 1932 Margaux with Jordan.[116]

The correspondents were clearly proud of their work and angered by the shortcomings they saw in that of others whose job it was to understand Russia. 'The foreign journalists of the last twenty years have been right ten times to every once that the diplomats have been right,' argued Jordan.[117] The time frame he identified would not reach back quite as far as the revolution, but he would have recognized the mistaken establishment belief then that Russia in revolution would continue to fight the First World War. His belief in the power of reporting was such that he even argued that if governments 'saw something more of contemporary life than did their diplomatic colleagues, there would be no war in Europe today'.[118] Cassidy was almost as dismissive and extremely perceptive about the way that the rise of the Soviet Union had come to influence expert and public opinion. 'It was something which one fervently approved or violently denounced. It was not something about which one knew a little or quite a lot. It was something about which one knew absolutely nothing or absolutely everything.'[119]

For this sharp division, one needed to look no further than Haldane. Dedicating *Russian Newsreel* 'To the Red Army', she later, perhaps ashamedly, told the story of correspondents being taken to see what was supposed to be captured German war materiel. The sharper-eyed amongst them noticed that the wheels had been made at the Stalin motor factory.[120] This was war, though – a propaganda war – and mistakes were inevitably made. There were also mistakes made in predicting the future: Werth hoped for the implementation of the Stalin constitution, which he compared to the Magna Carta[121]; Jordan rightly foresaw that Stalin would remain an autocrat, but believed this did not mean he opposed democracy.[122] Such predictions are notoriously difficult to get exactly right, and few foreign correspondents can truthfully claim never to have got one wrong. Werth's radio reports offer an insight, human details, which even today help to bring to life the 'Great Patriotic War'; Jordan's ambitious book, which he must have written very quickly, complements his reporting with its clear-eyed analysis of key themes. The reporting of the USSR's 'Great Patriotic War' was incomplete for a number of reasons, few of them the fault of the men and women who were trying to tell the story. 'Because our alliance with you was shattered at the war's end by the onset of the cold war, Americans never fully appreciated, until yesterday, the true extent of your sacrifice and its contribution to our common victory,"[123] President William J. Clinton told an audience in Moscow in 1995. He was speaking the day after a parade on Red Square to mark the fiftieth anniversary of the defeat of Nazi Germany. The Cold War would indeed shatter that alliance. Anyone seeking to understand what it had been like could have turned to the work of the war correspondents reporting from the USSR.

Secrets, censorship and cocktails with the Central Committee

Almost everything on one of Moscow's main streets has changed: shops, signs, even the street name. Traditionally Tverskaya, it became Gorky Street during the Soviet period, changing back as Soviet power waned. One constant is the half globe on the exterior of the Central Telegraph building. In Soviet times, this representation of the world – crowned by a red star, and supported by a hammer and sickle – was a rare, stunning, splash of colour among the general grey of the capital of world communism. With the end of that system came competition for the onlooker's attention: capitalism meant advertising, and the socialist semi-globe no longer had a monopoly on colour. It no longer had a monopoly on communications with the outside world either, although during the early decades of Soviet power, and even into the 1960s, it controlled the technology, and so, to a large extent, the story, too. 'It was dreadful, because we had to go to the censor and go through the censorship system,' remembers Robert Elphick, who was posted to Moscow as a correspondent for Reuters in 1958. 'We had to conform to the rules and the rules were, you go to the central telegraph office, submitted your column or whatever it was you were writing, and you hoped for a favourable answer.'[1]

The alliance between Britain, the United States and the Soviet Union – plagued as it was by suspicions, even when the Allies were all pulling in the same direction – did not survive the post-war division of Europe. The Iron Curtain fell. It did not rise again for more than four decades. In 1953, Stalin died. His harsh brand of Marxism–Leninism did not expire with him, but nor was everything as before. One Western correspondent in particular was crucial to the way that news of that dramatic change in the Soviet leadership's thinking was brought to the world. This was also an era in which an event that has had much greater consequences in our own time took place. In 1954,

Crimea, which had been part of the Russian Federative Socialist Republic, was transferred to the Ukrainian Soviet Socialist Republic. At that time, it mattered little. Both Russia and the Ukraine were constituent republics of the USSR. Both had Moscow as their capital. Both were controlled by the Soviet government. Given the central role which the territory has played in the worst confrontation between Russia and the West since the end of the Cold War, it seems now like one of those moves made to ensure the Soviet Union would actually be very difficult to dismantle.

The Second World War correspondents had hoped that the alliance forged in the hardship of battle with Nazi Germany would endure. Their hopes were not realized. The Cold War was to be an extremely difficult time for correspondents in the Soviet Union. The bloodthirst of the Stalinist regime had not been entirely slaked by the millions of deaths in the Great Patriotic War, and the purges continued, albeit at a much lower level. That was little comfort for those who were 'repressed': among them, in 1949, 'baselessly',[2] Solomon Lozovsky, the urbane censor who amused and infuriated the Moscow foreign press corps during the war. His long-term loyalty to the regime could not outweigh the disadvantage of his being Jewish during one of the periods of official anti-Semitism which stain and shame Russian history. Lozovsky had lived in the 'House on the Embankment', the enormous Moscow apartment block built for civil servants and their families. As many as 806[3] of the house's residents were arrested. Many were put to death. Today, a small museum to their memory occupies a couple of rooms on a corner of the ground floor. Its windows have a view of the towers of the Kremlin: across and along the Moskva River. Perhaps Lozovsky, on his way to spin for Stalin, looked at the red walls and golden cupolas and wondered some mornings if the system which had its centre there would ever turn against him. In 1952, three years after his arrest, and by then aged seventy-four, he was shot. In his book, *Russia at War*, published the following decade, Werth regretted the fate of the 'old *boulevardier*' he had known. It was a reminder to the correspondents of the pressures and risks under which the Soviet citizens who had contacts with them were forced to operate.

Stalin's successor was Nikita Khrushchev. He presided over what came to be known as the 'thaw', a period for Soviet writers 'when reform-minded journals would dedicate themselves to "truth telling" about past and present'.[4] As any would-be reformer in Russian history realized, part of change was to alter people's perception of the present and evaluation of the recent past. Yet this was a thaw within the confines of the Soviet system. Foreign correspondents then were still subject to pre-publication censorship (although that was to change), and the Soviet Union was not a society in which difficult issues – especially those relating to the political elite and the Communist Party – could readily be discussed openly and extensively in public. The fact that the way this new thinking was announced to the world is still today known as the 'secret speech' shows how sensitive the subject was. Yet it ended up in the Western public domain by a curious, circuitous, route that not even the journalist who got the world exclusive was ever entirely able to establish, even much later in the last century when a new wave of reforms – the last that the Soviet Union would ever set in motion – was well underway.

In 1956, John Rettie was based in Moscow for Reuters. In 2006, Rettie, who died three years later, set out, in an article for the *History Workshop Journal*, his best understanding of how the extraordinary events at the centre of which he found himself had unfolded. He began by describing the night of 24 February that year, when the windows of the Moscow headquarters of the Central Committee of the Communist Party 'ablaze with light until the early hours, with the great black limousines of the party elite parked all around it'[5] (there seems to be a conscious echo here of John Reed's description of the Smolny at night, in the throes of the October revolution). As the Twentieth Party Congress had formally ended that afternoon, there seemed no obvious explanation for the nocturnal activity. The account which Rettie himself gave of what happened in the period which followed this unusual burning of the midnight oil was in itself a great story – but it did not have the global political significance of the story which, after a good deal of careful consideration of the risks and consequences, Rettie did write and Reuters did publish. It was a sensational scoop, an account of 'a turning point in the USSR's politics'.[6]

For the Twentieth Party Congress had been the stage which Khrushchev had chosen to make a speech on 'the Cult of the Individual and its consequences'[7] – in other words, an attack on Stalin and his leadership of the Soviet Union. In the words of Robert Service, 'Khrushchev stressed that Stalin was a blunderer as well as a killer'[8] – producing an overall effect on his audience of Party delegates that left some 'so shocked by the contents of the closed session speech that they fainted'.[9] The fact that Khrushchev was speaking to a closed session of the Congress meant that this came to be known as the 'Secret Speech'. However, while the speaker might have wished to limit the audience for the speech, it would not have been made at all had the speaker not wanted its message to spread. That was where Rettie and Reuters came in. The Soviet authorities played the game of international relations through the media very cleverly. Rettie was never able – even decades later – conclusively to establish who his ultimate source had been. The risk that the report was not credible was largely contracted out to the news agency, which was also counted on to get the news to the target audience in the West.

It was not just the late-night activity at Party headquarters which alerted the correspondents to the fact that something was up. Rettie later recalled that, in the days which followed, 'inflammatory rumours' and 'scarcely credible tales' began to do the rounds, suggesting that Khrushchev 'had made a sensational speech denouncing Stalin for serious crimes'[10]: an astonishing story by any measure, meaning that there was all the more pressure on a correspondent, especially one working for an agency with the international reputation and subscriber network of Reuters. Even if the story were true, the Soviet leadership's media strategy meant that it would not permit it to be filed through the usual channels. Rettie's Reuters colleague, Sidney Weiland, did try but in that time of prior censorship nothing was allowed through. Weiland was not the type to be put off. Helen Womack – from a later generation of Moscow correspondents – was trained 'very ably' by him and remembered being 'devoted to him'.[11] She also remembers her first impression. 'He used to chain smoke enormous cigars and it was said that he used to in a rage throw typewriters at his trainees. I was to begin with very frightened of him.'

The rest of Rettie's account illustrated the complexity of ethical editorial decision making on a story such as this. Kostya Orlov, a Soviet source whom Rettie had come to know in Moscow, came to him one evening with two stories: one which broadly confirmed the rumours about the secret speech and a second which told of riots when word of the speech had reached Stalin's native Georgia. Rettie was due to leave Moscow the next day for a holiday in Sweden. That meant both that he had to decide quickly what do to with his explosive material and that he had a chance to bypass Soviet censorship and file it. Rettie discussed his predicament with Weiland, the two agreeing to meet in the street (away from any microphones hidden in apartment or bureau), outside the Central Telegraph. In the end, they decided that he would file the story from Stockholm. The coming departure of a *New York Times* correspondent, who would be able to file a report on the rumours, was also a factor.[12] While the Soviets had long-tolerated reports which might displease them being published in Latvia and elsewhere, no one based in Moscow had really tried this in the sterner years of Stalinism. In fact, Rettie was so nervous that he decided to file his copy over the phone to Reuters 'having fatuously assumed an American accent'[13] – although the copy-takers were not fooled. The stories ran under Bonn and Vienna datelines: the secret speech was secret no more, even if Rettie could not publicly take credit for his exclusive.

The despatch itself was widely printed; the account of Khrushchev's remarks duly attributed to 'Communist sources'. Rettie's 2006 account did note that Orlov 'never appeared to have any difficulty getting past the militiamen' who guarded the entrance to Rettie's block of flats, in which only foreigners were allowed to reside. This strongly suggests that Orlov was on a mission sanctioned by higher authority than that enjoyed by the uniformed officers whose duty it was to keep ordinary Soviet citizens from mixing with foreigners. The despatch itself was a striking account of Khrushchev's criticism of Stalin's responsibility for purging army officers in the decade before the war, and for his refusing to believe that war was coming, as everybody else knew.[14] Stalin, Khrushchev further suggested, 'was ruled by a mixture of persecution mania and gross conceit'.

Rettie's later speculation as to why he was chosen, and on the identity of his ultimate source, offers an insight into the methods of a Kremlin administration that seemed to be using secrecy to be open. Such was the contradictory way the authorities dealt with foreign correspondents during this brief 'thaw' in their relations. The late Stalin period had seen a rapid disappearance of the relative goodwill that had characterized the war years. Between 1949 and 1953, there were only four American correspondents in Moscow.[15] Cost was a factor. Internal BBC correspondence from 1948 – which discussed the desirability or otherwise of trying to retain the services of Alexander Werth from Moscow – referred to increasing costs, and to the fact that censorship made working there extremely difficult.[16] In one of Werth's own letters to the BBC later the same year, he wrote that 'working conditions have become much worse than they have ever been'.[17] Yet by the time that Rettie was wondering whether and how to use the sensational leak he had been given, Khrushchev's Kremlin had changed things. Yes, the censorship remained a major headache, as Sidney Weiland discovered when he tentatively tried to file his few paragraphs on the secret speech – but, on the other hand, this was an era when correspondents were able to talk to Soviet leaders as never before. Elphick remembers Khrushchev chatting about relations with US President John F. Kennedy – 'it was before the Cuba business, you see' – at a reception given for a visiting head of state. Khrushchev 'loved foreign correspondents,' Elphick says, 'so he always liked to have a coterie of us about because he could talk to us and we could then report stuff and he would get kudos in the Politburo.' Such frequent access to senior figures is impossible to imagine now – and equally impossible, given the great challenges that correspondents of the 1920s and 1930s faced to get even the briefest face-to-face encounter with Stalin, to imagine before. Rettie wrote that he 'was quite well known to Khrushchev and other members of the Party Presidium' because they met 'at diplomatic and Kremlin receptions – often as much as once a week'.[18] Rettie believed that it was 'inconceivable' that Orlov really was acting alone, as he insisted. Even when he returned to Moscow in 1990, and put this to Orlov, he got nowhere. The suspicion remained that it came from the top, but naturally nothing was ever written down, and no one would confirm it. Rettie concluded that he was chosen because the authorities wanted the story out, in a way which they could deny being the source, and knew that he was due to go on holiday.[19] Elphick's memories of dealing with the Soviet authorities then echo the curious mixture of making public and keeping secret that characterized the leaking of the secret speech. 'They had this ordinary system of openness in some ways and closedness in other ways.'

It was not until months later that *The New York Times* wrote a story about the secret speech, sourced to a 'document released by the State Department'[20] (for which, read a copy which Khrushchev had arranged to be leaked to the CIA[21]). Harrison Salisbury, who had until 1954 been Moscow correspondent (one of the tiny press corps which survived the outbreak of the Cold War), wrote a blistering top paragraph in which Stalin was described as a 'savage, half-mad, power-crazed despot' – but later admitted that many details of the speech were known already from 'earlier unofficial versions of the address published from March 16 onward'.[22] Rettie's own time in Moscow ended soon afterwards. While he suffered no direct consequences on his return to Moscow for his reporting of the 'Secret Speech', he was soon invited to regular lunches with a KGB officer. Fearful that he was being lined up for retaliation, he asked to be moved from Moscow – returning only in the twilight of the Soviet period when he tried, unsuccessfully, to get to the bottom of the source which had delivered him his great scoop. Orlov's refusal to admit to acting on anything else than his own initiative led Rettie to wonder what hold the KGB might have had over him, even as the collapse of the USSR drew near.[23]

Fear of the Soviet State ran deep among any Soviet citizens working with foreign correspondents throughout the Soviet period, and Orlov may well have been subject to it himself. Even during my first assignment to Moscow in the early 1990s, I recall an incident in the bureau of one Western news organization when Soviet staff decided that one of their number was a KGB informer. They demanded that the bureau editor – a Westerner – dismiss him. Then, as was always the case until after the collapse of the USSR, Western news organizations had to hire all their local staff through GlavUpDK – the Soviet acronym for the agency which served the Diplomatic Corps. Rettie's block of flats – as with all those used by foreign correspondents in the Soviet era – would have been owned and administered by them. GlavUpDK staff were carefully vetted for their political reliability. They would have been expected to answer any questions the KGB might have had about the activities of their Western employers. Some of them would have been KGB agents themselves: one former KGB officer, visiting a Western news bureau in the 1990s to give an interview, half-jokingly pointed out a Russian staff member who, he suggested, was an agent for the security services. In particularly fearful times, the risks which Soviet staff had to run were considerable. When he arrived in Moscow during the Second World War, Quentin Reynolds was assigned a Soviet secretary, Sophiana. Reynolds casually mentioned to his reader that Sophiana had served seven years in a Labour camp – after having been found guilty of spying when she had been working for the American Chamber of Commerce in Moscow.[24] It may have been she to whom Harold Denny referred in an article about the arrest of his own secretary, Valentina Snigirevskaya, when she was assisting him in his coverage of the 1938 show trial. In a terrifying reminder of the conditions in which all Soviet citizens lived, 27-year-old Snigirevskaya was herself taken from her home in the dead of night. Denny did not report the arrest until 20 March, twelve days after Snigirevskaya had been seized – hoping 'that it was an inadvertency that would soon be corrected'.[25] Denny's article reflected on the fact that Snigirevskaya's disappearance during the trial 'inconvenienced and handicapped many correspondents'[26] – presumably not as much as it troubled her, however – but Denny's piece did go on to pay tribute to Snigirevskaya and her peers for the 'unusual combination of abilities' required to do her job. Two days later, *The New York Times* published a photograph of Valentina Snigirevskaya at work. She was not mentioned again. Denny himself completed a five-year posting to Moscow, with the coverage of the show trials the biggest story of his time. He died in July 1945, aged fifty-six. His obituary[27] was a reminder of the remarkable lives lived by correspondents in the first half of the last century: he had fought as an infantryman in the First World War and was taken prisoner during the Second. Captured by the German Afrika Corps in 1941, he was interrogated by the Gestapo in Berlin, before being sent back to the United States. His obituary also mentioned an assignment to Nicaragua in the 1920s, on campaign with the US Marines, 'traveling by automobile, horseback, muleback, native canoe, motor launch, and ocean-going tug'.[28] Moscow tended to attract the determined, enterprising and resilient.

Harrison Salisbury, correspondent for *The New York Times*, was one such. He had first been in Moscow during the war, coming to cover for Henry Shapiro of UPI when he went on holiday.[29] Keen to work for *The New York Times*, he accepted their challenge: if he could get a visa, they would make him Moscow correspondent. He was helped in his quest by the fact that Edwin L. James, *The New York Times*' managing editor, came up with the creative decision to write and publish an 'open letter' to Stalin, arguing for the paper to be given a correspondent visa.[30] It worked. In 1949, Salisbury returned to Moscow as *The New York Times*' correspondent – a role in which he would witness the end of the Stalin era and find himself the target of concerted attacks from a left-wing colleague who had taken against his reporting and the editorial line of his newspaper. He would complete his posting set to win a Pulitzer Prize.

Salisbury arrived in the Soviet capital as the last glow of goodwill that had resulted from wartime alliance was fading. Censorship was as onerous as it had ever been. The CBS correspondent, Ed Fleming, was expelled after being accused of 'tearing up a heavily edited script and throwing it in the face of a censor'.[31] This must have been a rare encounter. Part of the correspondents' frustration and fascination with the whole system was its facelessness, although Elphick does recall a rare attempt at humour. 'The only joke I ever came across from the censor was when one of my American colleagues talked about Khrushchev as "one of the greatest men in the world,"' he says. 'I think they changed to "the greatest man in the world"'. The Russian author and journalist, Masha Gessen, whose grandmother Rozalia worked as a censor, wrote of the Central Telegraph building as a place where, 'shielded by a curtained door, the censors do their work openly but invisibly'.[32] Elphick recalls an attempt to find out what went on there – after a correspondent's three-year-old daughter was invited in. 'She went into the room with the green curtain and we all waited for her to come out again and tell us all about it – but she was too shy and never said a word.'

This was the time when the BBC was finding cost and censorship too great to merit keeping Alexander Werth's services. All in all, the Western press corps was dwindling from expulsion and frustration. Salisbury managed five years. The Cold War was beginning. In September 1949, Salisbury reported on *Pravda*'s mockery of President Truman for a suggestion he had made that the Soviet Union would lose the 'Cold War'[33] (the phrase was new enough then that it appeared in inverted commas in the article) but he also found time that first year to report on economic and infrastructure issues such as housing; Soviet fashion (spring/summer promised 'longer skirts, close-fitting bodices'[34]); and shopping. In these apparently softer stories, Salisbury managed to bring the Soviet experience to American readers in a way that harder political news could not: what the *Guardian* correspondent of a later era, Jonathan Steele, would call 'the three-dimensional quality'[35] of Soviet life. Salisbury also seems to have gained the admiration of at least one of those whose task it was to make his job more difficult: Gessen wrote that her grandmother 'loves translating Salisbury: he is a good and intelligent writer'.[36] Yet it was only after his departure, in 1954, that Salisbury's reporting received recognition at the highest level. The following year, he won a Pulitzer Prize. *The New York Times* introduced Salisbury's 'Russia re-viewed' series of articles on 19 September 1954, with the explanation that they could be published because Salisbury was free of the censorship which had hampered him during his time in Moscow.[37] Over the next two weeks, Salisbury covered subjects as diverse as the Soviet nuclear programme, crime, anti-Semitism, the prison camp system. Fittingly enough, his final report, published on 2 October, dealt with censorship. In a long article, he described the system as erratic, noting that his last two despatched from Moscow had been 'killed in entirety', whereas the first six submitted to the censor by his successor had been passed. One of his 'Russia re-viewed' articles which would have been worth even trying to get past Soviet censorship concerned the possibility that Stalin was murdered by 'the group of his close associates who now run Russia'.[38] Salisbury was honest enough to admit, at the beginning of the second paragraph, that there was 'virtually no way of proving this'.[39] The series as a whole was impressive, the work of a correspondent who had worked hard to understand the country in which he had been based and to communicate it to the outside world. Some of the pieces, such as the Stalin death one, do have a speculative element. Even Salisbury's obituary, when he died in 1993, mentioned that 'some of Mr. Salisbury's fellow journalists whispered that he sometimes exaggerated in his reporting'.[40] The Soviet authorities would no doubt have found this a feeble understatement. In January 1956, *The New York Times* reported that the Soviets had refused Salisbury a visa, although they would grant one to another correspondent.[41] Salisbury himself was clearly the problem. While, as Salisbury's obituary suggested, there may have been occasions on which he veered towards not letting the facts get in the way of a good story, his achievement remains impressive. Even those stories from his five-year posting which told of Soviet daily life – such as shopping and housing – would have been hard to get. Salisbury was to cross another ideological border the following decade, on perhaps his most famous assignment of all. During the Vietnam War, by then in his late fifties, he managed to get permission to report from Hanoi – all but impossible for a correspondent from the United States. Salisbury's coverage gave the lie to the Pentagon's insistence (not for the first or the last time) that its bombing raids destroyed infrastructure without causing civilian casualties. His obituary called him 'intrepid, enterprising and indefatigable', and he needed all of those qualities to report on the last years of Stalin's Russia.

Salisbury's work annoyed not only the Soviet authorities, but their sympathizers. This was an age when – despite those excesses of the Stalin regime which were already known in the West – the USSR had plenty of supporters outside. Those who, like Muggeridge, Lyons, and Haldane, had gone to the USSR because they shared its ideology had their post-war counterparts. One of Salisbury's first stories after his arrival in 1949 concerned the British editor of a Soviet journal who had renounced his British citizenship in favour of becoming a citizen of the USSR.[42] Salisbury's award-winning series provoked a furious attack from a fellow member of the Moscow press corps: Joseph Clark. Clark, the Moscow correspondent for the US-based *Daily Worker* (at this time there was also a British newspaper of the same name), published a pamphlet, *The Real Russia*, the same year as Salisbury's series appeared. Its purpose was to 'expos(e) the slanders and distortions'[43] which Clark saw in Salisbury's work. Correspondents covering the same story often have differing opinions. Disagreements can deteriorate into clashes where ink is flung like verbal vitriol. Reporting Russia seems to take this to extremes. In the same way that those covering the revolutions of 1917 became divided along political lines, the growing division between the capitalist and communist camps that would mark out the ideological battle of the Cold War created a new split. Clark was very clearly on the socialist side. In his pamphlet, he revealed that he was banned from briefings at the US embassy. He did not say why, but compared his lot with that of the 'capitalist press correspondents'[44] – so presumably his ban resulted from his own anti-capitalist views. Clark variously accused the US embassy of censorship of American correspondents' work,[45] with a further set of restrictions imposed by the 'editor censors' at *The New York Times*. The latter's main desire, in Clark's view, was to 'arouse hatred and enmity'.[46] Salisbury himself was accused of 'inventing characters for his articles'[47] and of having such poor Russian that he could barely speak to his servants, who were in any case the only real Russian workers he knew.[48] It was a remarkable attack – a reminder that at this, like any period in Russian history, the country had the ability sharply to divide the opinions of those who reported on it. As the Cold War continued, ideology underpinned and expanded differing editorial lines.

Clark's 1950s British counterpart was Sam Russell. In an interview recorded in 1992, Russell explained that he had first joined the Communist Party as a student in London in 1935. Sir Oswald Mosely's 'Blackshirt' movement was on the rise. For Russell, the Communist Party was 'the only organization that was aware of the dangers of fascism'.[49] For Russell, this was no idle student activism. By late October 1936, he was in Spain, having joined the International Brigades. Wounded on the Cordoba front, he crawled two kilometres to get help. He did not leave Spain until the eve of Barcelona's fall to General Franco's forces in January 1939. He escaped to France. In Paris, he took up the post of correspondent for the *Daily Worker* – a connection that was eventually to bring him to Moscow in 1956. Not surprisingly, given his own Communist convictions (he remained in the British Party until 1991,[50] when it was disbanded in the aftermath of the end of Soviet power in Russia), and his paper's ideological bent, Russell's reporting approved of pretty much everything he saw. A story on the setting up of new boarding schools in the Soviet Union (one of the solutions the state proposed for educating the large numbers of orphans left behind after the Great Patriotic War) gave a glowing description of the facilities the pupils would enjoy[51]; remarks by Nikita Khrushchev reaffirming 'international working class solidarity' were considered newsworthy enough to merit a story in their own right, under the headline 'World's Workers as United as Ever'.[52] Russell's politics did help with access. In the summer of 1956, he was able to travel to Siberian grain-producing regions to report on the harvest: with resulting headlines such as 'They're beating their own grain output plan'[53] you can see why the Soviets might have given him permission. Russell's personal politics were a product of his time and circumstances. That should not detract from reporting which also showed a willingness to discuss social issues such as divorce 'present laws and court practice have completely failed',[54] and lighter items such as how Moscow Zoo prepared animals for winter.[55] Overall, though, Russell's work was defined by ideology: his own; that of the *Daily Worker*; that of the Soviet authorities. While being correspondent for a Communist paper did bring some benefits in terms of access, it closed other doors. Elphick remembers Russell – 'one of the honest Communists' – in Moscow, but adds, of his communist counterparts in the press corps, 'The embassy distrusted them, so we never saw them in the British embassy.' Communist journalists did have an advantage of sorts with censors. For them, censorship was lifted in 1955[56] – presumably because the Soviet censors thought they could trust them – and only in 1961 for 'bourgeois' ones. It also denied Russell what might have been his biggest scoop: the secret speech. In his 1992 interview, Russell told the story of how he had phoned in a version – based on his own sources – which would have beaten Rettie. The *Daily Worker* did not publish it.[57]

If the mid-1950s were a time of change in the USSR, there were also developments in British journalism. Shelley Rohde, aged just twenty-two, became, after Charlotte Haldane, one of the first women to be assigned to the Soviet capital as a correspondent. Her departure was even reported on the front page of the paper for which she went, the *Daily Express*.[58] Rohde's first story appeared a few days later.[59] It was an account of a party which Soviet officials had given for the families and children of foreign diplomats. Rohde was honest enough to admit that she had not herself been there – she had arrived during the weekend with football supporters, whose team, Wolverhampton Wanderers, was in the USSR for a series of matches – but she had obviously done an admirable job of piecing together accounts of what had gone on. Later in the month, there were stories on shopping[60] (together with careful conversion of the prices of fur coats) and nightlife.[61] The following year, she was back in Moscow to report on a show of British fashion.[62] The subjects of these stories may suggest that Rohde was confined to what were then seen as material of interest to women alone, but that is not the full picture. Rohde's time in Moscow also gave her some top-level contacts. She seems to have enjoyed good access to Soviet delegations visiting Britain (when Khrushchev visited in 1956, she even did a couple of articles on learning Russian phrases[63]); Georgi Malenkov even awarded her a 'blue and Gold Soviet peace medal'.[64] During the same visit, invited to a reception at the Soviet Embassy, Rohde reported on the absence of Stalin's portrait. The picture had apparently 'been sent for a spring clean'[65] – some two weeks after news broke of the 'secret speech'. Rohde's assignments to Moscow may have been brief, but, given her youth and gender, represent an important moment in the history of a press corps dominated by men. The sexism of the time was epitomized in a letter which Rohde received from her editor, Arthur Christiansen, in which he told her that Lord Beaverbrook judged her 'a very good girl' for her work in Moscow.[66] There was further praise for the story about Stalin's portrait, although, in a memo to Beaverbrook, Christiansen did raise the concern that it would 'make enemies for us at the Russian Embassy, when we might need friends'.[67]

Radio having established itself during the Second World War as the prime medium for international communication and propaganda, this was an age in which the broadcast media were challenging the authority of print as never before. The broadcasters wanted representation in Moscow – even if internal BBC documents from the time show that questions remained over how much a correspondent would actually be allowed to do. 'I must confess I have always doubted the value of having a resident correspondent in Moscow who, it seems to me, would either find it impossible to report freely or else fall out with the authorities', wrote the head of Talks to the Foreign Editor in October 1961.[68]

Now the opportunity looked as if it might present itself – after times in which the BBC had either been refused permission or declined to seek it, seeing it as not worthwhile. There followed an extensive internal debate as to the value or otherwise of trying to get permanent representation in Moscow. The BBC Central Europe correspondent, Ian McDougall, had offered his own negative views: 'I think that all Moscow cover is a waste of time except for very special occasions.' These were cited in a memo circulated by the foreign editor. McDougall further pointed out the problem which had been experienced as far back as wartime: all the news that was allowed to be published was already available in London on the wire service of TASS; all the news that was not allowed to be published was unavailable anyway. The fact that a permanent correspondent could be 'slung out … [took] a lot of the fun out of the removal of censorship' (which had been formally lifted earlier that year).[69] BBC journalists of later generations might also recognize the lack of agreement between the Corporation's TV and radio arms. The former suggested, 'a man be sent there on an experimental basis – say, for six months'.[70] The latter retained the view that 'the Russian situation can best be covered from outside'.[71] Even if Khrushchev's 'thaw' had led to some more openness, there was still a Cold War – and the BBC's internal debate about opening a bureau in Moscow reflected their part in it. The thaw had its limits. After the Soviet Union's military intervention in Hungary in 1956, BBC Russian Service broadcasts were jammed. In response, the BBC refused Radio Moscow broadcast facilities for sporting events, including the England against the USSR football match at Wembley Stadium in London in October 1958.[72] After the game, the Kremlin may not have been so sorry. The USSR lost 5–0.

It was not only on the football field that this was an era of intense competition. Elphick's experience of two stories symbolizing the competition of the Cold War illustrates perfectly the 'openness' and 'closedness' which formed the correspondent experience. In 1960, with a summit being planned between Khrushchev and President Dwight D. Eisenhower, the Soviet Union shot down a U2 spy-plane in Soviet airspace.[73] 'They brought the wreckage of the U2 to Gorky Park and made a kind of exhibition of it,' Elphick remembers. 'Khrushchev appeared, as we thought, he climbed onto a chair and denounced President Eisenhower.' Elphick says that he had expected this to happen, so he had gone to the Central Telegraph to get a phone line ready, while his colleague, John Miller, had gone to Gorky Park to watch what unfolded. 'Miller came rushing back and I heard what he'd said, I repeated a hundred words quickly to London and then they cut us off. Everybody. All the correspondents were cut off.' Normal links were not restored 'for about four days', Elphick remembers.

'But nothing bad happened because I was doing what Khrushchev wanted.' The following year, Yuri Gagarin became the first man in space. 'It certainly worried the Americans,' Elphick says, 'and that was what it was all about. About the competition.' Elphick remembers meeting Gagarin later at a reception in the Kremlin, and another detail: oranges for sale – a treat for Soviet shoppers not used to fruit from faraway climates. 'We had never seen oranges in Gorky Street,' Elphick says, giving Tverskaya the name it bore for most of the Soviet period.

The BBC's internal debate continued through 1962, with editors seeking information from American Moscow correspondents and former correspondents visiting London. Over lunch, BBC editors tried to glean enough information to take a decision on whether to go ahead with opening a Moscow bureau. One such meeting, with Stanley Johnson of the Associated Press, reflected the Corporation's perceived influence in the Cold War era: the BBC correspondent, Johnson reportedly suggested, 'would probably be considered the next most important British personage in Moscow after the ambassador'. His wife – there was no question then that the correspondent would be a man – would need at least fifteen cocktail dresses for all the receptions she and her husband would be expected to attend. On living conditions, there was also a warning against 'uneatable' (sic) Russian food which 'stank'.[74] In a reflection of how sensitive such conversations were considered, this, like another memo about a lunch with Donald Connery of *Time* magazine, was marked 'Confidential'. In the latter, Connery told the story of a *Newsweek* correspondent who had got in trouble for cabling a joke about Khrushchev – although Connery suggested that the reporter might have got away with it had he sent his despatch by post.[75] It is hard to imagine anyone risking reporting a joke about Stalin by either means, but perhaps no one dared to make one which the correspondents could have reported anyway. Despite all the disadvantages, the BBC decided to go ahead. In 1963, Erik de Mauny became the first BBC Moscow correspondent, moving into a flat on Sadovo-Samotechnaya in central Moscow. The flat, which the BBC kept until the early twenty-first century, was in a building housing many other foreign correspondents – a building which, in consequence, was especially closely watched by the militia, as the Russian police were then called. De Mauny's reports showed a deep interest in Russia and its culture, and an ability to pick out the everyday details about life behind the Iron Curtain which so fascinated audiences on the other side of it (remember John Steinbeck's intention to find out what people ate and wore). In a despatch for the BBC programme *Woman's Hour*, broadcast in August 1963 (de Mauny had arrived in May), de Mauny satisfied some of that curiosity: describing food supplies in the markets (erratic when it came to fruit and vegetables), summer fashions and the number of Soviet women doing manual work. de Mauny called the last 'a rather moving spectacle – a reminder that the last war robbed Russia of almost an entire generation of young men'.[76] Towards the end, de Mauny said that the 'chief recompense' of life in the Soviet capital was 'the chance to get to know Russians better'. That, alas, remained far from straightforward. Those Soviet citizens who did approach foreigners either did so with official sanction or at great risk. The tension of the times meant that de Mauny was not only a pioneer but, for a while, an exception. When he left, the Soviet authorities refused to grant a visa to Elphick, whom the BBC had put forward as de Mauny's successor. The BBC was once again without a resident correspondent.[77]

By this time, the Soviet Union had made a permanent change. In 1964, 'a peaceful plot'[78] had been hatched to remove Khrushchev – significant, in terms of Russian and Soviet history, in that there were 'no guns, no executions'.[79] Alongside the thaw, Khrushchev's time as leader of the USSR also saw, in 1954, the transfer of the Crimea to Ukraine. This was not a big story at the time, although *The Manchester Guardian* did report it, their unnamed correspondent shrewdly noting that this 'purely administrative measure' was 'of less significance than the propaganda accompanying it'[80] – the propaganda being 'to give honour to Ukraine and to increase its interest in the maintenance of the Soviet order'.[81] Sixty years later, Vladimir Putin would take it back by force of arms in order to give honour to Russia. Khrushchev's successor, Leonid Brezhnev, would lead the USSR for almost twenty years – a time which came to be known as the 'era of stagnation'. For correspondents, closed off in their foreigners' compounds and subject to the vicissitudes of the changing political relationship of the Cold War, it was often an era of frustration. There were very few foreigners in the Soviet Union at the time. Tourism was limited to organized groups, often in cooperation with Soviet-friendly clubs or societies in the west. The planned Marxist–Leninist economy was hardly a magnet for businesspeople. This meant that almost all the Westerners in the USSR were diplomats, students or journalists. With the USSR so difficult to visit, and yet, during the Cold War, looming so large in Western lives (and, for many Westerners, their fears) there was a tremendous interest in learning about what went on there. Hedrick Smith, in his bestselling 1970s book *The Russians*, reflected on how difficult it was for correspondents to get to know Russians personally[82]; he mentioned train journeys as an environment in which people might become more relaxed.[83] Steele agrees, 'Trains were a good place. Somehow, there seemed to be less inhibition about chatting to foreigners on a train'. Audiences found the insights which emerged from these casual conversations illuminating. As Barbara Walker has put it, 'American readers wanted to know all about "real life" behind the Iron Curtain, even more than about political affairs in the heart of the enemy.'[84] Because access to this 'real life' was so limited by the correspondents' living and working conditions, they often found that interaction with that section of Soviet society that really wanted to speak to them – dissidents – was the best that they could do. Often members of intellectual elites, the dissidents were also that part of Soviet society which most admired the West. In extreme circumstances, such as cases of imprisoned activists, when they might seek help in the form of diplomatic pressure from the outside, correspondents might be persuaded to arrange to get material to the West[85]: the dissident got their voice heard; the correspondent got a story. Some dissidents were tempted to play an especially risky game: indulging in activism that might get them imprisoned in the hope that the authorities would exile them abroad instead. Western correspondents' reporting on such activism, and giving it publicity, was an important part of the overall strategy.[86]

In a sense, this was an adaptation of techniques used by the Soviet authorities themselves. Often hostile and suspicious during the Cold War, they were willing to use the Western media – especially those smaller news outlets which shared their Marxist–Leninist ideology – to communicate with the outside world. Russell's experience with the secret speech is telling. Even with access such as he apparently enjoyed, the Soviets knew that an international news agency, based in London, one of the strongholds of international capitalism, was going to be a more effective vehicle than those news media which shared their views. While it is impossible to be certain of the initial source of Rettie's scoop, his hypothesis that 'the order had been given by Khrushchev'[87] is perfectly plausible. Russell – although he seems to have had very good sources of his own – was not chosen as the conduit. Unlikely as it may have seemed during this stagnant, secretive, era in Soviet history, stagnation and secrecy would not endure. The Soviet Union itself would not even last a half-century after its victory over Nazi Germany – but, before it collapsed, it would offer foreign correspondents unprecedented opportunities to report on it.

A window on the country: Reporting reform and ruin

The rush hour traffic gave way to the demonstrators. They marched along Tverskaya which, by then, had regained its pre-Soviet name. Gleeful, enthusiastic, smiling under the hot sun of late afternoon in high summer, the throng shouted its support for Boris Yeltsin, candidate in the election for the first president of the Russian Federation. Yeltsin's rising role in Russian politics would be both disruptive and decisive. He generated massive media attention: almost completely positive in the West; largely, but not exclusively so, in what was still nominally Soviet Russia. Names were changing fast, reflecting changing politics and a new Russian, rather than Soviet, sense of identity. The day that Yeltsin was elected, 12 June 1991, the people of Leningrad, city revered through the Soviet era as the cradle of the revolution, voted to change its name back to Saint Petersburg. The day of the demonstration in Moscow, the international and Soviet news media were out in force to follow the crowds. The BBC Moscow correspondent, Martin Sixsmith, stood on top of an idle trolleybus to get a better position for his piece to camera. It seemed to symbolize the new freedom to report on Russia. It had all happened very quickly.

When Leonid Brezhnev died in 1982, he was succeeded by the head of the KGB, Yuri Andropov, whose 'ideological severity was emphatic'.[1] There was little immediate prospect that the working conditions for correspondents would improve under the new leadership. Then in my teens, I was at school in Manchester. I had started to write for the school newspaper and to learn Russian. I did not yet imagine that both those skills would play such a large part in my future professional life. We were taught Russian conversation by a woman who had emigrated from Soviet Union. Her response to the news of Andropov's accession to the post of general secretary was more direct than Professor Robert Service's measured view, cited above. 'When a bastard is a clever man, it is worse.'

Andropov was clever enough to understand that the USSR needed to reform if it was to succeed. Andropov, though, was in poor health. He did not live long enough really to make a difference. Crackdowns on public drunkenness and absenteeism at work did send a message to a Soviet population that the Brezhnev era – 'drink up and shut up' and 'they pretend to pay us, and we pretend to work' being popular sayings – was over. Andropov died in early 1984. He was succeeded by Konstantin Chernenko, a long-time associate of Brezhnev. Chernenko was himself in poor health. He died in March 1985. Chernenko's successor shared one characteristic with his predecessor: a deep conviction of the need for reform. Yet, fifty-four years old when he became Soviet leader, Mikhail Gorbachev also had one quality which neither of these short-lived general secretaries had enjoyed: relative youth, a distinguishing characteristic among the gerontocracy of the Soviet Union's political elite.

In news terms, the speed with which the succession was announced was remarkable. The deaths of previous leaders had been followed by lengthy deliberations over who was to take their place. Gorbachev was named the same day. Both *The Times* in London and *The New York Times* put the story on the front page: both used the word 'swift' in the headlines.[2] The latter, precise as ever, calculated that a mere four hours and fifteen minutes had elapsed between the announcement of Chernenko's death and the news that Gorbachev would take over. *The Times'* correspondent, Richard Owen, wrote – after a round of vox pops, including the views of a police officer hoping for a 'young and vigorous boss' – of the expectation that Gorbachev would 'at last open up the country to badly needed reforms'. Owen also noted 'pessimism' that such reforms could succeed 'in a country weighed down by centuries of bureaucracy and inertia'.[3] In a profile of the new leader, *The New York Times* quoted the famous verdict on Gorbachev given by the then British Prime Minister, Margaret Thatcher, during Gorbachev's visit to London the previous year: 'I like Mr Gorbachev. We can do business together'.[4] The article concluded with a reference to one element of Gorbachev's approach to power which would be integral to his reforms: his desire to court the news media. Turning up the previous month to cast his vote in a Soviet parliamentary election, Gorbachev had 'bantered easily with foreign correspondents'.[5]

The speed of the breaking story seemed to anticipate the new general secretary's enthusiasm for change. Two Russian words entered English, and many other languages, in the era which was to follow: *glasnost'* and *perestroika*. The former is usually translated as 'openness' (its linguistic root is an archaic form of the Russian word for 'voice'). The latter means 'reconstruction' or 'rebuilding'. In the six years which followed, Western correspondents in the Soviet Union would experience unprecedented access to a country where so much had been off limits. They would cover one of the biggest stories of the entire twentieth century. 'It was an amazing time, like windows flung open, doors, you could practically talk to anybody, fear dissipated, it was an extraordinary time,' remembers Fred Weir, who first arrived in Moscow in 1986, the year after Gorbachev came to power, and has been there since. 'I don't expect to ever see the like of it again.'[6]

The Cold War had guaranteed Western media interest in events in the USSR. The fact that the USSR itself might be on the threshold of radical and irreversible change made it even more interesting. Gorbachev's reforms were not only in the domestic sphere. Despite the United States' determination to press ahead with its Strategic Defense Initiative (known more commonly as 'Star Wars'), Gorbachev 'went out of his way to plead the case for global peace and for a process of disarmament.'[7] Curiosity about what was to come drew in newcomers to the Moscow press corps. Weir was among them: one of the first new correspondents in the *glasnost'* era; one of the last of another kind: the Communists. When he arrived in 1986, Weir did so as the correspondent for the *Canadian Tribune,* the publication of the Communist Party of Canada. Despite coming from a Communist family, and having five relatives married to Soviet citizens, Weir 'didn't want to be here – I didn't really like it here – until Gorbachev came to power'. At that point, Weir said, he 'desperately did' want to be in Moscow to see Gorbachev 'turning the Soviet Union upside down, democratizing that system, but from the bottom up'. Weir noted that Communist correspondents had always been 'in a different cage from the so-called bourgeois correspondents'. The last vestiges of that system endured even then. In the 1980s, as an accredited correspondent with a Communist publication, Weir found himself in a separate system. He was overseen not by the Foreign Ministry, but by a minder from the Central Committee of the Communist Party of the Soviet Union.[8] In an echo of the fate of his Communist counterparts of an earlier age, Weir found he was not welcome at the US embassy, or at that of Canada, his own country, which 'never accepted me in those days'.

Others began their reporting careers in this era sensing that something remarkable was about to unfold, whether or not they shared Gorbachev's hopes that the system could be reformed and survive. Bridget Kendall had been in the Soviet Union as a graduate student but, feeling that some of the Western correspondents she encountered living 'in these compounds with a policeman on the door' knew much less about the country than she had been able to learn from time in the provinces, was not sure that she wanted to join them. While she wanted to be a journalist, she worried that it would be 'very frustrating' to be a correspondent in Moscow.[9] The arrival of perestroika era changed that. Returning in 1986 as a journalist with the BBC, Kendall found people in think tanks and institutes who were close to Gorbachev willing to talk. Journalists' hearts often sink when they are offered only the 'official line'. In Moscow at that time, however, Kendall remembers, 'the official line was very interesting'. Those less connected to the new policies were more wary. In 1987, Kendall went to try to make a radio programme in a school – not normally the kind of place where a radio producer is stuck for sound effects. This was different. The children were 'all very inhibited'. The school bell between lessons was about all that could be recorded. A visit to another school two years later seemed to show how society was changing. The pupils there 'were all chattering and making noise and happy to talk, just like Western children were'.

Restrictions remained, however, for bourgeoisie and Bolshevik sympathizers alike. The new leader of the USSR may have been burning with energy to launch his reforms, but the 'bureaucracy and inertia' of which Richard Owen had written in *The Times* still weighed heavy on Soviet society. Travel restrictions on foreign journalists remained in place up until the end of Soviet power, and beyond. Correspondents were required to give forty-eight hours' notice of any trips outside the capital: in effect, beyond the ring road which encircles Moscow. Jonathan Steele is one former Moscow Bureau chief who has extensive experience of road travel in the Soviet Union. He first went there in the early 1960s in a Land Rover. After several reporting trips during the 1970s and 1980s for *The Guardian*, he took up a permanent post in Moscow in 1987. *Glasnost'* had been official policy for two years, but that did not mean correspondents were encouraged to be too curious. Unauthorized travellers were unlikely to reach their intended destinations. The authorities saw to that. 'They were on all the main roads out of Moscow,' Steele remembers. 'There were police checkpoints and you had special licence plates on your car if you were a foreign correspondent, so it was easily visible. Even a different colour of license plate: yellow.'[10] The licence plates also had letters identifying the car as belonging to a correspondent (they began with the letter 'K', the initial letter of the word in Russian) and numbers which indicated the correspondent's country of origin. These licence plates outlasted the travel restrictions, but still made foreign correspondents highly visible, especially to Russia's inquisitive – and occasionally rather menacing – traffic police. Kendall remembers being turned back at the city limits when she was driving out to the countryside to go for a walk. 'Things were still very restricted'. Seeking to go even further afield might trigger rules which bordered on the absurd. Trying to fly to Baku, in the then Soviet Socialist Republic of Azerbaijan, in order to cover anti-Soviet protests, Kendall encountered rules designed to keep her in Moscow. 'We were told you can't get a ticket until you have a visa and the Foreign ministry said you can't have a visa until you have a ticket, in order to stop us going.' Steele had similar experiences. 'It was a paradox, because you would want to go because something was happening, but precisely because something was happening, they wouldn't give you permission to go.' Weir had similar memories. 'The Soviet Union was a special place. People tell different stories about it, but the bottom line was that you were very limited in your movements. Official contact was difficult, and any travel had to be cleared in advance.' Some stories definitely fell into Steele's 'because something was happening, they wouldn't give you permission to go' category. One of the biggest stories of the early Gorbachev period definitely fell into that category. Correspondents' experience of it showed both that old Soviet methods of stonewalling silence still existed and that times had changed enough for it to be challenged.

On the night of 25–26 April 1986, there was an explosion at the Chernobyl nuclear power station in what was then the Soviet Socialist Republic of Ukraine. The resulting radiation was carried on the wind far beyond the borders of Ukraine: far beyond the borders of the USSR. It was from far beyond the borders of the USSR that the story was first reported. *The Times'* front-page headline of 29 April 'Huge nuclear leak at Soviet plant'[11] appeared over a story written by the paper's Science correspondent and a reporter from Stockholm. Not until the disturbingly high radiation levels had been detected in Scandinavia did the world learn of the disaster. In Moscow, the seat of the government and of the entire system which was ultimately responsible for the catastrophe, there was silence.

Philip Taubman was a correspondent for *The New York Times*. He had arrived in Moscow the previous fall to begin a three-year posting. Like many of the correspondents for the longer-established news organizations, he lived in the foreigners' apartment block at Sadovo-Samotechnaya. *The New York Times'* bureau chief, Serge Schmemann, lived in the same building, which also housed their office. The arrangement was convenient for correspondents who did not need to battle the winter weather to get to work. It was even more convenient for the Soviet security services who wanted to keep an eye on foreign journalists. Schmemann and Taubman would return to the bureau in the evenings to watch the main Soviet TV news bulletin, *Vremya* ('Time'): broadcast then, as now, at 21:00. Taubman remembers the evening that the

Soviet authorities decided to announce the accident – although not initially for the reason you might imagine. 'Neither of us was paying any attention,' he says of his and Schmemann's viewing that night, 'because typically there was nothing worth reporting on Vremya'.[12] It was only when Schmemann's wife, Mary, asked the two whether they had seen the item on a nuclear accident. Then, says Taubman, 'suddenly we sort of woke up, and started paying attention'. It is not surprising they missed it. As Schmemann later wrote, the TASS wire was '44 bland words'[13] – a grudging admission offered only after extensive enquiries from the governments of those Western countries, Sweden in particular, who had realized that something terrible had happened. *Glasnost'* in this case did not carry its primary non-political meaning of 'publicity'. As Steele remembers, plane crashes and other accidents in the Soviet Union were 'complete taboo' as far as the media were concerned. 'Anything that was bad news was ignored.' This could work when the media were controlled, and the accident was on Soviet territory. It was harder to control when clouds of radioactivity were rolling across Europe, and foreign media were getting information from their own governments and scientists. Still, as Martin Walker's report from Moscow for *The Guardian* on 30 April showed, the Soviet authorities did – in the first days after the accident, at least – manage to keep the worst of the news from their own population. Walker wrote of the disaster area being 'enclosed by a wall of official silence'. He did manage to contact a British schoolteacher, Sue Parminter, who was visiting Minsk, the capital of Belarus (then also part of the Soviet Union, and one of the countries worst affected by the radioactive fallout of the explosion[14]). Parminter had heard the news of the disaster on the BBC World Service, but when she asked people at the university about it, she was met with 'absolute incomprehension'.[15]

The Soviet authorities realized that, with the news being confirmed by sources outside the USSR, they had to respond. Their media management system was crude and ultimately ineffective – even drawing dissent from news media they might usually have been able to rely on. There was a clumsy attempt by one Soviet commentator to dismiss reports of mass casualties as 'inventions of the bourgeois mass media'. Schmemann also noted that the terse announcement on the Soviet official media that confirmed the accident had happened was followed by wire reports recalling nuclear accidents in the West.[16] Taubman remembers it being 'very frustrating' to try to write about Chernobyl in the initial period after the story broke. 'There was a very memorable news conference at the foreign ministry led by a group of Soviet officials and the Head of the National Academy of Sciences,' he recalls. 'They threw out a lot of data which was kind of meaningless because there was no context for it [...] They were deliberately trying to obscure what was going on.' They did not succeed. Taubman remembers the news conference being memorable for another reason, too: 'Eastern European correspondents, and I believe some Soviet reporters in the audience, actually pushed back very hard, saying "You're giving us all of this gibberish about data that we can't understand."' Reporters who would normally accept what they were told were suddenly challenging the official line, 'So it turned into a very combative news conference.' For Taubman, it was 'one of the first times' he saw his journalistic colleagues from the Communist bloc, 'angry at the lack of candour'. This was something new. As Steele points out, 'In previous periods, there were nuclear accidents that were completely suppressed, never appeared in the Soviet media. And the same with train crashes or any kind of disaster.'

The greater licence afforded to, and boldness shown by, the Soviet press could not but help their Western counterparts. Taubman's experience of watching *Vremya* in the Soviet period, and seeing little that was newsworthy, was typical – but, as *perestroika* advanced, Gorbachev made more and more use of the Soviet press to promote his cause, often in opposition to those conservative elements of his own party that sought to thwart his reforms. The Western press benefitted, too: there was more in the Soviet media which was truly newsworthy, especially in publications such as *Ognoyok* ('Little Flame'), *Argumenty i Fakty* ('Arguments and Facts') and *Moscow News* 'the flagship of glasnost'[17] in Steele's phrase. *Ogonyok*'s joining the cause of promoting *perestroika* 'had one obvious advantage: it was so reactionary and anti-Western that any shift to a more liberal and pro-Western position was immediately noticeable',[18] as Arkady Ostrovsky put it. This book's focus is Western reporting of Russia and the Soviet Union, but in this age perhaps more than any other, the Soviet media – so often the main or only source upon which foreign correspondents could draw – were actually sought after because there was genuine news in them, such as discussions of episodes of Soviet history not previously talked of publicly. On my own first visit to the USSR, as a language student in the summer of 1987, one of our party was bold enough to ask the guide what people thought of Trotsky. They were tersely informed that he was 'an enemy of the people' and so was not spoken of. It is important to emphasize, for an understanding of the era, that whatever its ultimate consequences, *perestroika* was launched as 'a return to a modernised version of several major strands in the Soviet past', as R.W. Davies put it. 'On this basis, Gorbachev argued, the "socialist choice made in 1917" would be reaffirmed and renewed.'[19] The Soviet news media were an integral part of

Gorbachev's reforms. They were enlisted to spread the message. In a way, this too was a return to an aspect of the Soviet past. Lenin himself identified 'propaganda, agitation, and organization'[20] as the key functions of political media. Gorbachev adapted Leninist use of the media not to prevent people from challenging the system, but actually to give journalists licence to question it. The result was an unprecedented era of Soviet media freedom: a time when, 'with the sanction of the general secretary, journalists also attacked the party establishment'.[21]

That gave foreign correspondents plenty to write about. For they were able, in the Soviet Union of that time, to write about not only a new present, but also a new past: one which had been hidden for decades, but was now being revealed. Taubman reported for *The New York Times* on the issue of new history textbooks: ones which did not portray the 1930s purely in terms of economic growth and industrial progress, while omitting mention of purges – as had been the case thereto. Family stories mass incarceration and execution – previously only talked of in guilty whispers at home – could now be mentioned in the classroom.[22] Taubman still remembers the chance to cover stories such as these as 'the electricity of going out and watching, and then writing about the breakup of Soviet control over Soviet society. It was really an electrifying experience'.

As foreign correspondents discovered during this era, there were also elements of the experience which could be terrifying. As with the initial attempt to cover up the nature and scale of the disaster at Chernobyl, there were times when – apparently feeling that they were being challenged to show their strength on the world stage, or their authority at home – the Soviet authorities reverted to the tactics of an earlier era to maintain their control over the international press. Even in the most liberal version of Marxist–Leninist society that the Soviet Union produced in its entire history, the Stalinist belief that all Western correspondents were really spies seemed to endure. Even in this time of openness and change, they were sometimes treated accordingly. In the newspaper archives from the *perestroika* period, alongside stories of schoolbooks recognizing the murderous chapters in Soviet history, there are also stories of correspondents themselves being persecuted. Perhaps the most unnerving example is that of Nicholas Daniloff, Moscow correspondent for *U.S. News and World Report* in the 1980s.

In Daniloff's 1988 memoir, *Two Lives, One Russia*, he recounted what happened to him in the late summer of 1986, as he prepared to leave the Soviet capital, his posting there complete. 'For many years, correspondents have assumed that expulsion is the stiffest penalty they are likely to suffer,'[23] Daniloff wrote. His experience tested the assumption. In his case, it was false. Having been handed a packet by a Soviet contact – documents, Daniloff assumed, for a story – he was soon arrested. The packet contained classified material. Daniloff found himself in Moscow's Lefortovo prison, charged with espionage. Daniloff realized that his contact, Misha, with whom he had become acquainted on an earlier trip to Frunze (now Bishkek) in Kyrgyzstan, 'must have been working with the KGB'.[24] It was a classic case of entrapment. Following pressure from the US government – and an agreement that the United States would allow a Soviet citizen accused of spying to leave the country – Daniloff was released two weeks later. When he was freed, there was media speculation that this had been a direct exchange – although *The New York Times* cited an official in the administration of then President Ronald Reagan as pointing out that the suspected Soviet spy, Gennady Zakharov, had pleaded guilty, whereas Daniloff had been allowed to leave before he was put on trial.[25] For Taubman, news that Daniloff was on the way to Sheremetyevo airport to leave the country sparked a race to catch him, and the story, before he took off. Any sense of solidarity among the press corps which might have formed as they followed Daniloff's plight had quickly vanished. Taubman remembers arriving at the airport to be told by a rival correspondent that he was too late, that Daniloff was boarding his flight. No to be outdone, Taubman actually managed to get on Daniloff's flight – the only other reporter on board, as he explained, apart from Alison Smale of the Associated Press.[26]

Before his arrest, Daniloff, who is of Russian descent – his father had even served in the Tsarist Army as a junior officer – had been thinking of writing a book about one of his Russian ancestors, Alexander Frolov. Frolov had been imprisoned for his part in the Decembrist revolt against Tsar Nicholas I in the nineteenth century.[27] Thoughts of Frolov's grim experiences may have helped his descendant face up to his own predicament, especially when he could not be sure what form it would take, or how long it would last. Daniloff's experience, on the other hand, did not help his colleagues in the Moscow press corps whilst they covered the story of one of their own locked up in one of Russia's most notorious prisons. As Daniloff remained in gaol, with his fate still uncertain, Taubman himself wrote a long piece on the 'intense and volatile conditions' faced by Western correspondents working in the Soviet capital. You needed to have contacts with Soviet citizens to do your job. With each such contact, there was a risk you might be tricked and trapped.[28] Daniloff's case gained a notoriety, an ability to inspire fear, which outlived his departure from Moscow. Ordered to leave Moscow in 1989 in a 'tit-for-tat' expulsion (eleven Soviet spies had been expelled from London days earlier), *The Sunday Times* correspondent Angus Roxburgh admitted to being 'really scared' when the case against him threatened to take the form of espionage charges. It led him to wonder if he might share Daniloff's fate.[29] Summoned unexpectedly to the British embassy on a Sunday morning to hear the news (the ambassador himself having only been told late the previous evening), along with Jeremy Harris of the BBC, and Ian Glover-James of *Independent Television News* (the main provider of news to commercial TV channels in the UK), Roxburgh reflected in his later memoir, *Moscow Calling*, that this was 'a sting from the tail of the old Cold War, just as democracy was dawning'.[30] The fact that the Soviet Union itself would only last for another couple of years meant that Roxburgh was able to return as a correspondent in the 1990s, working then for the BBC, and again, in the 2000s, as a public relations advisor with a Western agency working for the Kremlin.

None of the Moscow correspondents, present or former, to whom I spoke, on or off the record, while researching this book admitted to having worked for any intelligence agency. If any were spies, to admit it would be poor spy craft. Many have stories to tell of being treated as spies even if their experiences do not compare to Daniloff's. Womack says she 'was approached and I said fuck off to both' British and Soviet intelligence. The British, she adds, did not try to recruit her but 'warned me that my Russian teacher might be a KGB agent and I told them to get lost. And I told the Russians to get lost as well.' Mary Dejevsky, who was Moscow correspondent for *The Times* in the late 1980s and early 1990s, remembers, after a year in the Soviet Union as a student, being 'summoned to what was then old Scotland Yard to go and discuss my report' but 'that was the only contact I had'.[31] Kendall remembers being 'pestered' when she was a student by someone who claimed to be able to get tickets for 'Swan Lake' at the Bolshoi. The person would frequently phone the hall of residence. Finally, having suspected that the mystery caller offering an evening at the ballet was KGB, Kendall got her roommate to put him off – enjoying the fact that one person who was reporting on her to the KGB, as her roommate almost certainly would have been, got rid of another wanting to do the same. Taubman, who had covered security issues before leaving the United States, remembers declining an invitation to visit the CIA before he left for Moscow, 'because I felt that this was the moment at which they might try to ask for some kind of favours.' He concedes, though, that there is 'a long history of American journalists – *The New York Times* wrote about it at one point – some of my colleagues actually – who had worked hand in glove with the CIA over the years'. Having turned down the chance to meet the CIA, he did have an encounter with the KGB. Allowed to witness an underground nuclear test, Taubman was in a desperate hurry to return to his hotel to write his story. He eventually overcame protests that there were no cars available. At the hotel, Taubman encountered an apprehensive *dezhurnaya* – the employee who looked after keys on each floor of a Soviet hotel and who foreigners usually thought of as a KGB informant. She tried to put him off going to his room. He insisted. There he found the door ajar and 'two guys in my room, one of whom has got a camera and is taking photographs of my phonebook'. They rushed out. Before being posted to Moscow, Taubman had written extensively on diplomacy and intelligence. He wonders to this day what the intruders thought of him after they had found a contacts book stuffed with the names and phone numbers of 'senior intelligence officials' in Washington. While Taubman's tale has an element of farce, those of Daniloff and Roxburgh – who feared he was about to be charged with spying after agreeing to a request from a Soviet 'friend' (his inverted commas) to bring him a Dictaphone from the West[32] – have an air of menace. Taubman also remembers a story of another American correspondent who planned to write an article on the fact that VHS videocassette players were starting to appear in Moscow and that people were using them to watch material smuggled in from the West. 'He was going to do a story on this, and he went to someone's apartment and they put on a pornographic tape and five minutes later the KGB stormed in. He was set up.' Pornography was illegal in the Soviet Union, so just by watching it the reporter was breaking the law.

Access to places and information had improved, but the Soviet police state had not withered away. It was there and could appear without warning. In Steele's view, part of the problem was that the Soviet authorities, and people, did not really ever know how to respond to foreign correspondents. 'We weren't spies, we weren't intelligence agents, we weren't detectives, but we were trying to make reporting of the Soviet life more three-dimensional.' That three-dimensional reporting became easier as Soviet society opened up, when, as Weir put it, reporters could 'go out and meet real people and talk to real people and they would tell you what they were really thinking'. Officialdom opened up too – in the shape of an international press centre. 'There was a podium and a press spokesman from the Foreign Ministry would actually give press conferences and sometimes, some different ministry … education or science or something, culture … would also give briefings,' Steele remembers. As Daniloff and Roxburgh discovered, however, any kind of crisis in diplomatic relations with the West – especially those involving expulsions over allegations of espionage – caused a quick reversion to the ways of the Cold War.

The same was true of disasters and crises within the USSR. The explosion at Chernobyl was one example. There were more as protests against Soviet rule spread in restive republics: protests which were brutally and bloodily put down. Foreign correspondents were kept away. Such unrest and disorder were occasions when the obstacles that both Kendall and Steele described above – the contradictions involved in trying to gather the correct permission to travel – were placed as obstructively as possible in reporters' way. Tbilisi in Georgia and Vilnius in Lithuania – now capitals of independent states, then capitals of Soviet republics – were two notorious cases: both for bloodshed and media control. In April 1989, a demonstration in Tbilisi demanding Georgian independence was broken up by Soviet troops. Nineteen unarmed civilians were killed.[33] Steele, like the other foreign correspondents, could not go. The city was closed off. Reporting was reduced to the techniques employed by correspondents waiting at the Latvian border in the early days of the Bolshevik regime. For his report for *The Guardian* on 13 April, Steele compared the accounts given in official Soviet media, based in Moscow, with those in the Georgian Communist Party paper, *Zarya Vostoka* (meaning 'Dawn of the East' in Russian). The former blamed 'provocation by extremists'. The latter held the army responsible.[34] A *Guardian* editorial the following week, noting that there was a 'worthy Information Forum', in which Soviet officials were participating, then underway in London, argued for Moscow correspondents to have 'the freedom to set off at the drop of a news story to any part of the Soviet Union'. The leader also included the grisly detail, which had by then become public, that troops had used 'truncheons and sappers' spades' to attack the demonstrators.[35] In January 1991, fourteen people were killed in Vilnius when Soviet troops stormed the television station. Official Soviet media coverage, in the view of *The Times* correspondent in Moscow, Bruce Clark, was a combination of 'deafening silence, half-truths, and sententious comments'. The headline suggested the 'hardline media' had dealt 'a crippling blow to glasnost'.[36]

This was the contradiction at the centre of which Moscow correspondents found themselves in the dying days of Soviet power. On the one hand, doors and windows on Soviet society had been flung open, allowing journalists to see more than ever. On the other, the repressive police state was still very much present and could quickly be mobilized when hardliners chose. For some of those Soviet citizens seeking freedom and independence, the consequences were deadly. The conflict between the liberal and conservative interpretations of Soviet communism would eventually give the correspondents one of Moscow's biggest stories of the entire twentieth century.

Before it did, the Soviet capital would witness the emergence of a new centre of power – a chaotic, unpredictable one – which would straddle the end of

Marxism–Leninism and the dawn of the bandit capitalism which followed. In May 1990, Boris Yeltsin, formerly a party boss in Sverdlovsk (now known by its pre-Soviet name, Ekaterinburg), became speaker of the Russian – as opposed to Soviet – parliament. The following year, in June 1991, he was elected president of the Russian Federation 'on a promise to enhance Russian sovereignty'[37] at the expense of Soviet authority.

Six days before polling day, I flew to Moscow as a producer for Visnews, a television news agency. It was my first international assignment. Visnews was owned by NBC, the BBC and Reuters, which eventually became its sole owner, and changed its name to Reuters TV. Visnews gathered TV news material for distribution across the world and cooperated closely with NBC and the BBC in Moscow: sharing a bureau with the former (the BBC's bureau was a few doors down) in a block of flats set aside for foreigners. *Glasnost'* had begun to ease some of the working conditions to which foreign journalists had been subject. Visnews had recently been permitted to send material to London from its bureau. Previously, foreign TV correspondents had had to take their reports (on videocassettes, as was standard then) to the television centre at Ostankino in northern Moscow for transmission. Satellite time – extremely costly satellite time – had to be booked by the receiving station. Any delay due to traffic jams or intransigent reception staff at the TV centre meant that the transmission slot could be missed. If that happened, the satellite time, the story, and a lot of money would be lost, too. Visnews' link was routed through Ostankino, so the authorities could still cut transmissions should they choose to do so. The fact that they did not at one crucial moment would prove to be a defining difference between media management of the dawn of Soviet power and that of its death.

In the early 1990s, all filming and editing for broadcast television news was done on videotape. The BBC then had separate offices for television and radio, the latter being in the same UpDK block in which De Mauny had set up the bureau in the 1960s, and where Taubman and his *New York Times* colleagues were also based. Kendall remembers the telex machine which received news agency reports printing out the wire copy in four colours, 'a blue, a pink, yellow and a white. We kept the white and the other three went to the *Los Angeles Times*, the *Christian Science Monitor*, and *The Daily Telegraph*, who all had offices in the same block as us'. Kendall also remembers huge cabinets where, at the end of each day, she filed wire stories for future reference. The telex was also the means of communicating with the authorities. In the Visnews office, there were computers. They were a huge advantage, as we were reminded on those occasions when they, along with the phone links, failed (this seemed to happen more often when it rained). The telephones were, in theory, set up to dial internationally. This was not standard for Moscow phones at the time. At the telephone exchange, however, there were a limited number of lines which went beyond Moscow. It was a question of dialing and hoping that one would be free. At the time of a major breaking story, it was unlikely. When the phone and computer links failed, there was the option of having a live 'conversation' with London by typing over the telex machine. Even if they worked technically, the phones would sometimes be cut off mid conversation. We were obviously being listened to. We would sometimes be warned to watch what we said. That summer, you could often see long queues for even basic foodstuffs. Once, over the phone, I told a friend in London that living conditions were tough for Soviet citizens. The line immediately went dead. Dejevsky remembers similar experiences. 'As you were typing into your ancient Telex machine, if you used, say, "KGB," the tape would cut out and you would have to start all over again.' Tough as the working conditions sometimes were – in addition, we journalists could not eat regularly because of the hours we worked, and there were very few places where you could get a quick sandwich or snack – the story was compelling; the interest from editors insatiable. David Remnick, who went to Moscow in 1988 as a reporter for the *Washington Post*, later wrote in his award-winning book *Lenin's Tomb*, of a time when he 'was filing three and four hundred stories a year to editors who would certainly have taken more'.[38]

A changing Soviet Union sought changes in international relations. In late July 1991, President George H.W. Bush came to the Soviet capital for a summit meeting. The aim was to reduce further the nuclear arsenals that the two Cold War foes had stockpiled against each other in less cordial times. There were discussions, too, of measures to aid the collapsing Soviet economy. The more perceptive correspondents, such as Serge Schmemann, understood the domestic challenges which such gestures raised for Gorbachev. Schmemann noted in one of his despatches that the Soviet leader had been criticized by 'Communist hard-liners for "holding his hat out" to the West'. The sense of humiliation which such requests provoked was to have dire consequences later that summer. It arguably casts a shadow over Russia's relations with the West to this day. While the summit for the most part went smoothly, Schmemann also reported Boris Yeltsin's decision not to attend a meeting with President Bush at which Gorbachev would also be present – Yeltsin's dissent a sign, as Schmemann put it, of Gorbachev's being 'in open competition with new political forces at home'.[39] The visit was also marred by more grave

Soviet press pass issued to the author for the Gorbachev–Bush summit, Moscow, July 1991.

confrontations than political manoeuvres in Moscow: six Lithuanian guards on the border with Belarus were gunned down in their newly established customs post[40] – the very existence of which was a challenge to Soviet sovereignty. The killers were never identified, but particularly bloody footage of the aftermath of the attack was transmitted to Moscow to be distributed among the massive press corps which had gathered for the summit. I went to the TV station in Ostankino to collect the material. The unedited footage of the corpses shot with automatic weapons was an eye-opener for a young journalist more used to sanitized British broadcast news.

Bush's visit ended, as Dejevsky wrote in a report for *The Times*, 'in an uncomfortable diplomatic no-man's land'.[41] Having said his official farewells to Gorbachev, the president made a six-hour stopover in Kiev, capital of what was still then Soviet Ukraine. The historian Serhii Plokhy later described the gesture as a sign that 'Bush believed negotiations in Moscow were not enough' in a time when constituent republics of the USSR were finding their own voice. For those members of the press corps who followed Mr Bush, there was a striking example of the way that the Soviet system was seizing up. A number of us boarded a flight to Kiev the evening before Bush's arrival. We waited for two hours on the tarmac at Moscow's Vnukovo airport while the flight crew pleaded with the airport administration to provide them with fuel – a dispute that one of the cabin staff explained over the public address system. Bush's visit also coincided with the introduction of rationing of some foodstuffs in some districts of Kiev, a story which Visnews reported the day he arrived.

It was the last visit by a president of the United States to the Soviet Union. Less than three weeks later, on the eve of what was due to be the signing of a treaty giving the Soviet republics ever greater autonomy from the centre – especially in respect of the ownership of natural resources[42] – Gorbachev's opponents made their move. Declaring that Gorbachev had resigned for health reasons, a group of hardline Communists opposed to his reforms said that they were now running the country. The attempted coup lasted only three days, but during that time there were tanks on the streets of the Soviet capital taking orders from the self-styled 'State Emergency Committee'. Soviet television broadcast a performance of Swan Lake – intended, presumably, to reassure. To any half-curious observer in the USSR or abroad, it was actually a sign that something was not right. It was the first of several media management mistakes which the plotters were to make.

'The drama of the 19th was amazing,' remembers Dejevsky, who, unlike many members of the press corps, was not on holiday. Having been alerted to the story by a 5 am phone call from a broadcast station in Australia, and, anticipating roadblocks, having checked her documents were in order, she was astonished to discover that the armoured personnel carriers transporting troops to secure the capital 'were mingling with the ordinary traffic. You got trolleybuses, buses, pedestrians, and this great column of military gear'. Remarkably, the coup leaders did nothing to prevent correspondents who were outside the capital, or outside the country, from returning. Nor was there any attempt to control their activities in Moscow. Foreign correspondents were able to gather and send material. With newspapers going to press in the evening or early hours of the morning the Moscow time difference was kind – at least in the sense that being three hours ahead of London and eight hours ahead of the East Coast of the United States meant that correspondents could include not only the news of the coup, but also the opposition to it, in their reports published on 20 August. 'Yeltsin challenges Kremlin coup' was the headline above Dejevsky's despatch in *The Times*.[43] 'Gorbachev absent, Yeltsin defiant' was part of a stacked headline on the front page of *The New York Times*.[44] The abiding news image of these days which decided Russia's future direction was the Russian president standing on a tank outside the government building known as the 'White House' in central Moscow. It became a rallying point for those opposed to the coup: a magnet for the news media. Dejevsky arrived at just the right time. 'Yeltsin was coming down the stairs with a couple of his advisors and a posse of Russian MPs,' she remembers. 'He walked down to the bottom of the steps and then – we've all seen the pictures – he got on the tank and gave his mini speech.' Still free to move around, Dejevsky was able to return late at night. 'There was a feeling of everybody being on edge and not knowing what was happening. They got priests in the White House and they were basically swearing in troops loyal to Yeltsin, young volunteers.'

If that was the location of the images which defined opposition to the coup, there was one which has come to do the same for the hapless conspirators. The plotters staged a bizarre news conference at the Foreign Ministry Press Centre. The trembling hands of Gennady Yanayev – who had proclaimed himself president in Gorbachev's stead – as he spoke became such a symbol of their incompetence (and, in this particular case, probably drunkenness) that it outlasted Yanayev himself. It was mentioned in his obituaries after his death in 2010.[45] Dejevsky remembers, 'the trembling hands', but also 'the very aggressive questioning from the Russian correspondents'. As Taubman had noted during the news conference after Chernobyl, previously docile journalists from communist media were no longer compliant.

The coup collapsed. Gorbachev returned to Moscow. Back in London by then after a two-month assignment in Moscow, I had been woken by my colleagues on the news desk at Visnews early on the morning of the 19th to come in to help to translate Soviet TV broadcasts. By the end of the week, I was back in

Moscow. The White House was still surrounded by defenders of Russia's new democracy. They were exhausted and nervous. A TV script I sent on Sunday 25th August told of barricades and Molotov cocktails being prepared to face an expected new tank assault. The rumour was false. Rushing to a nearby public phone to call the bureau, I was chased by one of Yeltsin's supporters. Fearing I was about to send information to their enemies, he threatened me with a stick as I lifted the receiver – but relaxed when he heard me speaking English.

The Soviet Union was all but finished. The decision was formalized by new political agreements between the republics, and Gorbachev's resignation, on 25 December 1991. In Russia, Orthodox Christmas is observed on 7 January, so 25 December is a normal working day. The resignation was itself a major media event, with CNN flying in a special team to cover it.[46]

So ended the most newsworthy era of Russia's modern history. Gorbachev had signed up the Soviet media to support his reforms. The new freedom which they came to enjoy benefitted international correspondents, who also had unprecedented access to people and places. Restrictions and sanctions dating from the Stalin era still existed, as the experience of Nicholas Daniloff and others who were expelled showed. This system may have moved into the background, but it stood there in reserve, ready to be deployed. The international media were involved in Soviet domestic politics and diplomacy as never before. Kendall tells the story of a visit to Socialist East Germany with Gorbachev. The Soviet leader chatted, in Russian, to local people in the park. Kendall helped to translate for West German journalists. They duly reported Gorbachev's words encouraging citizens of the GDR to choose their own path. Kendall is certain that, knowing the West German broadcast would be seen in East Germany, this was Gorbachev's way of getting his message to the citizens of the GDR. 'I think at times that we were used,' she admits now. In the last months of the USSR, the Soviet political elite seemed to care more than ever about how they were being reported outside. Kendall remembers a Soviet Foreign Ministry source telling her that the then Minister, Eduard Shevardnadze, 'had on his desk a translation of the BBC World Service radio news bulletin from 6 am, because they wanted to know what the world was saying and especially what the world was saying about them'. During his captivity at his holiday house in Crimea, Gorbachev learnt of his fate from listening to BBC and other Western broadcasts. His captors had not thought to keep him completely incommunicado.

One of the coup plotters' biggest mistakes was not to follow the precedent set by their revolutionary forebears, and cut Russia off from the outside world, as had been done in 1917. In the early 1990s, this would not have been too difficult. Instead, the foreign media were allowed to do largely as they wished. As Ralph Nicholson, then, as Visnews bureau chief, responsible for the links that carried much of the television material to the outside world suggests, in their handling of the foreign media:

> The coup plotters made three mistakes. They never shut down the TV Centre which allowed us (and others) to get a signal out of the country, they never shut down Sheremetyevo, which would have prevented us getting any further journalists, crews, equipment, etc, into the country. And they never shut down the rail stations, which meant we were able to move around the country.

Correspondents were also free to move around Moscow, as Dejevsky remembers. 'There were no restrictions. I'd gone out with all my documents, expecting to have a great big battle at every checkpoint. Nothing. You could go practically everywhere.' As a result, in contrast to the uncertainty and secrecy which surrounded events in 1917, Russia's new great political transformation was a massive media event – and not one which the would-be new government proved competent enough to control. As Nicholson puts it now, 'Frankly, shutting down a TV station and restricting international and domestic travel is Coup Plotting For Beginners.'[47] Russia's new beginning was to prove a challenging, chaotic and, sometimes, very dangerous and violent assignment.

'Free for all': The Yeltsin era

In mid-January of that year we stayed in a house in a town that lay east of Grozny and across the frontlines. The house was our sleeping quarters. Along with other journalists, we worked in a nearby kindergarten. The kindergarten was also a shelter for refugees. Boris Yeltsin's government had lost patience with lawlessness that had spread across the North Caucasus. There was widespread criminal activity, and, more worrying for the Kremlin, there were also demands for independence. On the last day of 1994, the Russian Army launched an operation to take back control of Grozny, the main city in Chechnya, a republic at the southern edge of the Russian Federation. The Russian Defence Minister, Pavel Grachev, had boasted before the operation that 'Grozny could be taken by a single parachute regiment in the space of two hours,' as James Meek, then in the city, reported for *The Guardian* on 30 December.[1] As the refugees left to escape the ground assault and air raids, journalists from across the world – enjoying the freedom to travel which had followed the end of the USSR – went in the opposite direction. By January, it had become extremely dangerous to work in Grozny. Cynthia Elbaum, an American photojournalist, had been killed in an air raid on 22 December while taking pictures on the streets of the Chechen capital.[2] Aside from the risk of injury or death, broadcasters and providers of broadcast facilities, such as the European Broadcasting Union (EBU), needed areas of relative safety to set up and operate large and expensive equipment, such as satellite dishes. Such equipment could not be moved easily or quickly should the need suddenly arise. There were some especially courageous freelancers who spent their nights in Grozny and gave their material to other correspondents visiting during the daytime. Most journalists, though, had set up bases further from the frontlines: either to the West, in Nazran in Ingushetia, or to the East, in Khasavyurt in Dagestan – about eighty kilometres away. The distance offered journalists safety and therefore a degree of reassurance – but also presented logistical challenges. Combined with the danger, this was a very tough assignment for many. I had started working for the BBC by then. It was my first assignment for them. I was a producer for TV and Radio news coverage, and I also did a live news report – a little nervously, not being used to speaking the language on air – for the BBC's Russian Service.

The kindergarten where we edited and from where we sent our television material via satellite was only one location where international newsgathering shared space with scared and traumatized families seeking safety from the war. A local sports complex had been similarly changed into a media centre and refugee camp. For us outsiders, the trappings of everyday civilian life were reminders of how much the people among whom we were working had lost. One of the rooms the BBC was using had been a teacher's office. As the teacher had lost their workspace, so the pupils had lost part of their education. The absence of local children, and presence of others who had fled from elsewhere, spoke of a kind of war which belonged to the century which was approaching, rather than the one which was ending – although with the indiscriminate bombing of civilian areas had plenty of precedent during the bloody twentieth century. 'This is worse than Beirut,' said an American photographer one morning in Grozny as he peered out from the doorway where he and other journalists were sheltering. The Lebanese Civil War of the 1970s and 1980s was remembered then – including by the news media who had covered it – as an especially grim kind of urban warfare in which civilians were inevitably killed. Yet in this post-Cold War world it found plenty of echoes in the former Yugoslavia, especially in Sarajevo. The new century would bring the horrors of war on city streets in Gaza, and, of course, in Syria. At the end of the war in Chechnya, the centre of Grozny would not only remind correspondents who went there not only of Beirut, but also of pictures they had seen of Stalingrad.

Boris Yeltsin's time in office as the first president of Russia will be remembered for many things. It was a time when Moscow and the West seemed to be putting Cold War enmity behind them. It was a time of greater openness to the West. It was a time of new freedoms for Russians. It was a time of extreme economic hardship alongside those new freedoms. Mr Yeltsin himself will be remembered: both for his courage in facing down the coup, and for later, embarrassing episodes of public drunkenness. On a visit to Germany in 1994, he seized the conductor's baton and began to conduct an orchestra, an incident which the German news magazine, *Der Spiegel*, recalled in Yeltsin's obituary.[3] For the journalists who covered Russia then, the ham-fisted military campaign in Chechnya, and the colossal carnage which it caused, will inevitably cast a shadow over whatever else they remember from the era. Yet the incompetent leadership – political and military – which plagued Russia then created a special kind of media environment for the Western correspondents: extreme risk and extreme freedom. As Lawrence Sheets, who was then Reuters correspondent in the Caucasus, puts it, it was 'total chaos, so nobody cared what you were doing, and they did not have the ability or the inclination to sort of monitor everybody. It was a free-for-all'.[4] The veteran *Sunday Times* correspondent, Mark Franchetti, uses exactly the same phrase, 'it was very dangerous, but in terms of access, or rather in terms of lack of access or the authorities creating problems for foreign journalists working in Chechnya, it was actually a free-for-all.'[5]

Journalists reporting from Chechnya in late 1994 and early 1995 could largely go where they wanted and talk to whomever they chose. Provided correspondents were willing to accept that they would be working with 'chaos' and 'danger', they could do whatever their instincts suggested, and their nerves permitted. For those based in Khasavyurt, the day began with the drive to Grozny. The 'free-for-all' nature of covering this war meant that the trip involved crossing checkpoints manned by Russian Federal Troops; local Dagestani forces (theoretically loyal to Moscow, but in the extended family culture of the North Caucasus, quite likely to have sympathies with, and possibly distant relatives among, the separatist fighters); and finally into territory then controlled by rebel Chechen fighters who had taken up arms to stop Moscow re-establishing control over the territory. None of these groups placed any real restrictions on reporters. They occasionally checked media accreditation, but identity documents which said 'Press' in the Latin alphabet would usually suffice to show soldiers, who might not be able to read freely in that script, that they were dealing with foreigners. That meant people who would either probably be little trouble to them, or, just possibly, more trouble than they were worth. Journalists came very close to the fighting. On my first day in Grozny with the BBC team, a Saturday morning in mid-January 1995, we were lucky to escape serious injury when Russian war planes attacked Minutka Square in Grozny. We had stopped there to talk to groups of fighters, and decide whether we wished to go any further towards the Presidential Palace, the headquarters of the Chechen rebels. At least two of the fighters to whom we had been speaking were killed in the air strike. We left as soon as the planes seemed to have gone. We, and the other journalists in Minutka that day, were able to get so close to the story that it had become dangerous – Jeremy Bowen, the senior correspondent in that BBC team, later described Grozny then as 'by far the most violent place I had ever been'[6] – and yet, in doing so, we had been able to gather insights, an understanding of the conflict, which we could not possibly have got had we been subject to greater control. I remember the composure of the Chechen fighters that day as they carried away their dead and cared for their wounded. I remember the lack of emotion on their faces a couple of days later as we watched – from a safe distance up a hillside – a rocket barrage hitting the city centre. However much they were outgunned, none of this suggested that they would be defeated. The real losers in the military confrontation were the civilians of Grozny. The ethnic Russians seemed to suffer most of all. They had no extended family to turn to, in the relative safety of the nearby countryside. The lot of the conscript soldiers in the Russian army was miserable, too. That morning in Minutka two soldiers were presented to us as prisoners, probably captured during the disastrous attempt to take Grozny on New Year's Eve. I have often wondered if they ever got home. Other Russian servicemen, the majority of whom were poorly trained teenaged conscripts like the ones we met, were killed in their hundreds. In their book on the war, the correspondents Carlotta Gall and Thomas de Waal wrote that the figure circulating among the troops was 2,000 dead on New Year's Eve alone.[7] Gall and De Waal also cite the experience of the French photographer, Patrick Chauvel, who was in Grozny on 1 and 2 January, when Chechen fighters took him 'for a long and dangerous tour of the battlefield'.[8] Chauvel estimated he saw 800 Russian dead[9] in the space of a few hours. Journalists could talk to combatants on both sides. They could talk to prisoners. They could cross territory held by different parties to the conflict. These were not impressions enough to say for sure how the battle for Grozny would end, but they were enough to see that it would not be over 'in two hours'. The lack of restrictions placed on reporting was a consequence of Russia's weakness in Chechnya. If the army could not control the news media, how could they direct an effective military campaign? There was another factor, too. This was a time when Yeltsin's administration, for all its flaws, did believe in, and encourage, a free press. Russian reporting of the campaign, fearless as much of it was (especially the coverage by the then new TV channel, NTV), did the political powers few favours. The experience would change the Kremlin's views on dealing with journalists.

Free though they were in the lawless war zone, correspondents still had to contend with the constraints of twentieth-century communications and technology. There were satellite dishes to send broadcast quality audio and video anywhere in the world, but they were at a distance from the story and did not travel with the journalists. For broadcast, newsgathering was on analogue tape and had to be edited in real time. There were no mobile phones – at least not portable ones – in Chechnya. Making an international phone call involved setting up a satellite phone, switching it on and finding a signal. Scripts were scrawled in notebooks. News agency wires relaying political developments beyond the war zone were read down the satellite phone by editors, during the two or three calls a day that were usually practical. It was around this time that Kendall remembers first being 'aware of computers with American correspondents, who began to have laptops' when travelling. Calling in to London or New York would often be a long process. In a large news organization, those many people who had been waiting to talk to the correspondent most of the day would try to take their turn on the phone. Reporting from rural Russia then, especially from a war zone, meant only making a few phone calls a day. There was no other communication. In an attempt to get news from Grozny one day, we even sought out an amateur radio enthusiast in Khasavyurt. His pastime had earned him the description of 'radio hooligan' during the Soviet era, and that was still the term used to refer to him. I spent some time in his flat listening to him trying to raise the 'hooligans' he had previously contacted in Grozny. There was no answer, but he did explain that he had been able to listen to some of the Russian Army's logistics networks (the command ones were apparently encoded) and occasionally shout obscenities at exasperated quartermasters before vanishing again into his hooligan anonymity.

The conflict eventually subsided. It would be wrong to say, in the light of what followed, that it ended. By the spring of 1995 – I returned for another

Grozny, Chechnya, April 1995.

assignment in April that year – it was possible to walk around Grozny, by day, at least. It felt very unsafe to stay as dusk approached, and those Russian soldiers we met on the streets strongly advised correspondents to make themselves scarce before night fell. It meant working as quickly and efficiently as possible in the hours of daylight, then retiring to the relative safety of the town of Nazran in Ingushetia, where we had rented rooms. People in Grozny were ready enough to talk to correspondents. Many whom we found there appeared to show signs of post-traumatic stress disorder (PTSD). One woman picked through a pile of rubbish on the street, looking for food. As she did so, she repeated Leninist exhortations about the need to work to build Communism. Some soldiers, especially the younger conscripts, were happy enough to chat. Other, older servicemen resented our presence. One turned on us as we filmed and, having learnt that we were from the UK, snarled, 'Go and film in Ulster! Quick march!' We left, not wishing to see whether he would risk either striking, or even shooting, us with the rifle he angrily brandished.

With Grozny under some sort of control, the conflict broke out in other ways. In June of that year, a group of fighters, led by the rebel commander Shamil Basayev, took over a hospital in the Russian town of Budyonnovsk, north of Chechnya, taking thousands of hostages.[10] The deadly drama played out in the media. Among Basayev's demands was that he be allowed to give a news conference.[11] In the late summer of 1996, a ceasefire was agreed. The Russian military had learnt some harsh, humiliating, lessons. The Russian government had learnt, to its cost, the kind of coverage that could result when correspondents were free to cover a badly conducted military campaign that was causing mass civilian and conscript deaths. When the conflict flared again in the fall of 1999, things were different. There was a new Russian leader, the energetic Prime Minister, Vladimir Putin. By the following spring, he would be president. There were lessons for correspondents, too: the value of their access – Moscow-based diplomats sought meetings with journalists, who, unlike them, had been to the war zone, to try to broaden their own limited perspectives – and the limits of their influence.

Anatol Lieven was one of the very few international correspondents staying in Grozny itself during December 1994, as Russian bombardment intensified in the run-up to the main assault on New Year's Eve. In his report published on 24 December, *The Times* described its correspondent as 'the last British correspondent in Grozny'.[12] A few days later, Lieven wrote that, after a direct hit on Grozny's power station had taken out all communications, 'the six remaining members of the western press corps in Grozny decided it was time to go'. In the same piece, Lieven also made reference to the fact that one of their number, Cynthia Elbaum, had already left in a coffin, 'a volley of shots fired over her by Chechens as a mark of respect'.[13] Lieven was not away for long, returning to report from Chechnya after the New Year. On 13 January, he made reference to 'the growing level of condemnation' of Russia's military campaign. The piece was revealing as to the nature of this condemnation. The German Foreign Minister, Klaus Kinkel, 'said that the Kremlin deserved "massive criticism"' – but also 'reiterated that it was 'an "internal Russian issue"'.[14] Courageous correspondents had run great risks to tell the world the story of what was happening in Grozny. The world's governments had only a weak response. Neither Russia, nor Boris Yeltsin, ever suffered any sanction for the mass killing of civilians. Journalists reporting the conflict then learnt a lesson in the limits of power of the press. The Cold War was over, and our governments did not wish to provoke a new confrontation with Russia – not even when thousands of people were being killed. However much civilian death and suffering was reported, nothing changed. It remained, in the view of the world's foreign ministries, 'an "internal Russian issue"' – and journalism could not change that when political will was absent.

Yeltsin's time as Russian president is rightly remembered as a freer one for foreign correspondents than almost any other in Russian history. Russia was also often a very dangerous place to work. The death of the Soviet Union occurred without a Civil War of the kind that had followed its birth, but the USSR did not perish without blood being shed. In the fall of 1993, Boris Yeltsin's presidency brought tanks back to the streets of Moscow. They attacked the very building where he had stood on a tank to defy the hardline plotters against Gorbachev. This time, the armoured columns on the streets of the Russian capital did not melt away. They stayed until they had enforced Yeltsin's will with shot and shell. The Ostankino television centre, to the north of central Moscow, broadcast to the entire former Soviet Union. It was the site of some of the most intense conflict. A total of six journalists[15] were killed covering the story. The centre of a European capital became a war zone. Correspondents' working conditions covering the events in Moscow in October 1993 anticipated those in Chechnya during the first war when it broke out at the end of the following year: almost total freedom, but great danger. The main difference was the access. While permission was not needed to go to Chechnya, the fact that it was a long way from a functioning airport or train station (at least once the war had started) meant that it was hard to get to. The fighting in Moscow in October 1993 was harder to avoid than to witness. In addition to the TV centre, the main battleground was the White House: then home to the Russian parliament, and right in the centre of Moscow. The White House was so close to the city centre that many foreign correspondents' offices and apartments were not far from the firing line. From a journalist's perspective, the political events which led to the bloodshed encompassed many of the challenges of reporting Russia throughout the ages: a long, slow-burning story that is hard to tell in day-to-day news terms, and yet is hugely significant for a country's political development. Then suddenly it flares into a breaking story, armed conflict, personal danger, death. Helen Womack, the veteran Moscow correspondent for Reuters, *The Independent*, and other Western news media, wrote later, 'Russian politics became extremely tedious in 1993.'[16] It was not to stay that way.

The roots of Russia's biggest and bloodiest post-Soviet political crisis lay in the parliament which Boris Yeltsin had inherited as president. Elected before the breakup of the Soviet Union, it contained many deputies who were opposed to his reforms. They did what they could to frustrate his legislative programme. Long sessions of the parliament, known still by its Soviet-era name 'The Congress of People's Deputies' during late 1992 and the spring of 1993, saw Yeltsin forced to withdraw his preferred candidate for prime minister, the radical economic reformer, Yegor Gaidar. By the early fall, there was in effect a system of dual power in the country – to the extent that Boris Yeltsin's deputy, the Russian Vice-President, Alexander Rutskoi, sided with the parliament against his boss. In September, Yeltsin issued a decree suspending the activity of the assembly which continued to defy him. The building in which it was meeting was surrounded by a police cordon.

The worst political street-fighting in Russia since the revolutions of 1917 followed. For correspondents, it demonstrated how quickly confrontation can turn into armed conflict. On Saturday afternoon, 2 October, an anti-Yeltsin demonstration on Moscow's 'Garden Ring' (the inner ring road, encircling the city centre) began to turn violent. I was then a producer for Reuters TV, contracted to produce news for GMTV, a breakfast news programme in the UK. I had gone to watch part of the demonstration to get a sense of what kind of opposition to Yeltsin it might represent. The demonstration turned violent. Protesters started throwing rocks and other missiles at the militia, as the Russian police were then known. By nightfall, the demonstrators had blocked the Garden Ring with burning barricades. Twenty-four hours later, the police cordon around the White House had been broken, and armed groups loyal to Yeltsin's opponents moved on Ostankino with the aim of taking over the airwaves. They failed. The next day, tanks fired on the White House to destroy the last resistance. The rebellion was over. A total of 147[17] people had been killed, including the cameraman Rory Peck – a veteran of war reporting in the Gulf, Afghanistan and the former Yugoslavia. He was shot dead in crossfire outside Ostankino. The uprising crushed, Yeltsin moved to strengthen his grip on power. The measures included controls on the press. Those newspapers which had supported the rebels were banned.[18] A curfew was imposed, although foreign correspondents were permitted to be out. The Reuters bureau was then in the Slavyanskaya Hotel, near the Kiev Railway Station. It was close enough to the fighting to hear the tanks drawn up on the bridge outside the Ukraine Hotel firing on the White House. The flat where I lived then, at the top of Kutuzovsky Prospekt, looked down on the bridge where the tanks were positioned. Returning home to rest briefly between the long shifts we worked then (I spend the night of 3–4 October in the bureau, unsure I would be able to return if I left), I watched a curious kind of new urban warfare unfolding. Civilians came out in the autumn sunshine to watch the fighting. In the evenings that week, I walked home warily. I had the right to be out, and the pass to prove it – but the streets were tense because they were empty. An encounter with a small group of soldiers, on patrol to impose the curfew, ended amicably – but after I had had to stand at gunpoint, with my

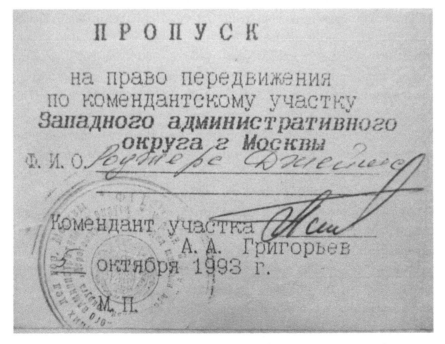

Curfew pass issued to the author by the Moscow Military Authorities, October 1993.

hands in the air, while I told them in which pocket they could find my wallet, and my curfew pass. The soldiers, young lads in their late teens, were nervous themselves, and I was grateful to be on my way home.

Yeltsin had consolidated power by force. The new democratic Russia demanded that he also did so at the ballot box. Three years later, in the summer of 1996, Russia held its first post-Soviet presidential election (when he was first elected president in the summer of 1991, the USSR still existed). A Yeltsin victory was uncertain, perhaps even unlikely. In parliamentary elections (the parliament had by now reverted to its pre-Soviet name, the Duma) in December 1995, Yeltsin's political opponents, the Communists and the extreme nationalist Liberal Democratic Party of Russia, had taken almost half the seats[19] in the 450-member assembly. The implication was clear: 'Communists begin drive for Russian Presidency'[20] as *The Daily Telegraph* headlined their story three days after the poll. The euphoria which had accompanied Yeltsin's election victory in the summer of 1991 had long since evaporated. Russia was a different country, and one in which many voters – worn down by the hardship and uncertainty of living through the transition from Marxism–Leninism to an extreme form of capitalism – missed the certainties of what had gone before. Opinion polls in the run-up to the presidential election (held over two rounds on 16 June and 3 July) put Yeltsin a distant second to his main rival, the Communist leader, Gennady Zyuganov. Helped by the considerable resources of those few who had got richer, rather than poorer, in the last few years – Russia's so-called 'oligarchs' – and by advisors from the United States, a massive media campaign was launched to turn the tide in Yeltsin's favour.[21] As Sarah Oates and Laura Roselle concluded in their study of Russian television coverage of the campaign, 'the main state and primary private channels were covering the elections in a very similar way, both promoting incumbent Russian president Boris Yeltsin over his challengers.'[22]

It worked. Yeltsin was re-elected, but Russian journalism, it might be argued, has never fully recovered from the time when so many news outlets, afraid of the return of Communism, decided actively to support him in the election.[23] The Western media also sensed that there was a lot at stake. With Yeltsin through the first round of the election, he still needed to beat Zyuganov in the run-off, 'No euphoria over Russia,'[24] cautioned *The Financial Times* in its editorial two days after the vote. *The New York Times* permitted itself to be a little more optimistic, commissioning a piece from the historian of the Russian revolution, Richard Pipes, after the first round. Pipes argued that Yeltsin had a 'slender but incontestable edge' as campaigning for the second and decisive round got underway. Pipes also referred to Yeltsin's 'control of television.'[25]

Reporting from Moscow, Alessandra Stanley noted that Yeltsin had 'wrestled loose' of election legislation banning campaigning on the eve of voting.[26] This latter physical activity may have been metaphorical, but there was plenty of real physical activity, too – Kendall recalls in particular television pictures of Yeltsin 'dancing in Siberia'. Womack herself had a TV experience: one which, as she wrote later, did little for her image.[27] Assigned to cover one of Zyuganov's main news conferences, she was taken ill with salmonella and had to leave the room to be taken to a medical centre for treatment.

Looking back, Womack is critical of the way that the Western press covered the campaign. 'There was a real chance that the communist Zyuganov would be elected,' she notes, but adds, 'in retrospect I think the western press should have encouraged a free election, and taken the risk that the communist was re-elected.'[28] Weir remembers, 'an incredibly dirty election. There were scandals even in pro-Yeltsin Russian media about shoeboxes full of money and so on.' There were also reports in the Western media. *Time* magazine's cover story on the 15 July promised 'The Secret Story of How American Advisors Helped Yeltsin win'. 'There were unbelievable torrents of black propaganda. Of course, the West made no secret of it because it was a case of a communist seeking to come back,' says Weir. 'It later came out about the American team of advisers holed up in the President Hotel in Moscow and so on. And yes, Americans sort of celebrated. I gather they made a movie about that in the early 2000s.'[29] All of that was after the fact, though. By the time it was widely reported, the election was over and won by Yeltsin – but the extent and nature of the support offered by the West may well raise an eyebrow in our own era, when Russia is so frequently suspected of seeking to influence the outcome of voting in the West.

I had not been based in Moscow since I was there for Reuters TV in 1993, but I had been on frequent short assignments: to Chechnya twice in early 1995; to cover the Duma elections in the December of that year; to cover the presidential elections in the summer of 1996. I returned in April 1998 to take up a post as a Senior Broadcast Journalist (producer/reporter) for the BBC. When I came back to Moscow that spring, part of me worried that there would not be enough to do. Compared with the earlier chaotic years of the Yeltsin presidency, Russia seemed calmer. There were mobile phones on which you could make direct international calls (only a few years earlier, you could not even call internationally from a fixed line unless it had been specially opened to make such calls). There were cash machines which worked, and which you could trust – although old habits from earlier in the decade died hard. Most of us Westerners still kept large sums of cash at home in case we ever needed to leave quickly. I always had at least US$ 1,500 in emergency funds in my apartment, although I never actually needed to use it. Many correspondents then still lived in UpDK blocks, but had not been obliged to do so since the end of the Soviet era. When based in Moscow from 1992 to 1993, I had rented a flat privately (the one at the top of Kutuzovsky Prospect, from the windows of which I saw the White House being shelled). There would be no more firefights on the streets of Moscow during that posting, but the appearance of order and progress was deceptive. For in the same way that pictures of Yeltsin's lively dancing during the 1996 election campaign had covered up the fact that he had serious heart problems (he had surgery later the same year), the Russian economy was in an extremely poor state – and, like the president of the country, would suffer a crisis.

In some postings, correspondents may use the term 'feast or famine' to describe editors' and audiences' interest in the story they are covering. Times which are quiet in terms of hard news are a challenge: there is still a story to be told, often a very important one, but nothing spectacular in terms of events which will really fire audiences' imagination. Russia in the spring of 1998 felt like just such a posting. I soon realized that my initial impressions – based on a return to Moscow – which, like capital cities the world over, is usually wealthier and better functioning than the rest of the country – were misleading. Trips outside the capital, especially by road, soon told another story. The economy had ceased to function to the extent that cash-strapped businesses were paying their employees in products, rather than roubles. Having worked to earn whatever they had made – pottery or glassware, for example – they might then have to go out onto the roadside to try to sell it. Those who did not have the option of doing that might even end up selling themselves – this happened even on the main roads approaching the outskirts of Moscow. In other words, you did not have far to go to see that Russia's brave new market economy was not delivering on its promise to make people richer and freer.

Yet it was still a difficult story to tell well. It was, after all, only seven years since the end of Soviet power. Even if the more radical reformers had foreseen rapid transformation, expectations had to be realistic. That Russia was failing to fulfil its potential, however, was beyond doubt. In July 1998, I worked with Allan Little and cameraman Andrew Kilrain to produce a report for the BBC's *Newsnight* programme.[30] Our brief was to make a report about the Russian economy. If you have read the book this far, you will realize that it is not my intention just to write about stories I have covered, but I will discuss this one in some detail because of what I learnt about journalism, TV news production and reporting Russia – and I would like to share those lessons.

We went to Rostov-on-Don, in southern Russia. In Soviet times, the city had benefitted from a large factory, Rostselmash,* making agricultural machinery. It had once made 80,000 combine harvesters a year, supplying the machines to the whole of the USSR, and other socialist countries. That year, it was expected to make 1,500. The workforce had been massively reduced. Those that remained were paid, in part, in jars of gherkins. The gherkins had come as part payment from a customer in Bulgaria that did not have sufficient cash to pay for their order. The factory let us film inside. There was little activity. A spokesman gave us an interview. We were able to speak to the workers. It took us more than one visit, but we were able to film people getting paid in gherkins. Aside from having to persuade the factory to give us permission, that was perhaps the hardest part of the whole assignment for one simple reason: the people involved were, understandably, and through no fault of their own, ashamed. It was an emotion we encountered frequently during the filming – so, even though no one's life was in danger from what we were doing, even though our contributors spoke to us willingly, there were still dilemmas of journalistic ethics. We had to be fair to those we filmed. We had to tell their stories without inviting our audiences simply to gawp at the absurd version of poverty in which our contributors found themselves. One worker, Nikolai Altansky, told us that the only cash income his household had was his mother-in-law's state pension. They survived on what he could grow on the small plot of land he owned outside the city. 'We're not expecting it to get better,' he told us. 'It will be even worse.'

He was right. In August that year, a month after our report was aired, Russia defaulted on its foreign debt. The rouble plummeted in value. Imported goods became scarce in the shops. Many people had lost their savings in the uncontrolled inflation that followed the freeing of prices at the end of the Soviet era. Many of those same people lost again. Others, their savings in dollars, survived. Writing in *The Times* the following weekend, Michael Binyon contrasted the fate of villagers outside Moscow with that of the newly wealthy who had built luxurious second homes nearby – the latter, having more to lose, seemed more nervous.[31] Reporting on Russia then often involved telling stories of loss. In December 1998, the governor of Chukotka, the arctic territory at Russia's far north-eastern tip, arranged a visit for Moscow correspondents. The idea seemed to be that international media coverage would attract investment. The region had gold mines. Instead, it was a look at the consequences of the failure of the Soviet system – made all the more dramatic by the fact that, at that

---

* The name is a combination of 'Rostov' and the Russian words for 'agriculture' and 'machine'.

time of year, temperatures approached minus 50 Celsius. Michael R. Gordon, *The New York Times* correspondent, saw 'the follies of planning at the Kremlin, 3,600 miles to the west'.[32] In *The Guardian*, James Meek wrote of severe food shortages.[33] Supply chains planned when they did not need to be part of an enterprise which made a profit were no longer fit for purpose. Workers who had come north in Soviet times, lured by promises of high wages and early retirement, had either fled, or were stuck. No one was there by choice. On the trip for the BBC, I remember being struck by how often I encountered the 'g' in Russian pronounced as 'h': a characteristic of accents from the south, or from Ukraine. It was a long way home.

Trips such as these showed correspondents what the reality of reform and economic resurrection meant in a country the size of Russia. It showed the scale of the task – giving them insights which policymakers in the West did not have; insights most likely equally unknown in the Kremlin so very far to the West. Chukotka was an extreme example, at the geographical extremity of Russia – and yet it told the story of the country as a whole, even if other regions' hardship was less dramatic and on a lesser scale.

Explaining the sense of humiliation which came with this was a vital task for correspondents, for it has since had major consequence not just for Russian domestic politics, but also for Russian foreign policy. During Russia's war with Georgia in 2008, coverage of which will be discussed in the next chapter, broadcast correspondents were frequently asked whether it was the worse point in the West's relations with Russia since the end of the Cold War. While the war in Georgia was undoubtedly a major crisis in relations, and also very significant for the role which the media played, it did not feel as difficult a time to be a correspondent in Moscow as the spring of 1999, when NATO unleashed a bombing campaign against Serbia over the conflict in Kosovo. As *The Economist* wrote in an editorial in April, 'ordinary Russians are deeply unhappy at seeing fellow Slavs being bombed.'[34] The editorial was headlined 'A New Cold War?' – perhaps one of the first times that idea emerged in the news media after the end of the real thing – and it certainly was a time when it could feel uncomfortable in Moscow to be a citizen of one of the countries involved in the attacks on Serbia. British residents were warned by their Embassy to keep a low profile. For us journalists, this was easier said than done, given that our cars then still had yellow licence plates (normal Russian ones have a white background) which identified us not only as foreign correspondents, but also indicated the country from which we came. Protests turned violent. Shots were even fired at the US embassy[35] on the Garden Ring Road. In *The New York Times*, Michael Wines wrote of Americans being 'denounced or harassed on the street'. Wines also wrote of the prevailing Russian view that, by the NATO action, the United States had 'rubbed Moscow's nose in its new second-tier status'.[36] If policymakers understood this at the time, presumably they felt it was a stage that would pass. To correspondents living in, and reporting from, Moscow then, though, it felt that something had changed. Yet before the 'new Cold War' narrative grew into the media phenomenon which it has since become, there was another war looming in Russia. In the late summer of 1999, there were a series of bombings of apartment blocks, including in Moscow. More than a hundred civilians were killed, many while they were asleep in their beds. The authorities blamed Chechen fighters,** who had recently re-emerged, under the command of Shamil Basayev, in the North Caucasus to mount an armed challenge to Moscow's rule in the region.[37] Soon a second war in Chechnya was underway.

The correspondents who went to cover it found very different working conditions from those they had known in the first war. 'During the second war, it was really difficult,' remembers Sheets. 'Because the Russians had gotten smart, to be honest with you, and you needed like eighteen documents and officially you had to go on official trips.' In theory, press accreditation from the Russian Foreign Ministry allowed the bearer to work anywhere in the Russian Federation, but an exception was made that fall for Chechnya, which was declared a zone of 'Counter Terrorist Operations', and was therefore off limits to foreign correspondents. Franchetti blames the fact that the Russian authorities, after the first war, had 'realized that, actually, this is a lot of bad press coming out of Chechnya they started – in the second war, certainly – becoming much more organized'. Franchetti also realized that stories – even hugely controversial ones – which had been possible before the second war, no longer were. In 1998, he went to Grozny to interview Basayev.[38] 'In the second war, let's say by the middle of the second war, you knew for a fact that if you interviewed – before he was killed – someone like Basayev or Khattab,*** or any of the leaders of Chechen terrorism, you would lose your accreditation.' Interviewing the masterminds of attacks on civilians (whether or not Chechens were responsible for the apartment bombings, their responsibility for Budyonnovsk is not in

---

** The armed Chechen groups always denied any involvement. Reports later emerged in the Russian media, and then in a book, *Blowing up Russia*, the co-author of which was the former FSB agent Alexander Litvinenko, that the FSB was actually responsible. The allegation was that the security forces had carried out the attacks to create a pretext for a new military campaign in Chechnya.
*** Another of the leaders of the armed Chechen groups, killed in 2002 by a poisoned letter sent to him by the FSB. http://news.bbc.co.uk/2/hi/europe/1952053.stm. Accessed 14 February 2020.

doubt) would not be permitted in many countries, and could well lead to action being taken against journalists. Russia is no exception in that sense – but it had not always been so strict. Attitudes to the foreign media were changing.

Franchetti's interview with Basayev also referred to another factor which severely limited reporting of the second Chechen war: kidnapping 'by gangs demanding ransoms of up to $1m'. At the time Franchetti made his trip to Grozny, two British hostages, Camilla Carr and Jon James, were being held in Chechnya. They were released in September 1998.[39] Later that year, four telecommunications engineers, three British and one New Zealander, who had been working in Chechnya, were beheaded.[40] Correspondents planning to cover the second Chechen war had to live with the threat that the same might happen to them. Getting to Grozny – legally, at least – was impossible. Many international journalists based themselves in Nazran. In the first weeks of the war, the fear of kidnap was so great that many stayed in the same hotel – sometimes sleeping five or six to a room – reasoning that there was safety in numbers. Those media organizations with sufficient budgets paid for local members of the security services to act as bodyguards. Eventually such measures were relaxed – but the great challenge in a war zone like that is that journalists can rarely be sure exactly who they are dealing with. One person whom the BBC had trusted to help fix

The author with the Russian Army in Chechnya, March 2000. Photo © Andrew Wilson.

travel arrangements decided one evening to tell my colleague Jonathan Charles and me that his family had held Russian soldiers hostage.

Even if it felt safer than the first war, it was extremely difficult to tell the story. Refugees crossing the border from Chechnya into Ingushetia were the main source of news. Their accounts of the dangers and abuses they had endured were consistent, and so could be used with due caution – but they were only part of the story. The real story lay not where they were going, but where they had come from – and few managed to get it. There were exceptions. The Marie Colvin, of *The Sunday Times* (later deliberately killed by government forces in the war in Syria), managed to get in to give an eyewitness account of the horrors which those we spoke to at the border had experienced as they fled.[41] She later escaped – in the dead of winter – over the mountains into Georgia.[42]

By the spring of 2000, with Moscow's grip on the territory stronger, the Russian Foreign Ministry organized trips for foreign correspondents. These were frustrating in that they were very time consuming. A week's trip might only produce two reports. There was no freedom to pursue your own stories. The minders were nervous. As I wrote on the BBC website at the time, we were told, 'when we say it's time to leave, it's time to leave'.[43] Matthew Chance, who went on similar trips for CNN – he has reported from Moscow for the network since the 1990s – was also struck by the way the trips were arranged, with little official regard for the fate of civilians in the ruined city. 'Twenty thousand people were said to be trapped in cellars, we never found out what happened to them, I assume that's one of the big mysteries of the Chechen conflicts and the recapture of Grozny.' Despite that, he remembers, Russian officials 'were proud. "Look what we've achieved," they said, "come in, CNN, see what we've done, we've recaptured Grozny."' There were also what seemed to be attempts to compromise correspondents. On one trip, we were taken to a winery that was supposedly getting back to normal after the war. We were offered a glass of wine. I declined, saying I did not drink alcohol during the working day. A photographer, who was with the minders, lowered his camera, apparently disappointed. I have always suspected that the plan was to show us drinking, and discredit our coverage. Being part of a media game – one which the Russian authorities were now starting to play, albeit rather clumsily – is just one of the drawbacks to agreeing to travel with an army. Yet, overall, there were advantages. Staying at the Russian camp at Khankala outside Grozny (we slept in a train carriage drawn up on a siding) offered a look at what conditions were like for the soldiers. We ate with the officers one night, and the food and facilities were poor. The conscripts must have been even worse off. I also overheard a junior officer's conversation about

Russian soldiers in Grozny, March 2000.

the army's illicit business dealings. Impressions like these were invaluable to get a fuller picture of the situation there. Reading the work of Anna Politkovskaya later made me realize I had not seen the half of it – the corrupt commerce one reason why the army was taking so long to prevail. Politkovskaya's murder in 2006 was a reminder to Western correspondents of the price that some Russian journalists had to pay for their tenacity, and greater insight. With patience, determination – and a realistic budget – there were ways round the restrictions. Sheets went on the official trips, then went back on his own. 'What I wrote were some really negative reports about what the Russians were doing in Chechnya,' he says now. 'But I also wrote that things are not as abnormal as you would think. Life carries on.' He concludes, 'My end impression was that they kind of appreciated that I am not fucking lying to them. If they wanted to find me, they could have. They didn't.'

In spring of that year we stayed in a run-down hotel where Russian officers, back from the front, spent the weekend with their wives and girlfriends. Mozdok was a garrison town established in 1763, as imperial Russia strove to expand its control southwards. On Sunday 26 March, we were flown by Russian military helicopter into Grozny, where we filmed voting in Russia's presidential election. Vladimir Putin won outright in the first round. He had been acting president since Boris Yeltsin resignation on the last day of 1999. His political career over, Yeltsin was only rarely seen thereafter. His era provided Western correspondents with some great stories, considerable challenges and matters to reflect on years later. 'I think in terms of the press, we underestimated in 1993 how very upset Russians were when Yeltsin shelled the parliament,' Womack says how. 'We basically gave Yeltsin a bit of a blank cheque. In retrospect, his shelling of the parliament was appalling and extremely undemocratic and we should have perhaps said so more at the time.' Yet the correspondents in this era – a time when access to Russian officials was often limited – gained insights with others, including policymakers, did not. By speaking to the people whose wages were not being paid, but who got jars of pickles instead, or nothing at all, they asked questions which would be fundamental to understanding Russia's future direction. As Womack puts it, 'For me, what really mattered were ordinary Russians, and this question, this constant question: are they living better? If not, why not?'

'A Russian without work is a bird without wings,' one of the underemployed workers at Rostselmash had told us, before turning walking away from camera into the cavernous gloom of the idle factory. 'What are the political consequences of shock and humiliation, of anger like this?' Allan Little asked in the script that followed. The answer was President Vladimir Putin. There were big changes to come in Russian politics, foreign policy and dealings with the news media, including foreign correspondents.

Becoming strong again?

The officer approached. He demanded the cassette from the camera. We had crossed the invisible line between what we were allowed to film and what we were not. A phone call to the Kremlin Press Service sorted things out. We explained that we were just trying to show how well Russia had prepared to host the biggest international summit of the year: the G8, in St Petersburg. The city had been founded three centuries earlier. It had started, and ended, the twentieth century with its original name: in between, it had also briefly been Petrograd, and then, for longer, Leningrad. The changes were prompted by war or revolution: the moments in history which kept correspondents coming to Russia. In the nineteenth century, the poet Alexander Pushkin had imagined the city's founder, Tsar Peter the Great, standing on the shore and picturing the magnificent capital which would be built there, a capital which the flags of the world would one day visit. In the summer of 2006, Vladimir Putin – himself born in Leningrad – had made the earlier Russian leader's poetic vision come true. Like Peter, he had relied in part on Western know-how to make it a reality. In Putin's case, Western public relations companies had been hired to burnish Russia's image, to tell the world that the chaos and bandit capitalism of the previous decade were over. The Putin era would be one in which the state fought hard to take control of the image of Russia which was presented to the world. Foreign correspondents found themselves drawn into that fight.

'The sense that we had then was that Russia really wanted to use this to portray itself as a partner of the west, and, you know, responsible member of the club and your reliable energy supplier,' remembers Neil Buckley, then Moscow Bureau Chief of *The Financial Times*.[1] On the day, 1 January, that Russia had taken over the rotating presidency of the G8 group of industrialized nations, the country had been headline news not for its return to prestige on the international stage, but for a dispute with its neighbour, Ukraine. The issue was payment for natural gas. The Soviet Union had ceased to exist some fourteen years before, and, although political ties between Moscow and its former satellites had loosened and broken since then, the infrastructure, and even elements of the socialist economy, remained. That meant that Russia's neighbours in many cases looked to their former overlord for gas – gas supplied below world prices. The contracts expired on New Year's Eve 2005. No new deal had been reached as the clock ticked round to midnight. Ukraine was not willing to agree to pay the new prices. So the next day, 1 January 2006, Russian TV suspended normal programming (which would usually be festive fare, New Year being in Russia the biggest holiday in the calendar) 'to show live pictures of technicians turning down the flow of natural gas to Ukraine', as Buckley reported it.[2] This was the G8 presidency which was supposed to have 'energy security' as its key theme – and yet, at its outset, Russia was turning off the gas taps as the coldest time of year drew close. 'It totally undercut the idea of them being your trusty, reliable, suppliers to the west,' Buckley says now. 'And I am not sure their image ever really recovered from that.'

Russia's relations with Ukraine would deteriorate even more drastically in the decade to come. This may be seen as the point from which the decline began. For although the dispute was supposedly about prices, and this is the way that Russia sought to portray it, politics lurked barely below the surface. In late 2004, Ukraine's 'Orange Revolution' had ended a period of post-Soviet stagnation, bringing to power a new government that had turned westward: towards, it hoped, eventual membership of the European Union, and perhaps even NATO. This was seen as a slap in the face of Moscow, especially as Vladimir Putin had made two widely publicized trips to Ukraine to support the candidate, Viktor Yanukovych,[3] who went on to lose the election. As Buckley wrote at the time, the move to charge world prices for gas was seen by some as 'a demonstration that life outside Russia's embrace can be harsh'.[4] While Moscow might have hoped this would send the required message to Ukraine, it did not play well with the wider world. It was not only a question of Ukraine's own energy supplies. The country's location meant that it was also a transit for supplies heading further west, to other parts of Europe. In consequence, Buckley says, for Russia, 'It was a massive PR failure, and a massive PR miscalculation. Because I really think they misguidedly believed that the Ukrainians would be seen as the bad guys here, and not them.'

Russia's international image had already suffered lasting damage from the collapse of its superpower status. The chaos of the 1990s, and the hardships faced by ordinary people, might have helped to elicit some sympathy from outside. It did not bring the respect that President Putin had sought to restore since the election victory that confirmed him in office in the spring of 2000. The early years of his presidency presented many challenges to that restoration of respect. In the late summer of 2000, disaster struck the Russian navy. During exercises in the Barents Sea, a nuclear-powered submarine, the *Kursk*, sank. All the 118 crew on board died. As if the loss of life were not bad enough, the Russian military establishment contrived to cover up for its own failings: firstly, in the fact that the accident occurred at all, and secondly in the fact that no one survived. Inept responses – including in dealing with the news media – guaranteed negative coverage. Initially, the authorities attempted to deflect public anger by suggesting that a NATO submarine, possibly British, had collided with the *Kursk*, causing it to sink.[5] It is perhaps hard to imagine now in a media world more used to summer pictures of Mr Putin engaged in various challenging outdoor pursuits,[6] but on this occasion he was anything but a man of action. 'Putin faces families' fury' was *The Guardian* headline when the president eventually arrived in northern Russia to meet some of the relatives of the dead submariners, after, in the words of correspondent Ian Traynor, 'maintaining an ill-judged low profile for the past 10 days'.[7] Perhaps not only to try to begin to compensate for the damage to the Russian navy's reputation, but also to try to establish himself as an international figure, Putin appeared the following month on CNN's *Larry King Live*, talking for about an hour through a translator. The fate of the *Kursk* was, inevitably, among the questions. Putin had learned from his mistakes. He appeared to regret the timing of his return from holiday, 'From the point of view of PR, that could look better.'[8] Something else which could have looked better was his answer to the question about what had happened to the *Kursk*. Putin replied simply, 'It sank'. Reflecting years later on the encounter, King – who by then had presented programmes for the Kremlin-backed TV channel RT – was generous enough to suggest that this had been 'a brilliant way to answer a difficult question'.[9] The Chechen conflict also returned: simmering in the territory itself and exploding beyond its borders. In October 2002, armed Chechens took over a Moscow theatre during a performance of a musical, Nord-Ost. With some of the attackers wearing suicide belts, and others having set explosives which could bring down the ceiling of the auditorium, they held the audience of at least 800[10] people hostage for three days before the venue was stormed by Russian special forces. Covering the story at the time, Franchetti noted that Putin 'to a great extent [owed] his election victory 2 ½ years ago to his tough stance in Chechnya'.[11] Now the Russian leader found himself faced with suicide bombers in the capital threatening to kill hundreds of hostages unless he called a halt to the campaign. Astonishingly, Franchetti was actually able to enter the theatre – twice – while the siege was ongoing. 'If you imagine an equivalent situation in London, where you've got 800 hostages held by ISIS, in the centre of London,' he asks, 'Would the British security services let in a foreign correspondent to go and interview the terrorists? Would they let him in the building?' Franchetti says now that the security services were 'delighted' to let him go. His report from the day after the siege ended included the leader of the attackers, Movsar Barayev, describing how his men had shot Olga Romanova, a woman who lived nearby, as they took control of the theatre 'because she did not listen to his men's orders'. When the security forces stormed the building, they did so in a way that tainted what might otherwise have been an unadulterated good news story. Before launching their assault, the Russian security forces pumped a strong narcotic gas into the theatre's ventilation system. Most of the 130 hostages who died perished from the effects of the gas.[12]

There was worse still to come – in the shape of an incident which would mark forever some of those correspondents who covered it. In September 2004, Chechen fighters took over a school in the town of Beslan, in the southern Russian region of North Ossetia. More than one thousand people – most of them schoolchildren – were taken hostage. At least 330 hostages, the majority of them children, were killed during the operation which ended the siege. The European Court of Human Rights later ruled there had been serious failings on the part of the Russian authorities. The security forces' use of 'powerful weapons', the court found, had 'contributed to the casualties among the hostages'.[13] Russia was largely dismissive of the findings.[14] For the journalists who covered it, including Zoya Trunova, a producer for the BBC, it was not so easily dismissed. 'I remember from the moment we landed the sound of women screaming,' she later told the BBC World Service's 'The Fifth Floor' programme. 'You wake up to that sound, and you go to bed to the sound of women wailing, and screaming.' More than eight years afterwards, she could not forget the impression covering the story had made. 'It was really disturbing. I have never seen anything like that, and I have been doing this job for many years, and I have covered lots of conflict before.'[15]

If Russia was to show the world that it had moved on from the disorder and poverty of the decade which followed the collapse of communism, the country, and its new leader, needed a better image. The BBC was offered a chance to be part of what may now be seen as the start of at least two important trends in the Kremlin's contemporary use of the media: firstly, to promote Mr Putin on the world stage, and secondly to show him ready and able to answer any questions that might be put to him. 'It was Putin's Kremlin who got in touch with us and said they wanted to do this big interview,' Kendall remembers, 'couched as an interview taking questions from the world'. The interview went ahead on 2001, with another, similar, one in 2006, before the G8. For the first 'webcast', in 2001, twenty-four thousand questions were submitted by email.[16] 'They did need at the beginning of Putin to tell the world about him, and to raise his stature locally. So the idea, I think, was to make him look like a globally connected Internet president.' The top news line which emerged from the interview also anticipated a third trend: the future direction of Russia's relations with the west under Putin's presidency. In this case, it was a warning that United States plans for a new missile defence system 'would jeopardise the entire international system of arms control'.[17] Putin used Western media – in this case, the BBC – to get his message across. Kendall sees a trend in Russia's offering access to its leaders at certain times of their careers. 'I think that, certainly in my time there, there's been a theme from Gorbachev onwards, that if you engage in the big Western interview, it can somehow increase your prestige at home if it goes well.' This Kremlin attempt to engage with the international media seemed to go fine for both parties. It showed that the new president was open to talking to foreign correspondents – the reasons perhaps including, as Kendall suggests, that a successful profile in the international media could play well at home. Not everything was going so well. As the Putin presidency progressed, he became more and more popular at home (he was re-elected president in the spring of 2004, with over 70 per cent of the vote[18]) – but disasters such as the Kursk, Nord-Ost and Beslan continued to dominate international reporting from Russia. In addition, there were growing concerns over freedom of expression in Russia, and fears over the longer-term implications of energy rows with Ukraine. At the same time, the Russian economy was looking more and more healthy, boosted by rising global prices for oil – and the Kremlin wanted to keep encouraging the investors who were seeking a slice of Russia's new wealth. The decision was taken to spend some of the cash on polishing the country's image.

Two and a half months before the G8 summit in St Petersburg, Buckley's front page story in *The Financial Times* reported that 'a multi-million dollar contract'[19] had been awarded to Ketchum, and 'a sister company, GPlus Europe'. Among the GPlus team was Angus Roxburgh: once expelled by the Soviet authorities, he was now back in Russia: in the Kremlin, to be precise, telling them how to deal with foreign correspondents. For one of my earlier books, I interviewed Roxburgh about his experience, 'We taught them what we could, but they came into it with strange ideas about how the western press worked,' he told me in 2010. 'I think they felt that everybody else did it, that all other governments had

PR people working for them as well – but didn't completely understand it.'[20] Nor, it seems, did they ask too many questions when seeking a suitable company to spin for them. Roxburgh later noted that the contact had been awarded without a tender[21]: one of those occasions that serve as a reminder that the same verb in Russian – стойть – may be translated as either 'to cost' or 'to be worth'. In that sense, the Russian language does not make a distinction between the concepts of value and price – and, on this occasion, the Kremlin and its new partners were not apparently inclined to haggle. Roxburgh put Ketchum's fee at 'almost $1m a month'.[22] The hiring of Ketchum and GPlus was a hugely significant decision in the history of Russia's dealing with the international news media. The Kremlin had decided to employ Western news management techniques, delivered by Western spin doctors, to promote its own view of the world. Used to a Russian presidential administration and government who were not usually especially open to talking to Western correspondents (the days of Nikita Khrushchev turning up at cocktail parties for impromptu news conferences were long gone), the Moscow press corps found the new approach helpful. 'Initially it was quite positive for all of the western media,' Buckley remembers, as the Western PR executives 'persuaded officials to come out and meet the western press'. I had returned to Moscow as BBC correspondent just weeks before the Ketchum deal was announced. The access was certainly something new. While there had been weekly – and hugely newsworthy, given the time when they were taking place – Foreign Ministry press briefings in the late Soviet period, they rarely produced much of note in the 1990s. Now senior figures were talking to the Western press on an unprecedentedly regular basis. If the Western PR advice was to offer a new openness to the Western news media, it also came with attempts at other elements of Western public relations with which the USSR might have been more comfortable: headlines planned, as far as possible, before the event, and duly delivered. As Roxburgh said, 'all other governments had PR people'. The novelty was seeing Russia deploy them. The novelty, too, was in seeing some of the officials who were persuaded to speak: among them, Vladislav Surkov. Surkov is a Kremlin advisor, who, as Peter Pomerantsev put it in a 2014 article, 'has directed Russian society like one great reality show'.[23] Surkov generally gave his directions from off stage, though. This was a rare sighting of him emerging from behind the red brick walls of the Kremlin. Within the walls, though, not all was well. The Kremlin may have paid the price demanded by Ketchum, but they did not necessarily seem to value the advice it bought. Roxburgh's account of his time working for them, in his 2013 book *The Strongman: Vladimir Putin and the Struggle for Russia*, is a story of being misunderstood, ignored and mistrusted:

the spin doctors were, for example, given the text of speeches at the same time as the media.[24] The experience as a whole, Roxburgh concluded, did little to change his journalist's view that PR 'was all charlatanism'.[25] From the correspondent's point of view, it was an improvement on what had gone before. Yet still there remained a fundamental misunderstanding not only of what western PR might be expected to achieve, but also of the way that the Western media worked. Reflecting on years of working in Moscow, Franchetti concludes, 'They always look at us thinking that someone is either feeding us stuff, and if it's not the intelligence services then we're being used by someone like Berezovsky.'*

This was an era in which such views came to dominate policy towards the Western media. In effect, the Kremlin believed that Western journalism was for sale (a view admittedly shared by many Western critics of 'Mainstream media'). They seemed also to believe that the millions of dollars they paid to Western PR firms would include the purchase of favourable opinions. Roxburgh concluded that what the Kremlin really wanted was for the PR's to try 'to manipulate journalists into painting a more positive picture of Russia'.[26] That was a hard enough task in 2006. It would become a lot harder as the Putin era went on. Western spin doctoring was not the only significant addition to the Kremlin's approach to dealing with the international media. The year 2005 saw the launch of *Russia Today*, an international English language TV news channel. Like many new media ventures, it had an inauspicious start. It was clunky and unimpressive to watch. For those of us correspondents based there then, it was interesting professionally – but more as a phenomenon, than as a source of information. Like the hiring of Western public relations executives, though, it was a significant development. Russia, tiring of what it saw as unfavourable international media coverage, was once again borrowing Western techniques – in this case, international, English language, television channels – to transmit its preferred message. *Russia Today* – which would later become simply *RT* – was borrowing the platform (international satellite news channel); the language (English); and, in many cases, the format (news in the first half hour; features and documentaries thereafter) pioneered by CNN and BBC World News. The mission to provide 'international audiences with a Russian viewpoint on major global events'[27] was underway.

I had returned in the spring of 2006 to a different Russia, with different working conditions for correspondents. Much of the wealth which had come to

---

* Boris Berezovsky, a Russian businessman who supported Vladimir Putin's rise to power, but later fell out of favour, and fled to the UK, where he became a vocal critic of Putin. In 2013, Berezovsky was found hanged in a mansion he owned outside London.

Russia from rising oil prices washed through the capital, leaving streets and shops transformed. Soviet planners had never foreseen anything like as many private cars as now clogged the city's streets. I liked to travel by Moscow metro anyway. Seeing the capital at rush hour gave ideas for stories. I now went to stories by metro too, at least when meeting contacts or reporting for radio with small, portable, equipment. Going anywhere by car for a TV story meant allowing lots of extra time for traffic jams. We Westerners no longer felt particularly well off, as had been the case in the late Soviet period and the 1990s. By 'we', I mean foreign correspondents. One of the ways in which Moscow had changed then was the massive influx of foreigners: oil executives, bankers, lawyers and accountants were flocking to Russia for a slice of the oil cash. Rents went through the roof. I had never been gladder for the right to take an apartment in a building owned by UpDK – an organization which had often been something of an obstacle for foreign correspondents, but which now represented a chance to get a flat at a reasonable rent. In the new century, correspondents did not live as well as Duranty apparently had in the 1930s, but nor did they have to ask their readers to imagine a city without running water (although the old Soviet habit of turning off hot water supplies for two or three weeks in the summer, to clean the pipes, endured). Diplomatic relations between Russia and the west were essentially good. Buckley, who had arrived the year before, remembers the way that Putin was generally seen at the time, as a kind of 'corrective after the Yeltsin years, that he kind of restored some control that was necessary, and some discipline, after the kind of chaos of the 1990s, and particularly the late Yeltsin era.'

This was the story which Russia wanted told at the G8 summit approached. St Petersburg had been specially spruced up to welcome the flags of the world. Peter the Great's dream was being fulfilled, in part, thanks to the techniques pioneered by a favourite of another Russian autocrat. The Potemkin village was being relaunched for the twenty-first century. It was not lost on the press. On a visit in early April, my BBC colleagues and I saw pavements being repaired along the road from the airport. In July, *The Daily Telegraph*'s Adrian Blomfield wrote of St Petersburg's homeless being told to make themselves scarce, and of the air force being ready to make rain clouds scarce[28] (a Soviet-era technique used to make sure that big parades were never washed out). There was one big story which was a significant propaganda boost – domestically at least – just the week before the summit opened. Russian federal forces in Chechnya killed Shamil Basayev. As I reported at the time,[29] Putin saw Basayev's death 'as deserved retribution against the bandits' responsible for attacks including Beslan. For all the time and trouble that had gone in to preparing the summit, the formal agenda – in this case, energy security – was to an extent overshadowed by war breaking out in Lebanon. For all the backslapping bonhomie among leaders, tensions did start to emerge. Even before the summit formally opened, Presidents Bush and Putin found plenty to disagree upon: in the view of *The New York Times*, a joint news conference 'highlighted growing tensions between former cold war rivals now jockeying for global position'.[30] 'Global position' is the key phrase. Much of the briefing to correspondents before the summit had suggested that Russia's membership of the World Trade Organization would be confirmed in St Petersburg. It was not. Russia would not join the WTO until 2012. Attempts to woo international public opinion through the news media could only go so far – especially when Russia continued to be at the centre of bad, if not shocking, news stories. On 23 November 2006, Alexander Litvinenko, a former FSB officer, died in London. The findings of an investigation into his death suggested that the cause of death was radiation poisoning. He had ingested polonium-210. The British official inquiry into Litvinenko's death, published in early 2016, agreed.[31] Two Russians, Andrei Lugovoi and Dmitry Kovtun, had met Litvinenko in London three weeks before he died. In 2007, the British Crown Prosecution Service concluded there was sufficient evidence to charge Lugovoi with Litvinenko's murder.[32] The British authorities sought Lugovoi's extradition from Moscow. Russia refused. Nothing since has suggested that situation will change – especially since Russia's refusal was based on the country's constitution, which does not allow for its citizens to be extradited.

Litvinenko's murder was an extraordinarily difficult story to report. The Moscow correspondents, British in particular, were under extreme pressure to send as much material as they could: there was insatiable editorial interest – and very few facts.* The story combined violent death by poisoning, the Russian security services and Kremlin intrigues. Into the latter category fell the fact that, when he first arrived in the UK, Litvinenko had been on the payroll of Boris Berezovsky. One of my years away from Moscow had been spent as editor of the BBC's website in Russian. One evening we had tried to contact Berezovsky for comment on a story. The producer who called said that Litvinenko had answered the phone. Litvinenko's extraordinarily public and painful murder – the poison was thought to have been given to him while he was taking tea with Lugovoi at a London hotel – meant that he was in the news more in death than ever he had been in life. Still we struggled to find anything new and substantial

---

* Any reader interested in learning more about the case itself should see Martin Sixsmith's book *The Litvinenko File.*

to say: although we did all we could. We staked out the hospital where Lugovoi was undergoing testing – something which seems now nothing more than a tactic to keep him away from the press. More than a decade later, Lugovoi does not seem to have suffered any health consequences from his part in the story. We happened across a team of British detectives – in town to investigate the case – on an evening out in a Moscow beer hall, 'friendly enough, but giving nothing away', I wrote in my diary. Days after Litvinenko's death, Yegor Gaidar was taken seriously ill with apparent poisoning. I got a phone call at home from a BBC editor who tried to put great pressure on me to write a story linking that incident with the death of Litvinenko. Gaidar has since died, but no such link was ever seriously suggested, let alone proven. A contact who had formerly been in the KGB suggested that Litvinenko had been killed as part of a business deal gone wrong. I did report that some weeks later, the interest in this story never waned – but as part of a story about differing views of who had been responsible for Litvinenko's death.[33] Many in Moscow then believed that Boris Berezovsky might have important information. Being one of the few 'oligarchs' who had made a fortune in the 1990s, he was never popular – and became even less so with both politicians and ordinary people after his leaving for London. He angered the Kremlin in particular by saying the following year he was planning a revolution to remove Vladimir Putin from power. The comments, made in an interview with *The Guardian*,[34] had consequences for the paper's then Moscow correspondent, Luke Harding, who told his fellow correspondents at the time, and later wrote, that he had been harassed by the security services following its publication.[35] Such incidents were not the norm, but the murder of Litvinenko damaged still further the image of a country which was trying to improve the way it looked overseas. As Womack says, 'Britain could not just ignore that. We couldn't just pretend it didn't happen. With the passage of time, there's been no apology, no acknowledgment.' Franchetti does see in some Western reporting, 'a relic of the Cold War, the knee-jerk reaction against Russia' but adds, 'let's not forget that if you're going to go and kill someone with polonium in the centre of London etc. etc. well, of course you have a problem'. Inaccessibility to sensitive sources on sensitive stories aside, this was one of the easier periods to be a correspondent in Moscow. Permission was no longer needed to travel (there were exceptions in parts of the North Caucasus); Moscow was a pleasant, if expensive, place to live; communications were generally good (internet and mobile telephony being as good as in any major world capital); Westerners were reasonably welcome, and often warmly received. 'Ordinary people were much, much, freer to talk,' remembers Buckley. For his newspaper in particular, there was plenty of corporate coverage in a Russia that wanted to show itself to be open for business. 'There was a western-style infrastructure of press people, public relations companies and so on. It's remarkable how that changed.'

Other things were changing, too. Re-elected president in 2004 by a huge majority, Putin was required by the Russian constitution to step down from the presidency in 2008, at the end of his second four-year term. Throughout 2007, speculation over his successor was a running story: with the prime minister, Dmitry Medvedev, and first deputy prime minister, Sergei Ivanov. Putin eventually nominated Medvedev. Medvedev duly won. On 2 March, he was elected president with 70 per cent of the vote,[36] meaning that there would be no need for a second round of voting. It had long been clear that Putin's chosen successor would win the election. The challenge facing correspondents was to determine the extent to which Medvedev would be president: this was the biggest question not only for reporters, but also for Western policy makers. One Western diplomat in Moscow pointed out to correspondents that Medvedev had survived and thrived on the 'snake pit' of Kremlin politics, and so must have some steel. The result of the election being beyond doubt, the story became speculation over the extent of Medvedev's eventual independence in office. *The Times* got into the game early in 2008, with the election still two months away, with a headline 'Stooge? No, This Is the Man to Push Putin Aside'.[37] The paper's then Moscow correspondent, Tony Halpin, offered a prediction then which has aged rather better. He wrote two weeks before voting that Putin, at his annual press conference, 'would retain control in Russia long after he stood down'.[38] An earlier despatch also hinted at one of the methods which might be deployed to retain that control. On 8 February, *The Times* reported that the Organization for Security and Cooperation in Europe (OSCE) had, complaining of 'unprecedented restrictions' on its election observers, 'cancelled' plans to send a mission to Russia to monitor voting.[39] On the evening of 2 March, the outgoing president and his successor sauntered down from the Kremlin to a stage next to St Basil's cathedral, where they were welcomed, in a well-choreographed media event, by crowds of cheering admirers. Medvedev had tried to dress tough – black leather jacket and jeans – but slightly spoiled the effect with shoes that seemed better suited to the lawyer's office for which he had originally trained.[40]

Security in Europe, and the toughness of leaders, dominated coverage for the rest of 2008 – a seminal year in Russia's use of the news media in international relations, and a year when Moscow correspondents found themselves once again writing about war. In May, for the first time in the post-Soviet era, tanks and missile launchers joined the Victory Day parade. The message sent by this inclusion of military hardware was much discussed at the time. What followed in August that year has since lent credence to the interpretation that it was a show of strength. Western correspondents were very much expected to cover the show. We had to present ourselves at 6.30 am in one of the streets, specially closed-off for the day, near Red Square. As always with an event where there was heavy security, there was a lot of waiting around. Thankfully, the authorities had also revived the Soviet-era technique of 'seeding the clouds' to prevent any rain from falling on Moscow that day. The day was a mixture of symbols. During the Soviet period, and into the era after Communism, the Defence Minister had traditionally been a serving officer. That day, Anatoly Serdyukov – a civilian – inspected the troops. Medvedev, formally inaugurated as president only days earlier, received the salute as head of state. The hammer and sickle of Soviet Russia could be seen on some of the military banners in the parade. There were also soldiers in replica uniforms from the tsarist era. The representation of contrasting and opposing political systems offered a unified message: Russia as a strong state, confident and respected – perhaps feared – by the world. *The New York Times* correspondent, C.J. Chivers, offered a nuanced assessment of what passed in front of the ranks of reporters: including the detail, observed by an eye experienced in military matters (Chivers is a former officer in the US Marine Corps), that some of the officers 'were visibly overweight'.[41]

The battle-readiness of Russia's military was subject to a sterner test in August. The military conflict was swiftly won. Success in the media battle, even with the Western spin doctors and the cheerleading of *Russia Today*, was less convincing. Nevertheless, the war which Russia waged in Georgia in the summer of 2008 may now be seen as a hugely significant staging post in the Russian authorities' approach to dealing with the international news media. The military campaign in Georgia may have been waged beyond Russia's borders – that, indeed is part of its significance – but it was planned and presented not only from the Kremlin, but also from the boulevards of Brussels. The greatest challenge of covering the war, as so often with armed conflict, was access: both to the area where the fighting was taking place, and to reliable information. Even now, more than a decade after the conflict, Russia and Georgia still blame each other for starting it. The official European Union-sponsored report[42] of the 'Independent International Fact-Finding Mission on the Conflict in Georgia' might have been expected to reach some kind of conclusion on where the blame lay. As the BBC's report on publication a year after the conflict noted, however, Russia was satisfied that the 'unequivocal answer' was that Georgia was to blame. Georgia, on the other hand, argued that the report's findings proved that Russia had been 'preparing for war all along'.[43] Before discussing the coverage of the conflict, therefore, it seems useful to offer the briefest of summaries of what happened. On the night of 7–8 August 2008, the Georgian army began an operation to take back control of the region of South Ossetia. South Ossetia, and another separatist area, Abkhazia, had been outside the control of the Georgian government since armed conflicts in the early 1990s. Russia intervened militarily to stop the Georgian advance, driving Georgian forces back beyond the administrative borders of South Ossetia, and advancing further into the rest of Georgia. After five days of fighting, a truce was declared. Eventually, Russia recognized the two regions as independent states. They remain outside the control of the Tbilisi government.

While Russia made progress militarily – the outcome of a conflict with its much smaller neighbour never seriously in doubt (although there were some problems with communications, and materiel[44]) – it fared less well with international public opinion. The main battleground on which the media battle was fought was international, English language, TV channels: principally the BBC and CNN, and also Al-Jazeera International. Russia's spin doctors were deployed. They strove to shape the coverage of the conflict and to tell a story in which the Kremlin was a peacekeeper, the protector of a small region against military aggression. Georgia had its spin doctors, too: Aspect, another Brussels-based company, that did its best to get Georgia's version of events accepted. These two companies, their offices only streets apart from each other in a very pleasant part of Brussels (I later visited them for a documentary my BBC colleague David Edmonds and I made about the PR war[45]), tried to persuade correspondents that they knew best what was happening in the heat of a bloody Caucasus summer almost 4,000 kilometres away.* In Moscow, GPlus first offered correspondents a conference call with the Russian Foreign Minister, Sergei Lavrov. Shortly afterwards, the offer was upgraded to one-on-one interviews. These were given to a small number of international news organizations, including the BBC.[46] It is a measure of *Russia Today*'s lack of influence then that they were not on the list. They were reduced to asking for the BBC's interview. This was agreed in return for an on-screen credit. Now, *RT* might be granted an exclusive.

There was a sense that Russia felt it was losing the PR battle. This kind of high-level access at a time of war was an attempt to alter the balance. As Chance

---

* Readers interested in a fuller account of the PR companies' work might wish to see Chapter 4 of my book *Reporting Conflict* (Palgrave Macmillan, 2012).

remembers, 'There was a moment, amid the Georgia war in 2008, where Russia was hiring an international PR company. They started putting out its message on international media, we had access to all sorts of people.' Correspondents covering the conflict, whether in the war zone itself – in Moscow and Tbilisi – were bombarded with conflicting sources of information. That in itself was nothing new in covering Russia in wartime. What was new was the extent of the sources of information. As Rick Fawn and Robert Nalbandov suggested in their study of the way the war was reported, 'The intensive communications and information networks now available risk becoming not sources of objective information but weapons in the war, obscuring causes and influencing consequences.'[47] Such were the dangers of the information war. There were dangers for correspondents covering the fighting, too. Sky News' Andrew Wilson had started his journey to Tbilisi feeling that he and his camera operator had spent too much time in the north of the country, 'trapped on the wrong side of the Russian advance, so our challenge was to get through the Russian lines.'[48] They managed, but only by putting themselves in almost fatal danger on the outskirts of the Georgian city of Gori. 'Gori was now empty because it had been shelled by the Russians,' Wilson remembers. 'We drove past a long line of Russian tanks parked up by the side of the road. They ignored us entirely, so we drove past those, and then there was the sound of small arms fire.' The situation was about to get a lot worse. Their car was soon cut up by one which sped past them, then stopped, blocking their way. They were robbed at gunpoint by three assailants whom Wilson describes as 'classic militia: headbands, Kalashnikovs, belts of ammunition around their shoulders, t-shirts, camouflage trousers'. Eventually, as Wilson was able to show his British passport and explain that he was a journalist, the attackers satisfied themselves with stealing the car and all the equipment it contained. The Kremlin was spending millions on Western public relations advice. The desire to improve Russia's image by helping the foreign press did not extend to the conflict zone. The Russian tank crews, Wilson remembers, 'could see these events taking place in front of them – where we were being threatened by these guys – and did absolutely nothing about it. They just watched it take place'.

To report the war in South Ossetia was to experience some of the best and worst of reporting from Russia. I was not in the region during the conflict itself – I was reporting from Moscow – but I had been there almost two years before, when the territory held a referendum on independence. I was also there some weeks after the war, in early October, when the Russian military took a group of correspondents there. They wanted to show that they were honouring their commitments under the ceasefire by relinquishing territory they had held since August. The first trip, in November 2006, was hugely instructive – but difficult to sell to editors. Yet going there, and spending a few days in South Ossetia with the separatist authorities, and a few more in Georgia, including time with the army, provided me with invaluable context when I had later to report on a conflict fought over a territory of which most of the world had never heard. It was one of those rare occasions when correspondents get to see both sides in a conflict; an opportunity which hardly exists for others doing different jobs. Hotel space being short, and taken by Russian election observers to the referendum, we stayed with a retired militia (Soviet police) colonel and his wife. Sharing their house for even a few days made us understand how little they wanted to be politically part of Georgia again. A day on an army base in Senaki, more time spent at a training camp outside Tbilisi,[49] and interviews with various officials in the capital made us realize how little the Georgian military and political establishment understood the views of people such as the colonel and his wife. When war broke out in 2008, I wondered over the fate of the idealistic young Georgian army officers who had given us lunch in the fall of 2006. The trip two years later, to see the partial Russian withdrawal, also offered insights into the state of the recently victorious Russian army. As we prepared to set off for our trip to South Ossetia (not permitted to spend the night there, we followed the route taken by the invading forces some weeks earlier, returning the same evening), the officer who was overseeing our arrangements asked if any of the journalists had a company mobile phone he could borrow. He wanted to make a call without using up his own credit. Inside South Ossetia, we were transferred from our bus to an armoured truck – ostensibly for safety. In reality, the intention seemed to be to stop us seeing properly the large-scale destruction of civilian property that we were able to glimpse from our obscured viewpoint.

Russia's position in the world had changed. Moscow had demonstrated that it would set red lines, irrespective of the way that was received by the west. The then Georgian administration of President Mikheil Saakashvili was strongly pro-Washington – some of the troops we had seen training were being prepared for deployment to Iraq – and had ambitions of joining NATO. From a Russian point of view, this was a threat. 'The logical conclusion is to destroy the military capacity of Georgia,'[50] said Dmitry Peskov, spokesman for Vladimir Putin, who was then prime minister. He may no longer have been head of state, but Putin was very much the leader. He flew back from the opening ceremony of the Beijing Olympics to take charge. Peskov too was in the ascendant: his decision to follow Putin to the Prime Minister's office paid off in the longer term, as Putin returned to the presidency in 2012, and Peskov continues to enjoy a high profile as presidential spokesman. He may have GPlus to thank for that, at least in part. 'They were also quite responsible I think for the rise of Peskov,' Buckley suggests. 'They promoted Peskov as the spokesman for the international press, and because he proved pretty effective in that role, he eventually kind of supplanted [Alexei] Gromov as the main spokesman.' Peskov's relaxed manner and fluent English had made him the natural choice for dealing with international correspondents, although Buckley recalls a rather frosty introduction. 'I remember going to my first meeting with Peskov to introduce myself and giving him my spiel about how I was a great Russophile and had studied Russia, was fascinated by Russia, wanted to tell the story fairly,' Buckley says of his arrival in 2005. 'Peskov looked at me and said: "Yes, but I think the problem is the West does not want to see Russia become strong again."'

Now Russia was becoming strong again – at least, if that meant reinforcing foreign policy with military action, and stamping out dissent at home. They set about the latter ignoring at least some of the expensive lessons in news management for which they had paid. The demonstrations organized by 'Another Russia' were a case in point. The leaders included the former world chess champion Garry Kasparov. The protests were sparsely attended rallies called to oppose Putin's policies. A Kremlin official once asked me why we covered them. I explained it was because they deployed so many police officers – in April 2007, Reuters reported the figure as 9,000[51] – to stop them. That was what made it a story. Roxburgh seems have had similar conversations.[52] Two thousand demonstrators in a city of ten million and more was not a story; their being blocked and beaten by four times as many riot police was. The Russia over which President Yeltsin had presided was in the past. In 2008, *The eXile*, an expatriate newspaper, closed. Admired by its supporters for its coverage of Russia, and for its mockery of established Western news organizations, it was also dismissed by its critics as juvenile and misogynistic. Its closure was a sign that the crazy days of the 1990s were over. In the first decade of Vladimir Putin's time at the top of Russian politics, Russia moved to improve its international image. It adopted a strategy which it would continue to pursue as social media's importance for newsgathering, distribution, and consumption increased dramatically in the decade to come. That strategy was to take Western media formats and technologies – public relations, satellite television, and, eventually, social media platforms – and use them to contradict or undermine Western reporting. Working conditions for correspondents became tougher as the political relationship between Russia and the west deteriorated, but it is important to put this in context: the restrictions were mild compared to what many of the Moscow press corps' predecessors had endured in the previous century. It became harder to know where the limits lay, though. One of my last assignments before completing my second and final BBC posting in 2009 was to Archangel, in northern Russia, to report on climate change. One of the locations where we wanted to film was a business growing roses under glass. We had not realized, but the greenhouses – although they were out in isolated countryside – were within the administrative boundaries of Severodvinsk. There is a naval dockyard in Severodvinsk. The town is therefore closed to foreigners without special permission. Shortly after we left the greenhouses, our car was stopped by the police. We spent the afternoon in a police station. The procedure was overseen by a slight young man in civilian clothes. He introduced himself as being from the interior ministry, but he was probably FSB. After signing a statement admitting that we had unintentionally ignored the restrictions, and being handprinted (fingerprints judged insufficient), we were released.[53] For the remaining two days of our trip, we were followed by unmarked cars. The local driver working with us became nervous, and quit. The first afternoon, when I realized that we were being detained, I called a contact in the Kremlin Press Service. There was nothing he would, or could, do.

10

Russia: My History

The story of Western correspondents in Russia is the story of Russia's attitude to the West. Since the revolution of 1917, Russia has at different times been open to Western ideas and contacts; cautious and distant; all but closed off. During the early years of Khrushchev's leadership, or during Gorbachev's *perestroika*, Russia's leaders have wanted to improve ties with the West. Access for correspondents improved. It was not just a question of the Kremlin wanting to make correspondents' lives easy. In both those periods of reform and lowering of tensions with the West, the Russian political elite also carefully calculated the benefits to be gained from greater openness. Exposure on major international news outlets has been useful to boost a Russian leader's standing in the eyes of the world, and, in consequence, in Russia, too. Moscow correspondents have been welcomed, offered assistance; obstructed, jailed, expelled. Cases of imprisonment and expulsion are rare. Being shut off from information has been more common, and, from the point of view of the Soviet authorities in the early years of the Cold War, effective. They did not want Western correspondents in the USSR, so made it expensive and unproductive: the Soviet understanding of capitalism apparently broad enough to realize that news organizations serving a market economy needed stories to sell. Without stories, there was not much point in having a bureau.

Dmitry Medvedev served only one term as president. He stepped down in 2012. Vladimir Putin returned to the Kremlin. In the meantime, the Russian constitution had been changed. Putin's election victory in 2012 won him a presidential term of six years, instead of four. He was re-elected in 2018, and is now due to be in office until 2024. By then, he will have been Russia's president or prime minister for a quarter of a century. During the 2008 presidential election campaign, a Russian politician close to the Kremlin suggested to me that, even though Putin was leaving the presidency, the 'Putin era [was] only just beginning'. They have been proved right. The Putin era has differed vastly from the Yeltsin era in relations with the West. This story of British and American reporting of Russia has taken the coverage of major events as its staging points. Since President Putin's return to power in 2012, there have been at least four major, ongoing, news stories which have altered dramatically Russia–West relations: the 2014 annexation of Crimea; the shooting down later that year of Malaysian airlines flight MH17 over Ukraine; Russia's military campaign in Syria, launched in 2015 in support of President Bashar al-Assad; in March 2018, the poisoning in the English town of Salisbury of the former Russian military intelligence officer, Sergei Skripal, and his daughter, Yulia.

Russia has always denied any involvement in the Salisbury poisoning, but the British authorities named two Russians – who had entered the country on passports giving their names as Ruslan Boshirov and Alexander Petrov[1] – as suspects. The Bellingcat website later said that these were aliases, and identified the two as agents in Russian Military Intelligence, the GRU[2]. The Russian authorities did not accept the evidence which convinced British prosecutors. Others did. Russian diplomats were expelled from more than twenty countries.[3] To these incidents may be added suggestions that Russia, using social media, tried to influence the outcomes of both the 2016 presidential election in the United States and the referendum in June 2016 when the United Kingdom voted to leave the European Union. Although it is a phrase that has frequently been used since the end of the Cold War – not least in news reports – it does now feel that relations between Russia and the West are at their worst since the ideological confrontations of the last century. In short, it is exactly the kind of era in which Russia and the West might choose to expel journalists as well as diplomats. Contemporary Russia has taken a different approach. 'On the side of the actual reporting, now you can go pretty much where you want to. You can get into a plane and just leave and report the breaking story,' says Kate de Pury, the Associated Press' news director for Russia and the CIS[4]. Although there are still areas that are off limits without special permission – military sites, areas of 'anti-terrorist' operations in the North Caucasus – the bureaucracy of travel permits designed to control correspondents' movements has largely gone. Some commentators on Russia are keen to talk of a new Cold War, but, from the correspondents' point of view, the experience is different. In the sense that their experience is indicative of Russia's attitude to the West, this is a new kind of conflict, not a new Cold War. During the Cold War, the Soviet Union did its best to stop its people reading and listening to Western news media. In our age, they attack it instead. Western public relations techniques (practised by Westerners for hire) are one method – the creation of a Russian answer to the BBC and CNN, in the shape of RT, another. The ongoing political and security debate over the extent of Russian use or misuse of Western social media platforms is yet another. This is an era in which Russia has adapted Western media to its own ends. As Weir puts it, 'the Russian government has been proactive in developing vehicles like RT and Sputnik to get its message across'. This is openly declared official policy. 'The Foreign Policy concept of the Russian Federation', published in 2016, and available in five languages on the Russian Foreign Ministry website, lists to 'bolster the standing of Russian mass media and communication tools in the global information space and convey Russia's perspective on international process to a wider international community' among its 'main objectives'.[5] In his 2016 essay, *Should We Fear Russia?* Dmitri Trenin, the Director of the Carnegie Moscow Center, persuasively argued, 'Rather than hushing up criticism of Russia and its leaders, which the Soviet Union practiced all the time, the Russian state-run media attack this criticism immediately, head-on, and seek to demolish the western story'.[6] RT, with its slogan, 'Question More', and the Sputnik news agency are on the frontline of that attack. Buckley sees Russian reporting of Ukraine in 2014 as 'a real turning point. That was really my first experience of fake news'. He cites notorious examples such as the story of a child being crucified by the rebels[7] and refugees, 'streaming across into Russia because they were so afraid of this neo-Nazi regime that had come to power. It was complete rubbish. The borders were quiet'. Chance argues that the Russian authorities view Western journalists as combatants in this media war. 'We're seen more as hostile actors in their world,' he says. 'It translates into the way we're spoken to, into the access we've got, which is negligible, and just the general climate of distrust of the foreign media that is cultivated by the authorities and by pro-Russian outlets.'

It is not just a question of keeping correspondents at arm's length. Older methods have not been abandoned. In 2015, after three decades working in Russia, Womack was told that her accreditation would not be renewed. It was, she says, 'kind of a hybrid expulsion'. For decades, the same kinds of letters and documents had been sufficient for Womack to prove her journalistic credentials. Suddenly, they were no longer adequate. In particular, the Russian authorities required an assurance that one of the newspapers for which Womack was writing would meet all her expenses. No media organization would advance such a guarantee on behalf of a freelance. To the list of incidents which have contributed to the deterioration of relations between Moscow and the West should be added the Magnitsky affair: the death in custody of a Moscow tax lawyer who said that he had uncovered a $230m fraud committed by tax

officials and police officers. After Magnitsky's death, the United States passed
legislation targeting Russians it held responsible, the so-called Magnitsky act.[8]
Womack 'wrote quite a lot about Sergei Magnitsky. Particularly, I befriended
and wrote about Sergei Magnitsky's mother'. Womack also suspects a reason
related to shooting down of MH17. 'If you remember, Putin went to a summit in
Australia and [then Australian Prime Minister] Tony Abbott said he was going
to shirtfront* Putin over the death of the passengers. Putin was quite humiliated
at that summit and left early.' Other correspondents have been harassed. In at
least one incident, the media itself was the chosen tool. In February 2016, the
BBC's Steve Rosenberg and his colleagues, on assignment in Siberia, found
themselves the focus of the curious conduct of a Russian TV reporter. The
reporter followed Rosenberg and his team, accusing them of showing Russia
in a bad light, filming them and airing the results on the local TV channel. In
a report for the BBC's website, Rosenberg suggested that this bizarre attempt at
intimidation had been prompted by a BBC *Panorama* documentary, broadcast
shortly before, about alleged corruption in the Kremlin. Rosenberg and his
team were not involved in the making of the programme. The local TV station
falsely claimed that they were – presumably the reason why they were targeted.[9]
Franchetti also recalls a time when he 'suddenly had a problem with my visa, I
was called in for a chat, both with the FSB and then with the Foreign Ministry'.
This had been occasioned by something he wrote. His visa was eventually
granted (and he still lives in Moscow today). In fact, he confesses to a degree of
surprise that some things he has written have not caused him trouble. 'I have
many examples of stories over the years that you would think would maybe
create problems and then it didn't.' One long-serving Western correspondent
in Moscow relates a story of a more subtle, and more sinister, experience: 'We
haven't actually had court cases in Russia, but I have had those threats made to
me. I once had somebody send to me on WhatsApp statutes from the Russian
Criminal Code when we'd written something that they didn't like.' Another had
an experience which illustrated the fear of the security services experienced
by even members of the Presidential administration. Seeking to contact the
correspondent outside office hours, to complain about a story, Kremlin staff
were unable to call because they did not have the correspondent's mobile
phone number. The correspondent explained that they had willingly shared
their phone number on more than one occasion. It seems the officials had not

---

* A move in Australian Rules Football where one player barges another in the chest.

dared save the number in their own phones. Having Western correspondents' personal contact details might make them suspicious in the eyes of the Russian security services.

The story which had caused such offence in the first case – the one which prompted the menacing WhatsApp message – concerned the Soviet Union's role in the Second World War. Specifically, it concerned a reference to the Molotov-Ribbentrop pact which described that as an 'alliance'. 'We got into a discussion of whether it could be called a pact and what that meant,' the correspondent remembers. The Russian officials who had objected to the story 'insisted that it had been behind closed doors, so it wasn't in any sense a public alliance. Any kind of suggestion that their World War II record is not spotless is badly received here'. The correspondent adds, 'Their sensitivity is somewhat understandable given the fact Russia and the Soviet Union lost around 27 million military and civilian lives. It's still the Great Patriotic War here in modern Russia.'

This is a key lesson for understanding modern Russia. A correspondent seeking tell the story of a people or nation must first understand the stories that nation tells about itself. This is the case particularly when that national story, whether in interpretation or fact, differs from the one more usually told outside the country. Russia has been keen to take control of the way its story is told, even in people's leisure time. The country now boasts a series of exhibitions called 'Russia: My History'. I visited the one in Moscow while writing this book. It is a multimedia show. There are no physical objects. All was light, sound and digital images, still and moving. The aim is to impress upon the visitor the virtue of Russia following its own path, and not permitting itself to be threatened or deceived by outsiders. Today, Russia's most revered story is of a people proud of the Soviet Union's victory over Nazi Germany. As Tom Parfitt of *The Times* noted in his report on the Victory Day parade in Moscow in May 2019, Putin 'warned that there were attempts to rewrite history and diminish the Soviet people's heroic feat in 1945 in "saving Europe and the world from slavery, from destruction, from the horrors of the Holocaust"'.[10] For someone who grew up mostly in the United Kingdom, as I did, it jars slightly to see 1941–45 on war memorials across the former USSR. To me, whose grandparents' and their generation lived through the conflict, the war began in 1939. And yet, as Clinton noted when speaking in 1995, and I know having grown up in Western Europe in the later stages of the Cold War, the Western allies then rarely gave the USSR the credit it deserved in the defeat of Nazi Germany. Wartime correspondence between Churchill and Stalin shows the tensions which existed between the two countries even when they were allies.[11] Today, Russia and the West only grudgingly acknowledge each other's stories,

A Soviet-era crest of Lenin, Volgograd, 2019.

if at all. Correspondents need to understand that, and to be familiar with the differing narratives, too.

A visit to Volgograd in the spring of 2019, while I was researching and writing this book, was a reminder of how Russia sees its own story and the West's role in it. If Western Europe has tended to see, and its journalism often to portray, Russia as a large, threatening land to the East, then for Russia threats have come from the West, in the shape of Hitler's armies in the 1940s, and Napoleon's forces in the nineteenth century. In addition to this military aspect of Russia's story of itself, there is another strand of more recent history which still casts a long shadow: 1991, and the end of the Soviet Union. As the former British Ambassador to Moscow, Tony Brenton, wrote some years later, some Russians blame the West for 'inadequate financial support and insanely neoliberal economic advice which produced economic chaos and collapse'.[12] As Franchetti puts it, 'It depends which generation you're talking about. But if you talk to the generation that was forty when the Soviet Union collapsed, that was their country they lost.' The news media, he feels – echoing Womack's point about how upset many Russians were after the shelling of the parliament in 1993 – have not always appreciated this. Franchetti gives examples of stories of the Mir space station, 'how it's collapsing, it's going to fall on our heads'. Referring also to 'terrible stories' from Chechnya, and 'all these symbols they were so proud of suddenly being dragged in the mud', he says, 'It's a country that went through a terrible humiliation and, yes, we were not sensitive enough to these guys. If we want to work with them, we have to be a little bit more sensitive to what their grievances are.'

Many of the correspondents interviewed for this book feel that this has been a point which has been lost on Western diplomats and policymakers dealing with Russia since the end of the Cold War. Wilson, arriving in the 1990s in the aftermath of what many in the West had seen as a Western victory in the Cold War, summarizes Western thinking then as 'once the other contender in the standoff has surrendered, given up, lost in whatever conflict you're involved in, the natural reaction will be to default to a Western mentality'. He says the attitude spread to journalists, initially, at least. 'We thought that's what we would find: people warming up to become Westerners. We couldn't have been more wrong.' Still, he argues, 'my learning curve in that respect was a lot faster than that of the prevailing wisdom back in the UK, or the States or anywhere in Europe.' Dejevsky refers to earlier trends, in the late Soviet period, when 'mass demonstrations in Moscow' took place on Saturday afternoons. The significance of these rallies was that the crowds 'were listening to unofficial politicians. The actual atmosphere of these things was unprecedented. I think that was appreciated more by the journalists than it was by diplomats.' She recognizes, however, that journalists 'were much freer to talk to Russians, including politically active Russians from unofficial groups, from Parliament, from all sorts of levels.' Especially in the later Soviet period, when Boris Yeltsin was emerging as a challenger to the overarching, Soviet, political system, Dejevsky concedes, 'that made life very difficult for diplomats, who deal with the established authorities'. Franchetti, reflecting on more than two decades of observing British and American policy towards Russia, says that, 'at the beginning, it was triumphalism and basically the only real priority was to make sure that Russia doesn't implode and there isn't some terrible nuclear weapon that goes off, or that some terrible weapon ends up in the hands of terrorists'. What followed was an approach which said, '"we're going to ignore Russia, because it's no longer a player." And that's fine, but it was a very short-sighted approach.' de Pury is even more forthright, seeing Western policy in general as 'unprepared, venal and, apart from the Germans, showing very little real understanding of Russia and Russian culture. I would say the Germans and the French have done best, in my view, in terms of understanding Russia'. The current state of diplomatic relations, she admits, means that 'Western diplomats are not on the inside at all'. Dejevsky, on the basis of a career of reporting and commenting on international affairs, says of journalists and diplomats, 'what we're actually looking for are very similar things', but with one major difference. 'We're looking for the bad news and the conflict and the dissonance, and they're looking for the points in common, the concord and the continuity. Our wish list is almost completely opposite.'

Opposites, too, are Western correspondents' views of themselves and the way they are seen by their Russian hosts. Suspicions of espionage have been constant. There is no sign that will change. The Russian authorities' view that Western correspondents have their views dictated to them endure, too. Buckley notes that, at *The Financial Times*, 'part of our credo and ethos is that we support liberal democracy, open markets, human rights'. Still he insists, 'No one in a senior position on the FT ever said to me "you must report the story in this way" or "you may take this line on this story, we really want to have a go at them over that."' His denials cut no ice in the Kremlin. 'This is something that the Russians, particularly in government, have difficulty accepting. They don't believe it.' Franchetti relates similar experiences. 'They believe there's a conspiracy. There is no conspiracy. It's just what we know and it's what sells.' This gulf of suspicion and misunderstanding is not so new, either. The urbane Lozovsky's remark to Philip Jordan in the 1940s, 'You do not write as journalists, but as politicians,'[13] finds its twenty-first-century echo in the suave, Marlboro-smoking Peskov's remark to Buckley that 'the problem is the West does not want to see Russia become strong again'. Today's press corps also has its version of the rows between the believers and non-believers in the causes of the twentieth century. It does not, perhaps, reach the heights of the row between Morgan Philips Price and Robert Wilton, but Franchetti admits to 'having a huge issue' with one in particular of the many Western correspondents who have passed through Moscow in his time there. Chance reflects that 'journalism is a profession that is absolutely packed to the seams with charlatans and that's the trouble with it. And that's why it's important to identify who is not one. Very smart charlatans'. Today, he argues, 'this idea that people are pro-Russia or anti-Russia has become much more pronounced. There are very few people, in which I include myself, left straddling that middle ground, who strive to be dispassionate and impartial'.

Those who have told Russia's story are not only critical of some of their peers, but capable of reflective self-criticism, too. 'I think we were all just naive to think that Russia could be reformed overnight. It's a vast and complicated country. It takes time,' says Womack. Franchetti, almost equally long serving, mentions that eternal journalistic challenge of context – but suggests that such an article would be hard to sell to editors. 'That kind of piece, by someone who's been here for a very long time and really has not gone native, but might give you a different perspective, that, they're really not interested in.' Perhaps in consequence, as Shaun Walker of *The Guardian* wrote when reflecting on the image of Russia when it hosted the football World Cup in 2018, 'I do wonder if us foreign correspondents could have done a better job of explaining the country.' He added, in an echo of Franchetti's and Womack's remarks in a previous chapter, 'In the end, Russia's bad press is largely of its own making.'[14] Imperfect correspondents sending bad news? There are plenty of examples, it is true – but Moscow correspondents have also brought to wider audiences that which only the individual traveller might otherwise learn. 'I think one of the big questions – and you can only really answer it properly if you're living in Russia – is to find out whether what Putin is doing has support from people,' says Steele. 'If you are living in the country and have the opportunity to talk, which you do much more freely in Russia now than you did in the Soviet Union, you can find out what people think.'

Correspondents in Russia have done that by talking to people at all levels of society. Amongst the political elites they have been able to seek signs of coming change when divisions emerged, both at the dawn and the demise of the Soviet Union. They have acted, though their reporting and personal contacts, as bridges between Russia and their own countries, as their policymakers sought to understand, respond to and influence Russian foreign policy, and, sometimes, domestic politics. They have been out to talk to the people among whom they lived, although at times this has been exceedingly difficult. Hobsbawm's tribute to Philips Price's 'talking to peasants, merchants, soldiers, overhearing conversations on Volga boats' is worth recalling here. It set the standard for first-rate reporting from Russia, or anywhere else. Price's mastery of the Russian language helped, just as it came to help those correspondents of later generations who also learnt Russian. Conversations with underemployed workers in near-idle factories in the 1990s could tell you much more about Russia's likely future political direction than any number of upbeat policy papers about democratic reform and the market economy. While there have been correspondents who have offered insights into Russia without that mastery of the language, they worked at a disadvantage. The Russian language is a way into Russian culture and Russian life. Russians are not used to outsiders learning Russian, so even the most modest effort can prove an ice-breaker in a country known the world over for the proverbial cold of its winters. In a country justly proud of its achievements in literature, music, opera and ballet, those correspondents who have been able to draw on an understanding of Russian culture as well as politics, diplomacy, military affairs and business, have had an advantage.

From the revolutionary period of the First World War onwards, correspondents in Russia have striven to tell the story of a country known to few outsiders. Their stories have not always been well received by political elites, audiences and even editors in their own countries – but their accounts have been a huge influence on how the West understands Russia. Not always perfect, at times downright misleading, they have, overall, been immensely valuable.

At their best, Moscow correspondents have been driven by a desire to learn about, and to tell others about, a country and culture that for most in the West has been alien and sometimes menacing. They have been curious, open to new ideas, internationalist: values that are increasingly lacking in our global discourse today. We are poorer for that.

Notes

Introduction

1 https://www.theguardian.com/politics/2018/mar/15/russia-ripping-up-the-international-rule-book-says-defence-secretary. Accessed 14 February 2020.
2 https://www.theguardian.com/world/2015/apr/22/any-analysis-of-russia-has-to-consider-effect-of-nato-expansion. Accessed 14 February 2020.

Chapter 1

1 'Federal'naya Sluzhba Bezopasnosti' (The State Security Service).
2 Broadcast on BBC1 at 1300 on 28 September 2006; at various other times on BBC World News.
3 Richard Pipes, *The Russian Revolution 1899–1919* (London: Harvill, 1997), 153.
4 Orlando Figes, *A People's Tragedy: The Russian Revolution* 1891–1924 (London: Pimlico, 1997), 213; Pipes, *The Russian Revolution 1899–1919,* 155.
5 Robert Wilton, *Russia's Agony* (London: Edward Arnold, 1918), 62.
6 Dates at this period of Russian history can be confusing. Until 1918, Russia used the Julian calendar, which was 13 days behind the Gregorian calendar in use in the West.
7 Donald Thompson, *Donald Thompson in Russia* (New York: The Century, 1918), 41. Thompson. When he gives the date as the 8 March, he does so according to the Gregorian calendar – so this is before the Tsar abdicates (see note 4, above).
8 Editors in London waiting for news from the Battle of Waterloo in 1815, for example, seem to have encountered difficulties which their counterparts in the First World War might still have recognized – at least where telecommunications were primitive, or suspended. See Brian Cathcart's *The News from Waterloo* (London: Faber & Faber, 2015).
9 *Daily Mail,* 14 March 1917.
10 *The New York Times,* 14 March 1917, 1.
11 *Daily Express*; *The Manchester Guardian,* 16 March 1917.
12 *Daily Mirror,* 20 March 1917.
13 *The Manchester Guardian,* 16 March 1917.

14 *The New York Times*, 14 March 1917, 1.

15 Thompson, *Donald Thompson in Russia*, 31.

16 Thompson, *Donald Thompson in Russia*, 57.

17 Thompson, *Donald Thompson in Russia*, 64.

18 Associated Press despatch printed in *The Manchester Guardian*, 17 March 1917.

19 *The Times*, 16 March 1917.

20 *The Times*, 16 March 1917.

21 *The Times*, 16 March 1917.

22 *Daily Mail*, 16 March 1917.

23 Robert Service, *A History of Modern Russia: from Nicholas II to Putin* (London: Penguin, 2003), 32.

24 *Daily Mail*, 16 March 1917.

25 Morgan Philips Price, *My Reminiscences of the Russian Revolution* (London: George Allen and Unwin, 1921), 21.

26 Morgan Philips Price, *Dispatches from the Revolution: Russia 1916–18*, edited by Tania Rose (London: Pluto Press, 1997), xi.

27 Bernard Pares, *Russian Memoirs* (London: Jonathan Cape, 1931), 428.

28 Philips Price, *Dispatches from the Revolution*, 41.

29 Buchan to Dawson, 1 May 1918. Times Newspapers Ltd Archive [TNL Archive], News UK and Ireland Ltd, TT/ED/GGD/2/.

30 Wilton, *Russia's Agony* (1918).

31 Philips Price, *My Reminiscences of the Russian Revolution*.

32 Philips Price, *My Reminiscences of the Russian Revolution*.

33 See Roland Chambers, *The Last Englishman: The Double Life of Arthur Ransome* (London: Faber & Faber, 2009).

34 Arthur Ransome, *The Crisis in Russia* (London: George Allen and Unwin, 1921), 12.

35 Ransome, *The Crisis in Russia*, 13.

36 Reuters, in *The Observer*, 18 March 1917.

37 Figes, *A People's Tragedy*, 413.

38 Zena Beth McGlashan, 'Women Witness the Russian Revolution: Analyzing Ways of Seeing'. *Journalism History*, Vol. 12, No. 2 (1985): 55.

39 Figes, *A People's Tragedy*, 419.

40 Figes, *A People's Tragedy*.

41 *The Financial Times*, 3 July 1917.

42 *The New York Times*, 3 July 1917, 1.

43 *Daily Mail*, 5 July 1917.

44 *The Sunday Times*, 1 July 1917.

45 Pipes, *The Russian Revolution 1899–1919*, 419.

46 Figes, *A People's Tragedy*, 421.

47 *Daily Mail*, 19 July 1917.

48 John Reed, *Ten Days That Shook the World* (London: Penguin, 1977), 21–22.

49 Figes, *A People's Tragedy,* 427.

50 Pipes, *The Russian Revolution 1899–1919,* 419.

51 A. J. P. Taylor, preface to John Reed, *Ten Days That Shook the World* (London: Penguin, 1977), xix.

52 Reed, *Ten Days That Shook the World,* 13.

53 Reed, *Ten Days That Shook the World,* 82.

54 In the preface to John Reed *Shaking the World: Revolutionary Journalism,* edited by John Newsinger; Preface by Paul Foot (London: Bookmarks, 1998), ix–x.

55 Reed, *Shaking the World,* 82.

56 Reed, *Shaking the World.*

57 Reed, *Shaking the World,* 85.

58 Eric Homberger, *John Reed* (Manchester: Manchester University Press, 1990), 133.

59 Thompson, *Donald Thompson in Russia,* 38.

60 Homberger, *John Reed,* 134–5.

61 Reed, *Ten Days That Shook the World,* 52.

62 R. H. Bruce Lockhart, *Memoirs of a British Agent* (London: Pan, 2002), 230.

63 Reed, *Ten Days That Shook the World,* 113.

64 Reed, *Ten Days That Shook the World,* 208.

65 Leon Trotsky, *The History of the Russian Revolution,* translated by Max Eastman (London: Pluto Press, 1977), 772.

66 A. J. P. Taylor, preface to Reed, *Ten Days That Shook the World,* vii.

67 Reed, *Ten Days That Shook the World,* vii.

68 Reed, *Ten Days That Shook the World,* xix.

69 Reed, *Ten Days That Shook the World,* xiv.

70 Trotsky, *The History of the Russian Revolution,* 1200.

71 *Daily Mail,* 9 November 1917, 2. For 'Cederbaum', see also *The Daily Telegraph.*

72 *Daily Mail,* 9 November 1917, 2. For 'Cederbaum', see also *The Daily Telegraph.*

73 *Daily Mail,* 9 November 1917, 2. For 'Cederbaum', see also *The Daily Telegraph.*

74 *The Times,* 9 November 1917, 7.

75 Dawson to Wilton, 9 November 1917, TNL Archive, BNS/3/.

76 Wilton to Dawson, 10 November 1917, TNL Archive BNS/3/.

77 *The Times,* 9 November 1917, 7.

78 *The Daily Telegraph,* 9 November 1917.

79 *The Daily Telegraph,* 9 November 1917.

80 *The Times,* 10 November 1917.

81 *The New York Times,* 9 November 1917, 1.

82 *San Francisco Bulletin,* 19 November 1917, cited in McGlashan, 'Women Witness the Russian Revolution', 61.

83 McGlashan, *Women Witness the Russian Revolution,* 55.

84 Philips Price, *Dispatches from the Revolution,* 92.

85   Philips Price, *Dispatches from the Revolution,* 88.

86   *Daily Mail,* 12 November 1917.

87   *The Times,* 12 November 1917.

88   *The Times,* 22 November 1917.

89   *The New York Times,* 9 November 1917, 1.

90   *The Sunday Times,* 11 November 1917.

91   Phillip Knightley, *The First Casualty* (London: Pan, 1989), 146.

92   Ariadna Tyrkova-Williams, *Cheerful Giver: The Life of Harold Williams* (London: Peter Davies, 1935), 188.

93   Kenneth O'Reilly, 'The *Times* of London and the Bolshevik Revolution', *Journalism Quarterly,* Vol. 56, No. 1 (1979): 70.

94   O'Reilly, 'The *Times* of London and the Bolshevik Revolution'.

95   Eric Hobsbawm, *The Age of Extremes, 1914–1991* (London: Abacus, 1994), 55.

96   Bruce Lockhart, *Memoirs of a British Agent,* 231.

97   Bruce Lockhart, *Memoirs of a British Agent,* 242.

Chapter 2

1   Knightley, *The First Casualty,* 146.

2   Arthur Ransome, *The Autobiography of Arthur Ransome,* edited by Rupert Hart-Davis (London: Century, 1985), 158.

3   See Hugh Brogan, *The Life of Arthur Ransome* (London: Pimlico, 1984), 79–90.

4   Brogan, *The Life of Arthur Ransome,* 91.

5   Brogan, *The Life of Arthur Ransome,* 96.

6   Ransome, *The Autobiography of Arthur Ransome,* 161.

7   Ransome, *The Autobiography of Arthur Ransome,* 167.

8   Charlotte Alston, *Russia's Greatest Enemy: Harold Williams and the Russian Revolutions* (London, Tauris Academic Studies, 2007b), 2.

9   Brogan, *The Life of Arthur Ransome,* 105.

10   Ransome, *The Autobiography of Arthur Ransome,* 163.

11   Cited in Brogan, *The Life of Arthur Ransome,* 105.

12   Available, for example, on the website of the Arthur Ransome Society at http://www.arthur-ransome.org.uk/?page_id=75

13   Pares, *Russian Memoirs,* 253.

14   University College London School of Slavonic and East European Studies website. Available at http://www.ssees.ucl.ac.uk/archives/par.htm. Accessed 10 July 2015.

15   Available at http://www.marxistsfr.org/archive/price/index.htm

16   Chief Passport Officer to the Manager, *The Times,* 21 May 1918. TNL Archive. MAN/1/Robert Wilton.

17　Wilton to Wickham Steed, 24 May 1918. TNL Archive. TT/ED/HWS/1/.

18　*The Times*, 242.

19　*The Times*, 244.

20　*The Times*, 244.

21　Wilton, *Russia's Agony* (1918), vii.

22　Wilton, *Russia's Agony* (1918), 99.

23　Figes, *A People's Tragedy*, 138.

24　Wilton, *Russia's Agony* (1918), 99.

25　*The Times*, 248.

26　Robert Wilton, *Russia's Agony* (New York: E.P Dutton, 1919), 141.

27　Wilton, *Russia's Agony* (1919), ix.

28　Dmitri Volkogonov, *Lenin: Life and Legacy*, translated and edited by Harold Shukman (London: HarperCollins, 1994), 81.

29　Wilton, *Russia's Agony* (1918), 261.

30　Wilton, *Russia's Agony* (1918).

31　Wilton, *Russia's Agony* (1918), 283.

32　Wilton, *Russia's Agony* (1918), 327.

33　Carl von Clausewitz, *On War* (Oxford: Oxford World's Classics, 2007), 32.

34　Bruce Lockhart, *Memoirs of a British Agent*, 288.

35　See, for example, Brogan, *The Life of Arthur Ransome*, 126.

36　Arthur Ransome, *Six Weeks in Russia, 1919* (London: Redwords, 1992), Kindle edition, 55.

37　Ransome, *Six Weeks in Russia, 1919*, 56.

38　Ransome, *Six Weeks in Russia, 1919*, 56.

39　Ransome, *Six Weeks in Russia, 1919*, 57.

40　Ransome, *Six Weeks in Russia, 1919*, Kindle edition.

41　Ransome, *Six Weeks in Russia, 1919*, Kindle edition.

42　Ransome, *Six Weeks in Russia, 1919*, 146.

43　Ransome, *Six Weeks in Russia, 1919*, 148.

44　Israel Zangzwill, *Hands Off Russia: Speech at the Albert Hall February 8th 1919* (London: Workers Socialist Federation, 1919).

45　Zangzwill, *Hands Off Russia*.

46　L. A. Motler, *Soviets for the British: A Plain Talk to Plain People* (London: Workers' Socialist Federation, 1919).

47　Motler, 'Soviets for the British'.

48　Ransome, *Six Weeks in Russia, 1919*, Kindle edition.

49　Ransome, *Six Weeks in Russia, 1919*, Kindle edition.

50　Ransome, *The Autobiography of Arthur Ransome*, 157.

51　Arthur Ransome, *The Truth about Russia* (London: Workers' Socialist Federation, 1918), 4.

52　Ransome, *The Autobiography of Arthur Ransome*, 229.

53　Ransome, *The Autobiography of Arthur Ransome*, 229.

54　W. P. Crozier to David Soskice, 2 October 1917, STH/DS/2/1/9 MG21.

55　Pipes, *The Russian Revolution 1899–1919*, 636.

56　*The Sunday Times*, 21 July 1918, 7.

57　Robert Service, *Trotsky: A Biography* (London: Macmillan, 2009), 215.

58　Ransome (1918), 18.

59　Ransome (1918), 18.

60　*The Manchester Guardian*, 20 February 1918. Cited in Philips Price, *Dispatches from the Revolution*, 118.

61　Philips Price, *My Reminiscences of the Russian Revolution*, 134.

62　Philips Price, *My Reminiscences of the Russian Revolution*, 134.

63　Philips Price, *Dispatches from the Revolution*, 148.

64　Philips Price, *Dispatches from the Revolution*, 148.

65　Philips Price, *My Reminiscences of the Russian Revolution*, 134.

66　Aylmer Maude to the Editor, *The Manchester Guardian*, 17 January 1917. Archive of *The Guardian* (formerly *The Manchester Guardian*) GB 133 GDN, University of Manchester Library. A/P53/16a.

67　Philips Price, *My Reminiscences of the Russian Revolution*, 297.

68　Figes, *A People's Tragedy*, 652.

69　Ransome, *The Autobiography of Arthur Ransome*, 228.

70　Philips Price, *My Reminiscences of the Russian Revolution*, 296.

71　Philips Price, *My Reminiscences of the Russian Revolution*, 298.

72　Philips Price, *My Reminiscences of the Russian Revolution*, 302.

73　Philips Price, *My Reminiscences of the Russian Revolution*, 302–3.

74　Philips Price, *My Reminiscences of the Russian Revolution*, 331.

75　Philips Price, *My Reminiscences of the Russian Revolution*, 331.

76　*The Guardian*, 21 September 1959. Republished online 21 September 2012. Available at https://www.theguardian.com/theguardian/2012/sep/21/khrushchev-visit-usa-disneyland-archive-1959. Accessed 11 July 2016.

77　Mikhail Gorbachev, *On My Country and the World* (New York: Columbia University Press, 2005), 40.

78　Scott to The General Manager, *Labour Monthly*, 24 February 1924. *Guardian* Archive MG A/P53/24.

79　*Guardian* Archive MG A/P53/10.

80　Philips Price, *Dispatches from the Revolution*, 141.

81　Philips Price, *Dispatches from the Revolution*, 141.

82　Reed, *Ten Days That Shook the World*, 13.

83　Philips Price, *My Reminiscences of the Russian Revolution*, 134.

84　Philips Price, *My Reminiscences of the Russian Revolution*, 134.

85　Alston, *Russia's Greatest Enemy*, 99.

86 Stanley Washburn, *On the Russian Front in WW1: Memoirs of an American War Correspondent* (New York: Robert Speller and Sons, 1982), 25.

87 Ransome, *The Autobiography of Arthur Ransome*, 267.

88 Ransome, *The Autobiography of Arthur Ransome*, 267.

89 Bruce Lockhart, *Memoirs of a British Agent*, 267.

90 Chambers, *The Last Englishman*, 8.

91 Bruce Lockhart, *Memoirs of a British Agent*, 266.

92 Chambers, *The Last Englishman*, 8.

93 Bruce Lockhart, *Memoirs of a British Agent*, 266.

94 John Ernest Hodgson, *With Denikin's Armies* (London: Temple Bar Publishing Co., 1932), 12.

95 Hodgson, *With Denikin's Armies*, 13.

96 Bruce Lockhart, *Memoirs of a British Agent*, 266.

97 Morgan Philips Price, *My Three Revolutions: Russia, Germany, Britain 1917–1969* (London: George Allen and Unwin, 1969), 12.

Chapter 3

1 John Steinbeck, *A Russian Journal* (London: Minerva, 1994), 4.

2 Walter Duranty, *I Write as I Please* (London: Hamish Hamilton, 1935), 106.

3 Robert Service, *A History of Modern Russia: From Nicholas II to Putin* (London: Penguin, 2003), 152.

4 Service, *A History of Modern Russia*, 152.

5 Service, *A History of Modern Russia*, 152.

6 Figes, *A People's Tragedy*, 317.

7 Sheila Fitzpatrick, *On Stalin's Team: The Years of Living Dangerously in Soviet Politics* (Woodstock (Oxfordshire, UK): Princeton University Press, 2015), 21.

8 Fitzpatrick, *On Stalin's Team*, 40.

9 Fitzpatrick, *On Stalin's Team*, 31–2.

10 Fitzpatrick, *On Stalin's Team*, 98.

11 Fitzpatrick, *On Stalin's Team*, 96.

12 *The New York Times*, 25 December 1919.

13 *The New York Times*, 25 December 1919.

14 *The New York Times*, 31 December 1919.

15 *The New York Times*, 31 December 1919.

16 *The New York Times*, 31 December 1919.

17 Whitman Bassow, *The Moscow Correspondents: Reporting on Russia from the Revolution to Glasnost* (New York: William Morrow, 1988), 34.

18 Bassow, *The Moscow Correspondents*, 34.

19 Service, *A History of Modern Russia*, 125.

20 Service, *A History of Modern Russia*, 170.

21 Service, *A History of Modern Russia*, 9.

22 Kazuo Nakai, 'Soviet Agricultural Policies in the Ukraine and the 1921–1922 Famine'. *Harvard Ukrainian Studies*, Vol. 6, No. 1 (March 1982): 55.

23 Figes, *A People's Tragedy*, 776.

24 Figes, *A People's Tragedy*, 776.

25 Figes, *A People's Tragedy*, 777.

26 Robert Conquest, *The Harvest of Sorrow: Soviet Collectivisation and the Terror-Famine* (London: Pimlico, 2002), 55.

27 Cited in Figes, *A People's Tragedy*, 778.

28 *The New York Times*, 17 July 1921, 10.

29 *The Times*, 18 July 1921, 9.

30 *The New York Times*, 24 July 1921, 2.

31 *The New York Times*, 31 July 1921, 2.

32 *The New York Times*, 31 July 1921, 1.

33 *The New York Times*, 24 April 1921, 18.

34 Marguerite Harrison, *Born for Trouble: The Story of a Chequered Life* (London: Victor Gollancz, 1936), 9.

35 Harrison, *Born for Trouble*, 159.

36 Harrison, *Born for Trouble*, 161.

37 Harrison, *Born for Trouble*, 161.

38 Harrison, *Born for Trouble*, 182.

39 Harrison, *Born for Trouble*, 182.

40 Harrison, *Born for Trouble*, 182.

41 Harrison, *Born for Trouble*, 173.

42 Harrison, *Born for Trouble*, 228.

43 Harrison, *Born for Trouble*, 186–7.

44 Marguerite Harrison, *Marooned in Moscow* (London: Thornton Butterworth, 1921), 316.

45 *The New York Times*, 4 August 1921, 6.

46 *The New York Times*, 24 August 1921, 1.

47 Bassow, *The Moscow Correspondents*, 38.

48 Bassow, *The Moscow Correspondents*, 42.

49 Bassow, *The Moscow Correspondents*, 42.

50 *The New York Times*, 24 August 1921, 1.

51 Duranty, *I Write as I Please*, 106, 108.

52 Conquest, *Harvest of Sorrow*, 55.

53 Bassow, *The Moscow Correspondents*, 39.

54 Duranty, *I Write as I Please*, 117.

55 Bassow, *The Moscow Correspondents*, 44–5.

56 S. J. Taylor, *Stalin's Apologist: Walter Duranty, The New York Times' Man in Moscow* (Oxford: Oxford University Press, 1990), 20.

57 Taylor, *Stalin's Apologist*, 254.

58 Duranty, *Search for a Key*, 1.

59 Taylor, *Stalin's Apologist*, 130.

60 Duranty, *I Write as I Please*, 8.

61 Duranty, *Search for a Key*, 115.

62 Taylor, *Stalin's Apologist*, 36–7.

63 Taylor, *Stalin's Apologist*, 122.

64 *The New York Times*, 1 May 1920, 17.

65 *The New York Times*, 27 May 1920, 17.

66 Walter Lippmann and Charles Merz, *A Test of the News*: A Supplement to The New Republic of August 4th, 1920, 3.

67 *The New York Times*, 23 January 1924, 1.

68 *The New York Times*, 26 January 1924, 5.

69 *The New York Times*, 28 January 1924, 1.

70 *The New York Times*, 23 January 1924, 3.

71 *The New York Times*, 25 January 1924, 16.

72 *The Times*, 12 March 1928, 14.

73 *The New York Times*, 17 March 1928, 8.

74 *The Observer*, 13 May 1928, 17.

75 *The Observer*, 13 May 1928, 17.

76 Service, *A History of Modern Russia*, 175.

77 Service, *A History of Modern Russia*, 175.

78 *The New York Times*, 7 July 1928, 30.

79 *The New York Times*, 7 July 1928, 30.

80 *The New York Times*, 7 July 1928, 30.

81 Eugene Lyons, *Assignment in Utopia* (London: George G. Harrap, 1938), 6.

82 Lyons, *Assignment in Utopia*, 8.

83 Lyons, *Assignment in Utopia*, 56.

84 Lyons, *Assignment in Utopia*, 67.

85 Lyons, *Assignment in Utopia*, 383.

86 Lyons, *Assignment in Utopia*, 385.

87 Lyons, *Assignment in Utopia*, 385.

88 Lyons, *Assignment in Utopia*, 388.

89 Lyons, *Assignment in Utopia*, 389.

90 Lyons, *Assignment in Utopia*, 397.

91 *The New York Times*, 1 December 1930, 1.

92 Malcolm Muggeridge, *Chronicles of Wasted Time: Volume 1, The Green Stick* (London: Collins, 1972), 205.

93 Muggeridge, *Chronicles of Wasted Time*, 206.

94   Muggeridge, *Chronicles of Wasted Time,* 215.

95   Muggeridge, *Chronicles of Wasted Time,* 215–16.

96   Muggeridge, *Chronicles of Wasted Time,* 216.

97   *The Manchester Guardian,* 1 November 1932, 7.

98   *The Manchester Guardian,* 1 November 1932, 7.

99   Muggeridge, *Chronicles of Wasted Time,* 221.

100   Muggeridge, *Chronicles of Wasted Time,* 227.

101   Malcolm Muggeridge, *Winter in Moscow* (Thirsk: House of Stratus, 2003 (1934)), 45.

102   Conquest, *Harvest of Sorrow,* 223.

103   Nicholas Hall, 'Gareth Jones, the Soviet Peasantry and the "Real Russia" 1930–1933'. *Russian Journal of Communication,* Vol. 8, No. 3 (2016): 242. doi 10.1080/19409419.2016.1213220.

104   Ray Gamache, 'Breaking Eggs for a Holodomor'. *Journalism History (0094–7679),* Vol. 39, No. 4 (2014): 208.

105   *The Manchester Guardian,* 30 March 1933, 12.

106   Stewart Purvis and Jeff Hulbert, *When Reporters Cross the Line: The Heroes, the Villains, the Hackers, and the Spies* (London: Biteback, 2013), Chapter 3.

107   *The New York Times,* 31 March 1933, 13.

108   *The New York Times,* 31 March 1933, 13.

109   Lyons, *Assignment in Utopia,* 572.

110   *The New York Times,* 31 March 1933, 13.

111   Lyons, *Assignment in Utopia,* 561.

112   Donald Read, *The Power of News: The History of Reuters* (2nd Edition) (Oxford: Oxford University Press, 1999), 227.

113   Lyons, *Assignment in Utopia,* 576.

114   Lyons, *Assignment in Utopia,* 575.

115   Gamache, 'Breaking Eggs for a Holodomor', 210.

116   Lyons, *Assignment in Utopia,* 575.

117   *The Manchester Guardian,* 25 March 1933, 13.

118   *The Manchester Guardian,* 25 March 1933, 13.

119   Muggeridge, *Chronicles of Wasted Time,* 258.

120   Muggeridge, *Chronicles of Wasted Time,* 268.

121   Muggeridge, *Chronicles of Wasted Time,* 231.

122   Douglas MCollam, 'Should This Pulitzer Be Pulled?' *Columbia Journalism Review,* November/December 2003, 43.

123   Taylor, *Stalin's Apologist.*

124   Duranty, *Search for a Key,* 213.

125   Duranty, *I Write as I Please,* 10.

126   Conquest, *The Great Terror,* 7.

127   Taylor, *Stalin's Apologist.*

128 Muggeridge, *Chronicles of Wasted Time,* 255.

129 Muggeridge, *Chronicles of Wasted Time,* 256.

130 Duranty, *I Write as I Please,* 12.

131 Lermontov, *A Hero of Our Time,* 130.

132 *The New York Times,* 25 November 1933, 1.

133 *The New York Times,* 25 November 1933, 1.

Chapter 4

1 The picture of Misha Shamonin which I saw that day is reproduced in this *Huffington Post* story, from 2016. https://www.huffingtonpost.com/lena-hades/ stalins-great-purge-boy-e_b_9535358.html?ec_carp=9030983708355874050&gucc ounter=1. Accessed 28 January 2019.

2 *War And Peace,* 1142.

3 At the time of writing, January 2019, a diary item which I wrote the following week for the BBC website and some of the BBC's coverage of that day are both still. Available at http://news.bbc.co.uk/1/hi/world/europe/6944834.stm and http://news. bbc.co.uk/1/hi/world/europe/6936478.stm. Accessed 28 January 2019.

4 'Vladimir Putin honoured the memory of the victims of political repressions', President of Russia website, posted 30 October 2007. Accessed 28 January 2019 http://en.kremlin.ru/events/president/news/43148

5 Service, *A History of Modern Russia,* 223.

6 'Vladimir Putin honoured the memory of the victims of political repressions', President of Russia website, posted 30 October 2007. Accessed 28 January 2019 http://en.kremlin.ru/events/president/news/43148. The NKVD comes from the initial letters, in Russian, of the 'People's Commissariat of Internal Affairs' (Народный комиссариат внутренних дел).

7 *The New York Times,* 7 July 1928, 30.

8 Fitzpatrick, *On Stalin's Team,* 115.

9 Service, *A History of Modern Russia,* 214.

10 Service, *A History of Modern Russia,* 214.

11 Fitzpatrick, *On Stalin's Team,* 116.

12 Service, *A History of Modern Russia,* 215.

13 *The New York Times,* 18 August 1936, 5.

14 *The New York Times,* 18 August 1936, 2.

15 *The New York Times,* 16 August 1936, 1.

16 *The Daily Telegraph,* 15 August 1936, 11.

17 *The Daily Telegraph,* 20 August 1936, 13.

18 *The Daily Mail,* 22 August 1936, 10.

19 *The Daily Mail,* 21 August 1936, 10.

20 *The Daily Mail*, 25 October 1924, 9.

21 *The Daily Mail*, 15 August, 19, 20, 21, 1936.

22 *The Daily Mail*, 21 August 1936, 10; *Manchester Guardian*, 21 August 1936, 9.

23 *The Manchester Guardian*, 26 August 1936, 12.

24 *The Times*, 26 August 1936, 7.

25 *The New York Times*, 21 August 1936, 11; *The Times*, 21 August 1936, 10.

26 *The Times*, 20 August 1936, 13.

27 *The Manchester Guardian*, 19 August 1937, 9.

28 *The Manchester Guardian*, 19 August 1937, 10.

29 *The New York Times*, 25 January 1937, 3.

30 *The New York Times*, 25 January 1937, 3.

31 *The Manchester Guardian*, 22 January 1937, 6.

32 *The Manchester Guardian*, 25 January 1937, 9.

33 *The Daily Mail*, 26 January 1937, 11.

34 *The Daily Mail*, 30 January 1937, 12.

35 *The Observer*, 31 January 1937, 7.

36 Conquest, *The Great Terror*, 167.

37 *The New York Times*, 24 January 1937, 28.

38 *The Observer*, 31 January 1937, 7.

39 Ransome, *The Autobiography of Arthur Ransome*, 295.

40 Conquest, *The Great Terror*, 165.

41 Fitzroy Maclean, *Eastern Approaches* (London: The Reprint Society, by Arrangement with Jonathan Cape, 1951), 57.

42 Maclean, *Eastern Approaches*, 57.

43 Maclean, *Eastern Approaches*, 58.

44 Maclean, *Eastern Approaches*, 58.

45 Maclean, *Eastern Approaches*, 57.

46 *The Times*, 28 February 1938, 14.

47 *The Daily Mail*, 28 February 1938, 13.

48 *The New York Times*, 28 February 1938, 1.

49 *The New York Times*, 1 March 1938, 9.

50 *The New York Times*, 3 March 1938, 1.

51 *The New York Times*, 3 March 1938, 1.

52 *The New York Times*, 4 March 1938, 1.

53 Maclean, *Eastern Approaches*, 64.

54 Maclean, *Eastern Approaches*, 56.

55 Maclean, *Eastern Approaches*, 96.

56 *The Daily Telegraph*, 8 March 1938, 18.

57 *The Daily Telegraph*, 8 March 1938, 18.

58 *The Daily Telegraph*, 4 March 1938, 15.

59 Fitzpatrick, *On Stalin's Team*, 125.

60 *The Daily Telegraph*, 3 March 1938, 15.

61 The *Manchester Guardian*, 11 March 1938, 12.

62 *The New York Times*, 1 March 1938, 9.

63 *The Daily Telegraph*, 16 March 1938, 15.

64 *The Daily Telegraph*, 9 March 1938, 14.

65 The *Sunday Times*, 6 March 1938, 19.

66 *The Sunday Times*, 6 March 1938, 29.

67 Maclean, *Eastern Approaches*, 95.

68 Maclean, *Eastern Approaches*, 88.

69 Maclean, *Eastern Approaches*, 93.

70 Maclean, *Eastern Approaches*, 96.

71 Muggeridge, *Chronicles of Wasted Time*, 21.

72 Quentin Reynolds, *Only the Stars Are Neutral* (London: Cassell, 1942), 57–8.

73 Robert W. Desmond, *Crisis and Conflict: World News Reporting between Two Wars 1920–1940* (Iowa: University of Iowa Press, 1982), 269.

74 Iverach McDonald, *A Man of The Times: Talks and Travels in a Disrupted World* (London: Hamish Hamilton, 1976), 21.

75 Muggeridge, *Chronicles of Wasted Time*, 228.

76 Desmond, *Crisis and Conflict,* 269.

77 Muggeridge, *Chronicles of Wasted Time*, 228.

78 *The History of The Times, Volume IV, Part II,* 911.

79 *The History of The Times, Volume IV, Part II,* 911.

80 *The History of The Times, Volume IV, Part II,* 912.

81 *The History of The Times, Volume IV, Part II,* 912.

82 *The History of The Times, Volume IV, Part II,* 911–12.

83 Fitzpatrick, *On Stalin's Team*, 98.

84 Lyons, *Assignment in Utopia*, 110.

85 Bassow, *The Moscow Correspondents*, 77.

86 Desmond, *Crisis and Conflict,* 441–2.

87 Desmond, *Crisis and Conflict,* 442.

88 *The History of The Times, Volume IV, Part II,* 911.

89 Desmond, *Crisis and Conflict,* 442–3.

90 André Gide, *Retour de l'U.R.S.S.* (Paris: Editions Gallimard, 1936) (extracts quoted here are translated by the author).

91 Gide, *Retour de l'U.R.S.S.* 48.

92 Gide, *Retour de l'U.R.S.S.*, 49.

93 Gide, *Retour de l'U.R.S.S.*, 39.

94 Lion Feuchtwanger, *Moscow 1937: My Visit Described for My Friends*, translated by Irene Josephy (London: Victor Gollancz, 1937), 18–19.

95 Feuchtwanger, *Moscow 1937*, 30.

96 Feuchtwanger, *Moscow 1937*, 47.

97 Feuchtwanger, *Moscow 1937*, 135.

98 Lyons, *Assignment in Utopia*, 106.

99 Lyons, *Assignment in Utopia*, 105.

Chapter 5

1 Dominic Lieven, *Russia against Napoleon* (London: Penguin, 2009), 9.

2 'Military Parade on Red Square' President of Russia Website. http://en.kremlin.ru/events/president/news/54467. Accessed 15 February 2019.

3 Reynolds, *Only the Stars Are Neutral*, 76.

4 Alexander Werth, *Russia at War* (London: Pan Books, 1965), 33.

5 Susan Carruthers, *The Media at War* (2nd Edition) (Basingstoke: Palgrave Macmillan, 2011), 72.

6 Philip M. Taylor, *Munitions of the Mind: A History of Propaganda from the Ancient World to the Present Day* (3rd Edition) (Manchester: Manchester University Press), 208.

7 Taylor, *Munitions of the Mind*, 246.

8 Taylor, *Munitions of the Mind*, 208.

9 Philip Jordan, *Russian Glory* (London: The Cresset Press, 1942), 107–8.

10 Rodric Braithwaite, *Moscow 1941: A City and Its People at War* (London: Profile Books, 2006), 95.

11 Braithwaite, *Moscow 1941*, 97.

12 Bassow, *The Moscow Correspondents*, 113.

13 Charlotte Haldane, *Russian Newsreel: An Eye-Witness Account of the Soviet Union at War* (London: Secker and Warburg, 1942), 95.

14 Haldane, *Russian Newsreel*, 46.

15 Haldane, *Russian Newsreel*, 46.

16 Werth, *Moscow War Diary*, 37–8.

17 Judith Adamson, *Charlotte Haldane: Woman Writer in a Man's World* (Basingstoke: Macmillan, 1998), 140.

18 Haldane, *Russian Newsreel*, 45–6.

19 Read, *The Power of News*, 259.

20 Henry C. Cassidy, *Moscow Dateline* (London: Cassell, 1943), 36.

21 Cassidy, *Moscow Dateline*, 44.

22 Haldane, *Russian Newsreel*, 44.

23 Reynolds, *Only the Stars Are Neutral*, 73–4.

24 Read, *The Power of News*, 258.

25 Knightley, *The First Casualty*, 251.

26 Haldane, *Russian Newsreel*, 50.

27 Knightley, *The First Casualty*, 246.

28 Werth, *Moscow War Diary*, 113.

29 Werth, *Moscow War Diary*, 71.

30 Jordan, *Russian Glory*, 106.

31 *The Daily Telegraph*, 25 September 1941, 4.

32 Haldane, *Russian Newsreel* (1942), facing 17.

33 *The Daily Telegraph*, 23 September 1941, 1.

34 *The Maisky Diaries*.

35 *The Daily Telegraph*, 24 September 1941, 3.

36 Haldane, *Russian Newsreel*, 70.

37 Haldane, *Russian Newsreel*, 70.

38 Haldane, *Russian Newsreel*, 71.

39 *The New York Times*, 25 September 1941, 4.

40 *The Daily Telegraph*, 25 September 1941, 4.

41 *The Daily Telegraph*, 25 September 1941, 4.

42 *The Sunday Times*, 28 September 1941, 8.

43 *The New York Times*, 25 September 1941, 4.

44 Haldane, *Russian Newsreel*, 79.

45 Geneva Convention of 27 July 1929 relative to the treatment of prisoners of war. Available at https://www.icrc.org/en/doc/resources/documents/misc/57jnws.htm. Accessed 25 February 2019.

46 Haldane, *Russian Newsreel*, 73–4.

47 Reynolds, *Only the Stars Are Neutral*, 86.

48 Reynolds, *Only the Stars Are Neutral*, 87.

49 Reynolds, *Only the Stars Are Neutral*, 87.

50 Cassidy, *Moscow Dateline*, 98.

51 Jordan, *Russian Glory*, 131–2.

52 Reynolds, *Only the Stars Are Neutral*, 76.

53 Reynolds, *Only the Stars Are Neutral*, 84.

54 Reynolds, *Only the Stars Are Neutral*, 84.

55 Reynolds, *Only the Stars Are Neutral*, 98.

56 Haldane, *Russian Newsreel*, 50.

57 Haldane, *Russian Newsreel*, 50.

58 Haldane, *Russian Newsreel*, 50.

59 David Reynolds and Vladimir Pechatnov, *The Kremlin Letters: Stalin's Wartime Correspondence with Churchill and Roosevelt* (Newhaven and London: Yale University Press, 2018), 54.

60 Reynolds and Pechatnov, *The Kremlin Letters*, 52.

61 Braithwaite, *Moscow 1941*, 245.

62 Reynolds, *Only the Stars Are Neutral*, 137.

63 Jordan, *Russian Glory*, 98.

64 Braithwaite, *Moscow 1941*, 242.

65 *Sir Stafford Cripps in Moscow, 1940–42*, 188.

66 *Sir Stafford Cripps in Moscow, 1940–42,* n66.

67 *The Daily Telegraph,* 27 October 1941, 5.

68 *The Daily Telegraph,* 28 October 1941, 1.

69 Reynolds, *Only the Stars Are Neutral,* 139.

70 Reynolds, *Only the Stars Are Neutral,* 141.

71 Reynolds, *Only the Stars Are Neutral,* 149.

72 Reynolds, *Only the Stars Are Neutral,* 144.

73 Reynolds, *Only the Stars Are Neutral,* 149–50.

74 *The Daily Telegraph,* 8 November 1941, 1.

75 Reynolds, *Only the Stars Are Neutral,* 169 ff.

76 Briggs, *The BBC: The First Fifty Years,* 194.

77 BBC Written Archives Centre, R13/264. Internal Memo from Assistant Controller Overseas, 26 August 1941.

78 BBC Written Archives Centre, R13/264. Internal Memo, 29 July 1941.

79 Reynolds, *Only the Stars Are Neutral,* 58.

80 Reynolds, *Only the Stars Are Neutral,* 58.

81 Sian Nicholas, *The Echo of War: Home Front Propaganda and the Wartime BBC* (Manchester University Press, 1996), 166.

82 Nicholas, *The Echo of War,* 171.

83 Werth, *Moscow War Diary,* 4.

84 BBC Written Archives Center, RCONT1 Werth, Alexander, Empire Talks Manager to Mr Titchener, 18 February 1942.

85 BBC Written Archives Centre, RCONT1 Werth, Alexander, Empire Talks Manager to Mr Titchener, 18 February 1942.

86 BBC Written Archives Centre, RCONT1 Werth, Alexander, Empire Talks Manager to Mr Titchener, 25 February 1942.

87 BBC Written Archives Centre, R47/973/1 Miss CGH Reeves to Miss A Kallinn, 17 November 1949.

88 Werth, *Moscow War Diary,* 34.

89 Werth, 'Britain Speaks', broadcast 31 January/1 February 1942.

90 Werth, 'Russian Commentary', broadcast 25 August 1942.

91 Werth, 'Russian Commentary', broadcast 15 September 1942.

92 Werth, 'Russian Commentary', broadcast 15 September 1942.

93 Werth, 'Russian Commentary', broadcast 9 February 1943.

94 Werth, 'Russian Commentary', broadcast 4 October 1943.

95 Knightley, *The First Casualty,* 262.

96 'Mauled Nazis Lag in Kursk Attacks', *The New York Times,* 14 July 1943, 1.

97 Werth, *Russia at War,* 180.

98 Reynolds, *Only the Stars Are Neutral,* 184.

99 Jordan, *Russian Glory,* 108.

100 Haldane, *Russian Newsreel*, 61.

101 Reynolds, *Only the Stars Are Neutral*, 193.

102 Reynolds, *Only the Stars Are Neutral*, 195.

103 Cassidy, *Moscow Dateline*, 250.

104 Jordan, *Russian Glory*, 108.

105 Haldane, *Russian Newsreel*, 61.

106 Haldane, *Truth Will Out*, 233.

107 Haldane, *Truth Will Out*, 237.

108 Jordan, *Russian Glory*, 1.

109 Cassidy, *Moscow Dateline*, 60.

110 Haldane, *Russian Newsreel*, 48.

111 Jordan, *Russian Glory*, 169–70.

112 Haldane, *Truth Will Out*, 216.

113 BBC News, 'Ofcom RT Ruling: Russia to Check BBC News in Response'. Available at https://www.bbc.co.uk/news/world-europe-46648010. Accessed 18 October 2019.

114 Haldane, *Russian Newsreel*, 29.

115 Werth, *Moscow War Diary*, 30.

116 Cassidy, *Moscow Dateline*, 74.

117 Jordan, *Russian Glory*, 106.

118 Jordan, *Russian Glory*, 106.

119 Cassidy, *Moscow Dateline*, 56.

120 Haldane, *Truth Will Out*, 217.

121 Werth, 'Britain Speaks', broadcast 31 January/1 February 1942.

122 Jordan, *Russian Glory*, 244.

123 William J. Clinton, Remarks to Students at Moscow State University, 10 May 1995. Available at https://www.govinfo.gov/content/pkg/PPP-1995-book1/html/PPP-1995-book1-doc-pg672.htm. Accessed 28 February 2019.

Chapter 6

1 Telephone interview with the author, London, 23 April 2019.

2 Note from the records of the 'House on the Embankment' Museum.

3 Figure from the 'House on the Embankment' Museum.

4 Fitzpatrick, *On Stalin's Team*, 237.

5 John Rettie, 'How Khrushchev Leaked His Secret Speech to the World'. *History Workshop Journal*, No. 62 (2006): 187.

6 Service, *A History of Modern Russia*, 339.

7 Service, *A History of Modern Russia*, 338.

8 Service, *A History of Modern Russia*, 339.

9   Service, *A History of Modern Russia*, 341.

10 Rettie, 'How Khrushchev Leaked His Secret Speech to the World', 187.

11 Interview conducted by Facebook video between Fanø, Denmark and Budapest, 21 May 2019. Unless otherwise attributed, all subsequent quotations from Womack are taken from this interview.

12 Rettie, 'How Khrushchev Leaked His Secret Speech to the World', 187.

13 Rettie, 'How Khrushchev Leaked His Secret Speech to the World', 190.

14 *The Manchester Guardian*, 16 March 1956, 1.

15 Bassow, *The Moscow Correspondents*, 125.

16 BBC Written Archive, R47/973/1 C.J. Curran to DT, 26 January 1948.

17 BBC Written Archive, R47/973/1 A. Werth to C.J. Curran, 2 May 1948.

18 Rettie, 'How Khrushchev Leaked His Secret Speech to the World', 192.

19 Rettie, 'How Khrushchev Leaked His Secret Speech to the World', 192.

20 *The New York Times*, 5 June 1956, 1.

21 Service, *A History of Modern Russia*, 341.

22 *The New York Times*, 5 June 1956, 1.

23 Rettie, 'How Khrushchev Leaked His Secret Speech to the World', 193.

24 Reynolds, *Only The Stars Are Neutral*, 109.

25 *The New York Times*, 20 March 1938, 1.

26 *The New York Times*, 20 March 1938, 1.

27 *The New York Times*, 4 July 1945, 13.

28 *The New York Times*, 4 July 1945, 13.

29 John Hohenberg, *Foreign Correspondence: The Great Reporters and Their Times* (New York: Columbia University Press, 1964), 399.

30 Hohenberg, *Foreign Correspondence*, 400.

31 Hohenberg, *Foreign Correspondence*, 400.

32 Masha Gessen, *Two Babushkas* (London: Bloomsbury, 2004), 211.

33 *The New York Times*, 10 September 1949, 6.

34 *The New York Times*, 18 May 1949, 34.

35 Interview with the author, London, 2 April 2019.

36 Gessen, *Two Babushkas*, 235.

37 *The New York Times*, 19 September 1954, E10.

38 *The New York Times*, 20 September 1954, 1.

39 *The New York Times*, 20 September 1954, 1.

40 *The New York Times*, 7 July 1993, 19.

41 *The New York Times*, 13 January 1956, 5.

42 *The New York Times*, 25 April 1949, 1.

43 Joseph Clark, *The Real Russia* (New York: New Century Publishers, 1954), 2.

44 Clark, *The Real Russia*, 14.

45 Clark, *The Real Russia*, 15.

46 Clark, *The Real Russia*, 32.

47 Clark, *The Real Russia*, 16–17.

48 Clark, *The Real Russia*, 17.

49 British Library. Russell, Sam (speaker, Male; Whitehead), Andrew (speaker, Male). *Sam Russell (Sam Lesser) Interviewed by Andrew Whitehead*, 1992.

50 'Russell, Sam (1915–2010) journalist, also known as Sam Lesser' Bishopsgate Institute website. available at https://www.bishopsgate.org.uk/Library/Special-Collections-and-Archives/Labour-and-Socialist-History/Russell-Sam. Accessed 12 April 2019.

51 *Daily Worker*, 10 August 1956.

52 *Daily Worker*, 16 July 1956.

53 *Daily Worker*, 11 September 1956.

54 *Daily Worker*, 7 October 1956.

55 *Daily Worker*, 17 December 1957.

56 British Library. Russell, Sam *Interviewed by Andrew Whitehead*. 1992.

57 British Library. Russell, Sam *Interviewed by Andrew Whitehead*. 1992.

58 *Daily Express*, 5 August 1955, 1.

59 *Daily Express*, 8 August 1955, 1.

60 *Daily Express*, 17 August 1955, 6.

61 *Daily Express*, 20 August 1955, 4.

62 *Daily Express*, 9 June, 5; 11 June, 2; 14 June, 5; 1956.

63 *Daily Express*, 16 April 1956, 6.

64 *Daily Express*, 22 March 1956, 7.

65 *Daily Express*, 31 March 1956, 5.

66 Letter sent to Rohde and shown to the author by her son, Gavin Weaver.

67 Arthur Christiansen to Lord Beaverbrook, 17 November 1955. Parliamentary archive, BBK/H/177 (Christiansen).

68 BBC Written Archives Centre R28/311 Head of Talks (Kenneth Lamb/J. A. Camacho) to FE (Foreign Editor), 10 October 1961.

69 BBC Written Archives Centre R28/311 Internal Memo from the Foreign Editor, 19 September 1961.

70 BBC Written Archives Centre R28/311 Editor Television News to Foreign Editor, 3 October 1961.

71 BBC Written Archives Centre R28/311 Chief Assistant (Current Affairs) Talks to Foreign Editor 6 October 1961.

72 BBC Written Archives Centre E1/2 434/1 F.R.H. Murray to Sir Beresford Clark, 10 February 1959.

73 Service, *A History of Modern Russia*, 353.

74 BBC Written Archives Centre R28/418/1 Acting Foreign News Editor to Editor News and Current Affairs, 10 December 1962. Confidential. 'Russia: Luncheon with Mr Stanley Johnson of Associated Press on 5 December 1962'.

75 BBC Written Archives Centre Acting Foreign News Editor (G.H.G. Norman) to E.N.C.A., 29 November 1962. 'Russian Coverage. Confidential. Account of lunch with Donald Connery'.

76 BBC Written Archives Centre, Programme as Broadcast, 'Woman's Hour', 14 August 1963.

77 BBC Written Archives Centre E1/2 457/1 Minutes from the BBC Board of Management, 23 May 1966.

78 Service, *A History of Modern Russia*, 377.

79 Service, *A History of Modern Russia*, 378.

80 *The Manchester Guardian*, 1 March 1954, 5.

81 Service, *A History of Modern Russia*, 367.

82 Hedrick Smith, *The Russians* (London: Sphere, 1976), 30–1.

83 Smith, *The Russians*, 36.

84 Barbara Walker, 'The Moscow Correspondents, Soviet Human Rights Activists, and the Problem of the Western Gift', in Choi Chatterjee and Beth Holmgren (eds) *Americans Experience Russia: Encountering the Enigma, 1917 to the Present* (1st Edition) (New York: Routledge, 2013), 141.

85 Walker, 'The Moscow Correspondents', 139.

86 Jonathan Steele, Interview with the author, London, 2 April 2019.

87 Rettie, 'How Khrushchev Leaked His Secret Speech to the World', 193.

Chapter 7

1   Service, *A History of Modern Russia*, 429.

2   *The Times*, 12 March 1985, 1; *The New York Times*, 12 March 1985, 1.

3   *The Times*, 12 March 1985, 1.

4   *The New York Times*, 12 March 1985, 16.

5   *The New York Times*, 12 March 1985, 16.

6   Interview with the author conducted via Skype between London and Moscow, 16 April 2019. All subsequent quotations from Weir come from the same interview.

7   Service, *A History of Modern Russia*, 444.

8   Interview with the author, 16 April 2019.

9   Interview with the author, London, 4 April 2019. All subsequent quotations from Kendall come from the same interview.

10 Jonathan Steele, Interview with the author, London, 2 April 2019.

11 *The Times*, 29 April 1986, 1.

12 Interview with the author conducted via Skype between London and Portola Valley, California, 25 April 2019. All subsequent quotations from Taubman come from the same interview.

13 *The New York Times*, 1 May 1986, 1.

14 Any reader interested in more about how the consequences of the disaster in the region where it caused the greatest loss of life and destruction should see Svetlana Alexievich's book, translated into English as either *Chernobyl Prayer* or *Voices from Chernobyl*.

15 *The Guardian*, 30 April 1986, 1.

16 *The New York Times*, 1 May 1986, 1.

17 Jonathan Steele, *Eternal Russia: Yeltsin, Gorbachev, and the Mirage of Democracy* (London: Faber and Faber, 1994), 3.

18 Arkady Ostrovsky, *The Invention of Russia: The Journey from Gorbachev's Freedom to Putin's War* (London: Atlantic Books, 2015), 69.

19 R. W. Davies, *Soviet History in the Yeltsin Era* (London: Macmillan, 1997), 6.

20 Elena Vartanova, 'The Russian Media Model in the Context of Post-Soviet Dynamics', in Daniel C. Hallin and Paolo Mancini (eds) *Comparing Media Systems Beyond the Western World* (Cambridge: Cambridge University Press, 2012), 128.

21 Ivan Zassoursky, *Media and Power in Post-Soviet Russia* (Armonk, New York and London: M. E. Sharpe, 2004), 11.

22 *The New York Times*, 20 October 1988, 1.

23 Nicholas Daniloff, *Two Lives, One Russia* (London: Bodley Head, 1988), 27.

24 Daniloff, *Two Lives, One Russia*, 24.

25 *The New York Times*, 1 October 1986, 1.

26 *The New York Times*, 30 September 1986, 1.

27 Daniloff, *Two Lives, One Russia*, 58.

28 *The New York Times*, 21 September 1986, SM59.

29 Angus Roxburgh, *Moscow Calling: Memoirs of a Foreign Correspondent* (Edinburgh: Birlinn, 2018), 191.

30 Roxburgh, *Moscow Calling*, 188.

31 Interview with the author, London, 29 May 2019. This and all subsequent quotations from Dejevsky are taken from that interview unless otherwise indicated.

32 Roxburgh, *Moscow Calling*, 191.

33 Service, *A History of Modern Russia*, 473.

34 *The Guardian*, 13 April 1989, 10.

35 *The Guardian*, 21 April 1989, 22.

36 *The Times*, 14 January 1991, 6.

37 Serhii Plokhy, *The Last Empire: The Final Days of the Soviet Union* (New York: Basic Books, 2014), 40.

38 David Remnick, *Lenin's Tomb: The Last Days of the Soviet Empire* (London: Penguin, 1993), xi.

39 *The New York Times*, 31 July 1991, 11.

40 Plokhy, *The Last Empire*, 50.

41 *The Times*, 2 August 1991, 11.

42 Plokhy, *The Last Empire*, 41.

43 *The Times*, 20 August 1991, 1.

44 *The New York Times*, 20 August 1991, A1.

45 See, for example, Jonathan Steele's obituary of Yanayev for *The Guardian*, posted on 26 September 2010. Available at https://www.theguardian.com/world/2010/sep/26/gennady-yanayev-obituary-communist-gorbachev. Accessed 3 May 2019.

46 See Ostrovsky, *The Invention of Russia*, 12 and Plokhy, *The Last Empire*, 374.

47 Email to the author, 1 May 2019.

Chapter 8

1 *The Guardian*, 31 December 1994, 14.

2 Committee to Protect Journalists website. https://cpj.org/data/people/cynthia-elbaum/. Accessed 10 May 2019.

3 https://www.spiegel.de/international/world/boris-yeltsin-rip-the-rise-and-fall-of-the-drunken-czar-a-479096-5.html. Accessed 14 February 2020.

4 Skype interview with the author conducted between London and Tbilisi, 15 April 2019. This and all other quotations from Sheets are taken from that interview.

5 Skype interview with the author conducted between London and Moscow, 16 April 2019. This and all other quotations from Franchetti are taken from that interview.

6 Jeremy Bowen, *War Stories* (London: Simon and Schuster, 2006), 211.

7 Carlotta Gall and Thomas de Waal, *Chechnya: A Small Victorious War* (London: Pan, 1997), 16.

8 Gall and de Waal, *Chechnya: A Small Victorious War*, 11.

9 Gall and de Waal, *Chechnya: A Small Victorious War*, 12.

10 Gall and de Waal, *Chechnya: A Small Victorious War*, 257.

11 Gall and de Waal, *Chechnya: A Small Victorious War*, 265.

12 *The Times*, 24 December 1994, 1.

13 *The Times*, 26 December 1994, 1.

14 *The Times*, 13 January 1995, 10.

15 Committee to Protect Journalists website. Available at https://cpj.org/data/people/rory-peck/. Accessed 21 May 2019.

16 Helen Womack, *The Ice Walk: Surviving the Soviet Break-up and the New Russia* (Ely: Melrose Books, 2013), 133.

17 Lilia Shevtsova, '1993: Russia's Small Civil War' Carnegie Moscow Center commentary. First posted 3 October 2013. Available at https://carnegie.ru/commentary/53189. Accessed 21 May 2019.

18 Jonathan Steele and David Hearst, 'Yeltsin Crushes Revolt'. *The Guardian*, First published 5 October 1993. Available at https://www.theguardian.com/world/1993/oct/05/russia.davidhearst. Accessed 21 May 2019.

19 Russia Votes website. available at http://www.russiavotes.org/duma/duma_elections_93-03.php. Accessed 22 May 2019.

20 *The Daily Telegraph*, 20 December 1995, 12.

21 Hélène Richard, 'Quand Washington Manipulait la présidentielle russe'. *Le Monde Diplomatique* (March 2019), 14–15.

22 Sarah Oates and Laura Roselle, 'Russian Elections and TV News Comparison of Campaign News on State-Controlled and Commercial Television Channels', *The Harvard International Journal of Press/Politics*, Vol. 5, No. 2 (Spring 2000): 31.

23 James Rodgers, 'From Perestroika to Putin – Journalism in Russia', in James Bennett and Niki Strange (eds) *Media Independence: Working with Freedom or Working for Free?* (Abingdon: Routledge, 2015).

24 *The Financial Times*, 18 June 1996, 15.

25 *The New York Times*, 19 June 1996, A23.

26 *The New York Times*, 16 June 1996, 11.

27 Womack, *The Ice Walk*, 188.

28 Interview conducted by Facebook video between Fanø, Denmark and Budapest, 21 May 2019. Unless otherwise attributed, all subsequent quotations from Womack are taken from this interview.

29 A reference to 'Spinning Boris', 2003 film directed by Roger Spottiswoode.

30 It was broadcast in the UK on BBC2 at 2230 on 15 July 1998.

31 *The Times*, 22 August 1998, 16.

32 *The New York Times*, 6 January 1999, A4.

33 *The Guardian,* 11 December 1998, 18.

34 *The Economist*, 17 April 1999, 19.

35 BBC News, 'Europe Protests Escalate into Moscow gun battle'. First posted 28 March 1999. Available at http://news.bbc.co.uk/2/hi/europe/306234.stm. Accessed 23 May 2019.

36 *The New York Times*, 12 April 1999, A1.

37 *The Daily Telegraph*, 6 September 1999, 10.

38 *The Sunday Times*, 22 February 1998, 18.

39 BBC News, 'UK Hostages Taste Freedom'. Available at http://news.bbc.co.uk/2/hi/uk_news/175919.stm. Accessed 23 May 2019.

40 BBC News, 'Chechnya Kidnap Victims Are Dead'. Available at http://news.bbc.co.uk/2/hi/europe/230215.stm. Accessed 23 May 2019.

41 *The Sunday Times*, 19 December 1999, 18–19.

42 *The Sunday Times* website, 2 January 2000. Available at https://www.thetimes.co.uk/article/escape-from-chechnya-to-a-trial-by-ice-78mpwtd66pk. Accessed 23 May 2019.

43 'Chechnya: Destruction Defying Description' BBC News website. Available at http://news.bbc.co.uk/2/hi/europe/780073.stm. Accessed 23 May 2019.

Chapter 9

1   Interview with the author, London, 29 May 2019. This and all subsequent quotations from Buckley are taken from this interview.

2   *The Financial Times*, 3 January 2006, 8.

3   'Outsiders Warned Off Ukraine Poll' BBC News website, originally posted 5 December 2004. Available at http://news.bbc.co.uk/1/hi/world/europe/4070389.stm. Accessed 4 June 2019.

4   *The Financial Times*, 3 January 2006, 8.

5   *The Daily Telegraph* website, Marcus Warren and Michael Smith. 'Divers End Rescue after Finding Kursk Flooded'. First posted 22 August 2000. Available at https://www.telegraph.co.uk/news/worldnews/europe/norway/1367181/Divers-end-rescue-after-finding-Kursk-flooded.html. Accessed 4 June 2019.

6   See, for example, the Reuters photo story 'Putin's Macho Image' published 5 December 2011. Available at https://www.reuters.com/news/picture/putins-macho-image-idUSRTR2UVJN. Accessed 4 June 2019.

7   *Guardian* website. First published 23 August 2000. Available at https://www.theguardian.com/world/2000/aug/23/kursk.russia. Accessed 4 June 2019.

8   'Putin Opens Up for CNN's Larry King.' Available at http://edition.cnn.com/2000/WORLD/europe/09/08/russia.putin.03/. Accessed 4 June 2019.

9   'Putin Has "It"' – Larry King'. RT website. Available at https://www.rt.com/news/larry-king-putin-interview-163/. Accessed 4 June 2019.

10 This was the figure given at the time. A later BBC report, prepared with the benefit of later information, put the figure at 912. See 'Moscow Theatre Siege: Questions Remain Unanswered.' Available at https://www.bbc.co.uk/news/world-europe-20067384. Accessed 4 June 2019.

11 *The Sunday Times*, 27 October 2002, 2.

12 'Moscow Theatre Siege: Questions Remain Unanswered.' Available at https://www.bbc.co.uk/news/world-europe-20067384. Accessed 4 June 2019.

13 'Judgement Tagayeva and Others v. Russia – Serious Failings in the Authorities' Response to the Beslan Attack'. Press release available at https://hudoc.echr.coe.int/eng-press#{'itemid':['003-5684105-7210070']}. Accessed 4 June 2019.

14 'Beslan Ruling: Moscow Slams ECHR's Claim That More Lives Could Have Been Saved'. First posted 13 April 2017. Available at https://www.rt.com/news/384607-echr-ruling-beslan-victims/. Accessed 4 June 2019.

15 BBC World Service, 'The Fifth Floor' First broadcast 29 December 2012. Available at https://www.bbc.co.uk/sounds/play/p012bp4x. Accessed 4 June 2019.

16 BBC News, 'Putin's Webcast Missile Warning'. 6 March 2001. Available at http://news.bbc.co.uk/1/hi/world/europe/1205664.stm. Accessed 4 June 2019.

17 BBC News, 'Putin's Webcast Missile Warning'. 6 March 2001. Available at http://news.bbc.co.uk/1/hi/world/europe/1205664.stm. Accessed 4 June 2019.

18 'Russia Votes'. Available at http://www.russiavotes.org/president/presidency_96-04.php. Accessed 11 June 2019.

19 *The Financial Times*, 1 May 2006, 1.

20 Rodgers, *Reporting Conflict*, 76.

21 Angus Roxburgh, *The Strongman: Vladimir Putin and the Struggle for Russia* (London: I.B. Tauris, 2013), 184.

22 Roxburgh, *The Strongman*, 185.

23 'The Hidden Author of Putinism: How Vladislav Surkov Invented the New Russia' *The Atlantic* website. First posted 7 November 2014. Available at https://www.theatlantic.com/international/archive/2014/11/hidden-author-putinism-russia-vladislav-surkov/382489/. Accessed 5 June 2019.

24 Roxburgh, *The Strongman*, 191.

25 Roxburgh, *Moscow Calling*, 304.

26 Roxburgh, *The Strongman*, 191.

27 'About RT'. RT website. Available at https://www.rt.com/about-us/. Accessed 6 June 2019.

28 *The Daily Telegraph* website 'Putin Cracks the Whip for Summit'. First posted 12 July 2006. Available at https://www.telegraph.co.uk/news/worldnews/europe/russia/1523717/Putin-cracks-the-whip-for-summit.html. Accessed 6 June 2019.

29 BBC News, 'Basayev Death to Profit Kremlin'. First posted 10 July 2006. Available at http://news.bbc.co.uk/1/hi/world/europe/5166664.stm. Accessed 6 June 2019.

30 'As Tensions Rise, U.S. and Moscow Falter on Trade'. *The New York Times* website. Available at https://www.nytimes.com/2006/07/16/world/europe/16summit.html. Accessed 6 June 2019.

31 *The Litvinenko Inquiry*, 185.

32 Crown Prosecution Service Press release 'CPS Announces Decision on Alexander Litvinenko Case' 22 May 2007. Available at https://webarchive.nationalarchives.gov.uk/20080612102021/ and http://www.cps.gov.uk/news/pressreleases/archive/2007/130_07.html. Accessed 6 June 2019.

33 'Moscow Diary: The Litvinenko Saga'. Available at http://news.bbc.co.uk/1/hi/world/europe/6332823.stm. Accessed 6 June 2019.

34 'I Am Plotting a New Russian Revolution'. Available at https://www.theguardian.com/world/2007/apr/13/topstories3.russia. Accessed 6 June 2019.

35 See https://www.theguardian.com/world/2011/sep/23/luke-harding-russia. Accessed 28 February 2020.

36   Russia Votes website. http://www.russiavotes.org/president/presidency_2008.php. Accessed 10 June 2019.

37   *The Times*, 2 January 2008, 15.

38   *The Times*, 15 February 2008, 37.

39   *The Times*, 8 February 2008, 39.

40   AP Video 'Medvedev Wins, Likely to Stay on Putin Path.' Available on YouTube. https://www.youtube.com/watch?v=jivsXVhSSfY. Accessed 25 October 2019.

41   *The New York Times*, 10 May 2008, A9.

42   Often referred to as the Tagliavini report. This can be viewed on the Council of Europe website. Available at https://www.echr.coe.int/Documents/ HUDOC_38263_08_Annexes_ENG.pdf. Accessed 10 June 2019.

43   BBC News, 'Georgia Started Unjustified War.' Available at http://news.bbc.co.uk/1/ hi/world/europe/8281990.stm. Accessed 10 June 2019.

44   See Timothy L. Thomas, 'The Bear Went through the Mountain: Russia Appraises its Five-Day War in South Ossetia', *Journal of Slavic Military Studies*, Vol. 22, No. 1 (2009), DOI: 10.1080/13518040802695241, 46.

45   The documentary 'The PR Battle for the Caucasus' is available for download from BBC Sounds. https://www.bbc.co.uk/programmes/p02sbq12. Accessed 10 June 2019.

46   The text of my interview 'Interview by Minister of Foreign Affairs of the Russian Federation Sergey Lavrov to BBC, Moscow, 9 August 2008' is available by searching on the Russian Ministry of Foreign Affairs website. http://www.mid.ru/en/main_ en. Accessed 14 February 2020, although the sentence construction in some of the questions leads me to suspect there may have been minor errors in transcription.

47   Rick Fawn and Robert Nalbandov, 'The Difficulties of Knowing the Start of War in the Information Age: Russia, Georgia and the War over South Ossetia, August 2008', *European Security*, Vol. 21, No. 1 (2012), DOI: 10.1080/09662839.2012.656601, 57.

48   Interview with the author, Elsfield, Oxfordshire, England, 3 June 2019.

49   BBC News, 'Georgia's NATO Bid Irks Russia'. http://news.bbc.co.uk/1/hi/world/ europe/6190858.stm. Accessed 11 June 2019.

50   BBC News, 'Russia Buoyed by Weakened Georgia'. First posted 12 August 2008. Available at http://news.bbc.co.uk/1/hi/world/europe/7556503.stm. Accessed 11 June 2019.

51   'Kasparov Defiant after Arrest in Moscow March'. First posted 14 April 2007. Available at https://uk.reuters.com/article/uk-russia-protest-kasparov-idUKL1451666820070414. Accessed 11 June 2019.

52   Roxburgh, *The Strongman*, 190.

53   I wrote about this later for my Moscow Diary on the BBC website. First posted 11 February 2009. Available at http://news.bbc.co.uk/1/hi/world/europe/7883539.stm. Accessed 11 June 2019.

Chapter 10

1 Crown Prosecution Service statement. Available at https://www.cps.gov.uk/cps/
   news/cps-statement-salisbury. Accessed 20 June 2019.
2 Their investigation was published later in 2018. Available at https://www.bellingcat.
   com/news/uk-and-europe/2018/09/26/skripal-suspect-boshirov-identified-gru-
   colonel-anatoliy-chepiga/. Accessed 20 June 2019.
3 The *Guardian* website, 'Western Allies Expel Scores of Russian Diplomats over
   Skripal Attack'. Available at https://www.theguardian.com/uk-news/2018/mar/26/
   four-eu-states-set-to-expel-russian-diplomats-over-skripal-attack. Accessed 20
   June 2019.
4 Skype interview with the author conducted between London and Moscow, 4 June
   2019. This and all other quotations from de Pury come from that interview unless
   otherwise stated.
5 Available at http://www.mid.ru/en/foreign_policy/official_documents/-/asset_
   publisher/CptICkB6BZ29/content/id/2542248. Accessed 19 July 2019.
6 Dmitri Trenin, *Should We Fear Russia?* (Cambridge: Polity, 2016), 93.
7 See https://www.stopfake.org/en/lies-crucifixion-on-channel-one/. Accessed 1
   November 2019.
8 Some details are available on the website of the US Treasury. https://www.treasury.
   gov/resource-center/sanctions/Programs/Pages/magnitsky.aspx. Accessed 20 June
   2019.
9 'How I Hit the Headlines on Siberian TV'. Available at https://www.bbc.co.uk/news/
   magazine-35668596. Accessed 20 June 2019.
10 *The Times, Russia: Vladimir Putin Shows Off Military Might at Victory Day Parade
   in Moscow*. Available at https://www.thetimes.co.uk/article/vladimir-putin-shows-
   off-military-might-at-victory-day-parade-d3b6wn7qw. Accessed 12 July 2019.
11 See, for example, Reynolds and Pechatov, *The Kremlin Letters*, 270.
12 'Snubbing Putin at Sochi Did Not Help Ukraine'. Available at https://
   standpointmag.co.uk/issues/march-2014/features-march-14-snubbing-vladimir-
   putin-at-sochi-did-not-help-ukraine-tony-brenton-kiev-protests/. Accessed 12 July
   2019.
13 Jordan, *Russian Glory*, 169–70.
14 Will the World Cup Finally Change How Russia Is Portrayed? Available at https://
   www.theguardian.com/football/2018/jul/12/will-the-world-cup-finally-change-
   how-russia-is-portrayed. Accessed 12 July 2019.

Bibliography

Adamson, Judith (1998) *Charlotte Haldane: Woman Writer in a Man's World* (Basingstoke, Macmillan).

Alston, Charlotte (2007a) 'British Journalism and the Campaign for Intervention in the Russian Civil War, 1918–20'. *Revolutionary Russia* 20: 1, 35–49. doi: 1080/09546540701314343.

Alston, Charlotte (2007b) *Russia's Greatest Enemy: Harold Williams and the Russian Revolutions* (London, Tauris Academic Studies).

Bassow, Whitman (1988) *The Moscow Correspondents: Reporting on Russia from the Revolution to Glasnost* (New York, William Morrow).

Bowen, Jeremy (2006) *War Stories* (London, Simon and Schuster).

Braithwaite, Rodric (2006) *Moscow 1941: A City and Its People at War* (London, Profile Books).

Briggs, Asa (1985) *The BBC: The First Fifty Years* (Oxford, Oxford University Press).

Brogan, Hugh (1984) *The Life of Arthur Ransome* (London, Pimlico).

Bruce Lockhart, R. H. (2002) *Memoirs of a British Agent* (London, Pan).

Carruthers, Susan (2011) *The Media at War* (2nd Edition) (Basingstoke, Palgrave Macmillan).

Cassidy, Henry C. (1943) *Moscow Dateline* (London, Cassell).

Cathcart, Brian (2015) *The News from Waterloo* (London, Faber & Faber).

Chambers, Roland (2009) *The Last Englishman: The Double Life of Arthur Ransome* (London, Faber & Faber).

Clark, Christopher (2013) *The Sleepwalkers: How Europe Went to War in 1914* (London, Penguin).

Clark, Joseph (1954) *The Real Russia* (New York, New Century Publishers).

Conquest, Robert (2002) *The Harvest of Sorrow: Soviet Collectivisation and the Terror-Famine* (London, Pimlico).

Conquest, Robert (2008) *The Great Terror: A Reassessment* (London, Pimlico)

von Clausewitz, Carl (2007) *On War* (Oxford, Oxford World's Classics)

Cripps, Stafford (2007) *Stafford Cripps in Moscow 1940–42, Diaries and Papers* (edited by Gabriel Gorodetsky) (London and Portland Oregon, Valentine Mitchell).

Daniloff, Nicholas (1988) *Two Lives, One Russia* (London, Bodley Head).

Davies, R. W. (1997) *Soviet History in the Yeltsin Era* (London, Macmillan).

Desmond, Robert W. (1982) *Crisis and Conflict: World News Reporting between Two Wars 1920–1940* (Iowa, University of Iowa Press)

Duranty, Walter (1935) *I Write as I Please* (London, Hamish Hamilton).

Duranty, Walter (1943) *Search for a Key* (New York, Simon and Schuster).

Fawn, Rick and Nalbandov, Robert (2012) 'The Difficulties of Knowing the Start of War in the Information Age: Russia, Georgia and the War over South Ossetia, August 2008'. *European Security* 21: 1, 57–89. doi: 10.1080/09662839.2012.656601.

Feuchtwanger, Lion (1937) *Moscow 1937: My Visit Described for My Friends* (translated by Irene Josephy) (London, Victor Gollancz) Left Book Club Topical Book.

Figes, Orlando (1997) *A People's Tragedy: The Russian Revolution 1891–1924* (London, Pimlico).

Fitzpatrick, Sheila (2015) *On Stalin's Team: The Years of Living Dangerously in Soviet Politics* (Woodstock (Oxfordshire, UK), Princeton University Press).

Gall, Carlotta and de Waal, Thomas (1997) *Chechnya: A Small Victorious War* (London, Pan).

Gessen, Masha (2004) *Two Babushkas* (London, Bloomsbury).

Gide, André (1936) *Retour de l'U.R.S.S* (Paris, Editions Gallimard).

Gorbachev, Mikhail (2005) *On My Country and the World* (New York, Columbia University Press).

Grossman, Vassily (2006) *A Writer at War: With the Red Army 1941–1945* (edited and translated by Antony Beevor and Luba Vinogradova) (London, Pimlico).

Haldane, Charlotte (1942) *Russian Newsreel: An Eye-Witness Account of the Soviet Union at War* (London, Secker and Warburg).

Haldane, Charlotte (1943) *Russian Newsreel* (Harmondsworth, Middlesex, Penguin).

Haldane, Charlotte (1949) *Truth Will Out* (London, Weidenfeld and Nicolson).

Hall, Nicholas (2016) 'Gareth Jones, the Soviet Peasantry and the "Real Russia" 1930–1933'. *Russian Journal of Communication* 8: 3, 242–55. doi: 10.1080/19409419.2016.1213220.

Harrison, Marguerite (1921) *Marooned in Moscow* (London, Thornton Butterworth).

Harrison, Marguerite (1936) *Born for Trouble: The Story of a Chequered Life* (London, Victor Gollancz).

Hobsbawm, Eric (1994) *The Age of Extremes, 1914–1991* (London, Abacus).

Hodgson, John Ernest (1932) *With Denikin's Armies* (London, Temple Bar Publishing Co.).

Hohenberg, John (1964) *Foreign Correspondence: The Great Reporters and Their Times* (New York and London, Columbia University Press).

Homberger, Eric (1990) *John Reed* (Manchester, Manchester University Press).

Jordan, Philip (1942) *Russian Glory* (London, The Cresset Press).

Knightley, Phillip (1989) *The First Casualty* (London, Pan).

Lermontov, Mikhail (1966) *A Hero of Our Time* (translated by Paul Foote) (London, Penguin Classics).

Lieven, Dominic (2009) *Russia against Napoleon* (London, Penguin).

Lieven, Dominic (2015) *Towards the Flame: Empire, War and the End of Tsarist Russia* (London, Allen Lane).

Lippmann, Walter and Merz, Charles (1920) *A Test of the News* A Supplement to The New Republic of August 4th 1920, Vol. XXIII. PART II. No. 296 (Washington, DC).

Lyons, Eugene (1938) *Assignment in Utopia* (London, George G. Harrap).

Maclean, Fitzroy (1951) *Eastern Approaches* (London, The Reprint Society, by Arrangement with Jonathan Cape).

Maisky, Ivan (2015) *The Maisky Diaries: Red Ambassador to the Court of St James, 1932–1943* (edited by Gabriel Gorodetsky) (New Haven and London, Yale University Press).

McCollam, Douglas (November/December 2003) 'Should This Pulitzer Be Pulled?' *Columbia Journalism Review* 42: 4.

McDonald, Iverach (1976) *A Man of The Times: Talks and Travels in a Disrupted World* (London, Hamish Hamilton).

McEwen, J. M. (1978). 'The Press and the Fall of Asquith'. *The Historical Journal* 21: 4, 863–83. doi: 10.1017/S0018246X00000728.

McGlashan, Zena Beth (1985) 'Women Witness the Russian Revolution: Analyzing Ways of Seeing'. *Journalism History* 12: 2, 54–61.

Motler, L. A. (1919) *Soviets for the British: A Plain Talk to Plain People* (London, Workers' Socialist Federation).

Muggeridge, Malcolm (1972) *Chronicles of Wasted Time: Volume 1, The Green Stick* (London, Collins).

Muggeridge, Malcolm (2003 (1934)) *Winter in Moscow* (Thirsk, House of Stratus).

Nakai, Kazuo (March 1982) 'Soviet Agricultural Policies in the Ukraine and the 1921–1922 Famine'. *Harvard Ukrainian Studies* 6: 1, 43–61.

Neilson, Keith (1995) *Britain and the Last Tsar* (Oxford, Oxford University Press).

Nicholas, Sian (1996) *The Echo of War: Home Front Propaganda and the Wartime BBC* (Manchester, Manchester University Press).

Oates, Sarah and Roselle, Laura (Spring 2000) 'Russian Elections and TV News Comparison of Campaign News on State-Controlled and Commercial Television Channels'. *The Harvard International Journal of Press/Politics* 5: 2, 30–51.

O' Reilly, Kenneth (1979) '*The Times* of London and the Bolshevik Revolution'. *Journalism Quarterly* 56: 1, 69–76.

Ostrovsky, Arkady (2015) *The Invention of Russia: The Journey from Gorbachev's Freedom to Putin's War* (London, Atlantic Books).

Owen, Sir Robert (2016) *The Litvinenko Enquiry: Report into the Death of Alexander Litvinenko*. Presented to Parliament pursuant to Section 26 of the Inquiries Act 2005 Ordered by the House of Commons to be printed on 21 January 2016. Available at https://webarchive.nationalarchives.gov.uk/20160613090757/ and https://www.litvinenkoinquiry.org/files/Litvinenko-Inquiry-Report-print-version.pdf. Accessed 6 June 2019.

Pares, Bernard (1931) *Russian Memoirs* (London, Jonathan Cape).

Philips Price, Morgan (1912) *Siberia* (London, Methuen).

Philips Price, Morgan (1918) *The Truth about the Allied Intervention in Russia* (Pamphlet published in Moscow by the Soviet Authorities).

Philips Price, Morgan (1921) *My Reminiscences of the Russian Revolution* (London, George Allen and Unwin).

Philips Price, Morgan (1969) *My Three Revolutions: Russia, Germany, Britain 1917–1969* (London, George Allen and Unwin).

Philips Price, Morgan (1997) *Dispatches from the Revolution: Russia 1916–18* (edited by Tania Rose) (London, Pluto Press).

Pipes, Richard (1997) *The Russian Revolution 1899–1919* (London, Harvill).

Plokhy, Serhii (2014) *The Last Empire: The Final Days of the Soviet Union* (New York, Basic Books).

Purvis, Stewart and Hulbert, Jeff (2013) *When Reporters Cross the Line: The Heroes, the Villains, the Hackers, and the Spies* (London, Biteback).

Ransome, Arthur (1921) *The Crisis in Russia* (London, George Allen and Unwin).

Ransome, Arthur (1985) *The Autobiography of Arthur Ransome* (edited by Rupert Hart-Davis) (London, Century).

Ransome, Arthur (1992) *Six Weeks in Russia, 1919* (Kindle Edition) (London, Redwords).

Read, Donald (1999) *The Power of News: The History of Reuters* (2nd Edition) (Oxford, Oxford University Press).

Reed, John (1977) *Ten Days That Shook the World* (London: Penguin).

Reed, John (1998) *Shaking the World: Revolutionary Journalism* (edited by John Newsinger; Preface by Paul Foot) (London: Bookmarks).

Remnick, David (1993) *Lenin's Tomb: The Last Days of the Soviet Empire* (London, Penguin).

Rettie, John (2006) 'How Khrushchev Leaked His Secret Speech to the World'. *History Workshop Journal* 62 (Autumn 2006), 187–93.

Reynolds, Quentin (1942) *Only the Stars Are Neutral* (London, Cassell).

Reynolds, David and Pechatnov, Vladimir (2018) *The Kremlin Letters: Stalin's Wartime Correspondence with Churchill and Roosevelt* (Newhaven and London, Yale University Press).

Richard, Hélène (2019) 'Quand Washington manipulait la présidentielle russe'. *Le Monde Diplomatique* March 2019, 14–15.

Rodgers, James (2012) *Reporting Conflict* (Basingstoke, Palgrave Macmillan).

Rodgers, James (2015) 'From Perestroika to Putin – Journalism in Russia' in Bennett, James and Strange, Niki (eds) *Media independence: Working with Freedom or Working for Free?* (Abingdon, Routledge) pp. 223–42.

Roxburgh, Angus (2013) *The Strongman: Vladimir Putin and the Struggle for Russia* (London, I.B. Tauris).

Roxburgh, Angus (2018) *Moscow Calling: Memoirs of a Foreign Correspondent* (Edinburgh, Birlinn).

Salisbury, Harrison (1959) *To Moscow and Beyond* (New York, Harper).

Salisbury, Harrison (1962) *A New Russia* (New York, Harper and Row).

Saul, Norman E. (2001) *War and Revolution: The United States and Russia 1917–1921* (Lawrence, Kansas, University Press of Kansas).

Service, Robert (2003) *A History of Modern Russia: From Nicholas II to Putin* (London, Penguin).

Service, Robert (2009) *Trotsky: A Biography* (London, Macmillan).

Sixsmith, Martin (2007) *The Litvinenko File* (London, Macmillan).

Smele, Jonathan (1995) 'What the Papers Didn't Say: Unpublished Despatches from Russia by M. Philips Price, May 1918 to January 1919'. *Revolutionary Russia* 8: 2, 129–65. doi: 10. 1080/09546549508575636.

Smith, Hedrick (1976) *The Russians* (London, Sphere).

Steele, Jonathan (1994) *Eternal Russia: Yeltsin, Gorbachev, and the Mirage of Democracy* (London, Faber and Faber).

Steinbeck, John (1994) *A Russian Journal* (London, Minerva).

Taylor, A. J. P. (1966) *The First World War: An Illustrated History* (London, Penguin).

Taylor, A. J. P. (1977) *Preface to Reed, John (1977) Ten Days That Shook the World* (London, Penguin).

Taylor, Philip M. (2003) *Munitions of the Mind: A History of Propaganda from the Ancient World to the Present Day* (3rd Edition) (Manchester, Manchester University Press).

Taylor, S. J. (1990) *Stalin's Apologist: Walter Duranty, The New York Times' Man in Moscow* (Oxford, Oxford University Press).

Thomas, Timothy L. (2009) 'The Bear Went through the Mountain: Russia Appraises Its Five-Day War in South Ossetia'. *Journal of Slavic Military Studies* 22: 1, 31–67. doi: 10.1080/13518040802695241.

Thompson, Donald (1918) *Donald Thompson in Russia* (New York, The Century).

The Times (1952) *The History of The Times, Volume IV, The 150th Anniversary and beyond 1912–1948, Part I, Chapters I–XII 1912–1920* (London, The Times).

The Times (1952) *The History of The Times, Volume IV, The 150th Anniversary and beyond 1912 The Times 1948, Part II, Chapters XIII The Times XXIV 1921 The Times 1948* (London, The Times).

Tolstoy, Leo (1985) *War and Peace* (translated and with an introduction by Rosemary Edmonds) (London, Penguin Classics).

Trenin, Dmitri (2016) *Should We Fear Russia?* (Cambridge, Polity).

Trotsky, Leon (1977) *The History of the Russian Revolution* (translated by Max Eastman) (London, Pluto Press).

Tyrkova-Williams, Ariadna (1935) *Cheerful Giver: The Life of Harold Williams* (London, Peter Davies).

Vartanova, Elena (2012) 'The Russian Media Model in the Context of Post-Soviet Dynamics' in Hallin, Daniel C. and Mancini, Paolo (eds) *Comparing Media Systems beyond the Western World* (Cambridge: Cambridge University Press, 2012) pp. 119–42.

Volkogonov, Dmitri (1994) *Lenin: Life and Legacy* (translated and edited by Harold Shukman) (London, HarperCollins).

Walker, Barbara (2013) 'The Moscow Correspondents, Soviet Human Rights Activists, and the Problem of the Western Gift' in Chatterjee, Choi and Holmgren, Beth (eds) *Americans Experience Russia: Encountering the Enigma, 1917 to the Present* (1st Edition) (New York, Routledge) pp. 139–57.

Washburn, Stanley (1982) *On the Russian Front in WW1: Memoirs of an American War Correspondent* (New York, Robert Speller and Sons).

Werth, Alexander (1942) *Moscow War Diary* (New York, Alfred A. Knopf).

Werth, Alexander (1965) *Russia at War* (London, Pan Books).

Wilton, Robert (1918) *Russia's Agony* (London, Edward Arnold).

Wilton, Robert (1919) *Russia's Agony* (New York, E.P Dutton).

Womack, Helen (2013) *The Ice Walk: Surviving the Soviet Break-Up and the New Russia* (Ely, Melrose Books).

Zangzwill, Israel (1919) *Hands Off Russia: Speech at the Albert Hall February 8th 1919* (London, Workers Socialist Federation).

Zassoursky, Ivan (2004) *Media and Power in Post-Soviet Russia* (Armonk, New York and London, M. E. Sharpe).

Archives

Archive of *The Guardian* (formerly *Manchester Guardian*), University of Manchester Library

The BBC Written Archives Centre

The Bishopsgate Institute

The Parliamentary Archives

Times Newspapers Ltd Archive [TNL Archive], News UK and Ireland Ltd

Index